To Know Her Own History

Pittsburgh Series in Composition, Literacy, and Culture
David Bartholomae and Jean Ferguson Carr, Editors

To Know Her Own History

Writing at the Woman's College, 1943–1963

Kelly Ritter

University of Pittsburgh Press

Published by the University of Pittsburgh Press, Pittsburgh, Pa., 15260
Copyright © 2012, University of Pittsburgh Press
All rights reserved
Manufactured in the United States of America
Printed on acid-free paper
10 9 8 7 6 5 4 3 2 1

Library of Congress Cataloging-in-Publication Data

Ritter, Kelly.
To know her own history : writing at the woman's college, 1943–1963 / Kelly Ritter.
p. cm. — (Pittsburgh series in composition, literacy, and culture)
Includes bibliographical references and index.
ISBN 978-0-8229-6186-4 (pbk. : acid-free paper)
1. Women's colleges—United States—History—20th century. 2. Academic writing—Study and
teaching (Higher) —Case studies. 3. Women—Education (Higher) —United States—History—20th
century. 4. Composition (Language arts) —Study and teaching (Secondary) —United States. I. Title.
LC1756.R58 2012
378.1'9822—dc23   2011039629

Contents

Acknowledgments

I WOULD LIKE to thank the many individuals who assisted in the shaping, revision, and publication of this book. First, I thank Betty Carter, Hermann J. Trojanowski, and Sean Mullin of the University of North Carolina–Greensboro Archives and Manuscripts, for their time and expertise in directing me toward relevant materials and locating items that I needed—sometimes multiple times—and always welcoming me back to their collections. I again thank Tim Driscoll and Michelle Gachette at the Harvard University archives for their assistance with this second project involving their collections; Sarah Hutcheon at the Radcliffe archives in the Schlesinger Library, who was extremely accommodating and helpful to me as a first-time visitor; and Diane Jensen, Peace College Archives Librarian, who helped me to fill in some historical holes regarding May Bush. I thank Jean Ferguson Carr and David Bartholomae at the University of Pittsburgh for their interest and faith in this project, and to Jean especially for her extensive reading of my draft chapters as I wrote them; I also thank Jessica Enoch for her reading of the article version of viii ∿ Acknowledgments

chapter 2 as well as her general support of and interest in this project. I thank my colleagues in the English department at the University of North Carolina–Greensboro, but especially Risa Applegarth, Anne Wallace, Jennifer Keith, Michelle Dowd, Amy Vines, Jennifer Feather, and Mary Ellis Gibson, each of whom were, and are, invaluable in their support of me and my scholarship. And I thank David Fleming at the University of Massachusetts–Amherst and Neal Lerner at Northeastern University for their support in being allied archival researchers in composition studies and presenting with me at the 2010 Conference on College Composition and Communication in Louisville, Kentucky, where I presented elements of this project.

I give heartfelt thanks to the women who shared their memories of the Woman's College with me and gave me important personal insight as to what it was like to be a woman college writer during this postwar era: Elizabeth Stanfield-Maddox, Lucy Page Wagner, and Jacqueline Jernigan Ammons. I also thank all of the women who were students and faculty at the Woman's College during the time upon which my research is based, but whom I never had the chance to meet, especially May Delaney Bush. All of you are in my thoughts and are the true inspiration for this book.

And as always, I give my particular thanks to my husband (and patient copy editor), Joshua Rosenberg, and my daughter, Sarah Rosenberg, for their infinite patience, love, and support.

Introduction

The History of Composition Is the History of Its People

I HAVE ALWAYS been interested in local history, but until the last few years I did not envision myself becoming a scholar of the local histories of writing. In my earlier scholarship, I had focused on the present and future of writing and rhetoric, concerned with breaking new ground rather than retooling the past. In graduate school, I decided against a concentration in literary studies precisely because I believed that this field of study would require me to tread over texts and documents already explored by numerous scholars in as many settings. I did not see, in my own work, the value of the old; I saw writing studies—broadly construed—as a place where the new is always taking place, where the emergent creation, not cold resuscitation, of the text was the focal point of study. I did not see the value of the documented narratives of my—or your, or even *our*—educational past.

My lack of interest in archival work was in stark contrast to my interest in the symbols of the past that had perpetually surrounded me. My doctoral work took place in Chicago, where history is a forceful presence that tells its tales in the architecture of the city. On my long daily bus rides to campus, I was transfixed by the turn-of-the-century skyscrapers on La-Salle and Michigan Avenues against the brutalist work of Cabrini-Green. On campus at the University of Illinois at Chicago (UIC), I was equally fascinated by the functionalist school buildings of concrete-in, concrete-out, riot-proof design. It was said that the UIC campus was built to "identify" with the Eisenhower Expressway to its immediate north. This identification was made possible largely by the razing of Maxwell Street and much of the Jane Addams Hull House mission. It was one of a series of pockets of contrast throughout Chicago: socioeconomic statements about historical erasures and new beginnings, creating human and community sacrifices, including those of history-changing women such as Addams. In history, there is always this measure of tangible regret, as there are always voices that long to be heard more forcefully, if ever heard at all.

As I graduated and left the city to begin my academic career, I did not forget my burgeoning interest in the physically represented past that was strengthened during my time as a student. Yet, for myself, I still did not see any clear connection between history and writing studies scholarship. I moved East to teach first-year composition and direct the first-year writing program of a regional university in Connecticut. This university had its origins as a late-nineteenth-century normal school: it was the Southern Connecticut State Teachers College for over seventy years. It then became, in 1959, the Southern Connecticut State College—newly coeducational and comprehensive in nature. Finally, in the 1990s, just a few years before my arrival on campus, it became Southern Connecticut State University. Older community members still referred to it as "the girls' school" or "SCSC," forgetting—or not recognizing—its new position as a regional university and its aim to move beyond undergraduate, single-sex education, even though this population had been our roots. The student body still was nearly two-thirds female, and the best programs were still in education and nursing—those fields that have historically attracted women students. But still it doggedly built shiny new buildings and put up bright new signs, advertising the future and eschewing the less-selective, less-inclusive past. Faculty spoke little, if at all, about the women who had founded the school. The university kept a limited archive; it had little physical, public evidence of our transformation from normal school to coeducational university, particularly within the academic departments' records. It was a blank slate upon which history was rewritten, in keeping with the shifting educational economy, every twenty or so years.

So when, after seven years in Connecticut, I began my first archival project on basic writing—falling quite by accident on the rich history of this subfield of writing studies as it had been hidden in, of all places, Yale University, some five miles from my campus—I came to a swift and unexpected consciousness regarding the ways in which composition and rhetoric, like cities and educational institutions, are heavily indebted to the stories and legacies of their past. As I discussed in my first book on archival histories, *Before Shaughnessy*, I saw through the Yale archives the insubstantiation of the histories of writing, particularly basic writers, who had had no real voice in the scholarship I had read, save their revoicing by well-meaning (and often vitally important) teachers and scholars. I began to understand—first through Yale's archives, and then through those at Harvard—that the history of the local was what ultimately moved composition studies as a field; that I had not thought deeply enough, in the first few years of my professional life, about how much composition in the present time is influenced by the students and teachers, and other stakeholders, of its past. I similarly began to understand that those histories that were the least told—such as those of basic writers, particularly those at prestigious universities, where they were doubly marginalized from within and without—were those histories that the archives could most effectively tell. Yet at the time, I did not anticipate finding still more voices to uncover.

In 2008, I moved to the University of North Carolina–Greensboro to direct its first-year composition program, leaving behind, but not forgetting, the vexing path of writing histories in Connecticut. In North Carolina, I would again be met by the vestiges of the past, and these fragments of history would also be part of the legacy of women's education to which I had seen so little homage at SCSU. Even though I was now teaching at a research-intensive university with a variety of doctoral programs, including one in the English department, the roots of my campus were still heavily steeped in its past as first a normal school, and then a general women's college. I was surrounded by a reverence for the past on campus and in my community. As a newcomer to the South and its histories, I inhaled all available stories about my institution.

Unlike the erasure of history and women's voices that I found at SCSU, I learned that our surviving alumnae from the Woman's College era of the University of North Carolina–Greensboro—1931–63—have been, in fact, our most vocal and valuable community members, and their histories fill the buildings and other gathering spaces of our campus. Hardly a day goes by that I am not reminded that once we were not just a teachers college, but one of the premier public colleges for women in the South. Our alumnae keep this memory alive in many ways; the class of 1952 endows a generous departmental research fund for senior faculty in English, and all surviving classes of this era—the WC graduates, as they are known—hold annual reunions that bring classmates together from far and wide. Our Woman's College alumnae are the most vital of all graduates in the history of the institution. Those who followed, the UNCG-era alumni, are certainly valuable and valued, but they have nowhere near the institutional investment that the WC alumnae do. We may be coeducational at this point in our history, but our campus is built solidly on the socioinstitutional stories of women—as students, teachers, and, important to this particular book, as writers. A full-sized statue of Minerva, the goddess of wisdom, stands outside our university library as a keen reminder of our (positively) gendered past.

In undertaking this book, which serves as a sequel to my focus on the local in *Before Shaughnessy*, I thus employ the rich history of women's education at my own institution as a vehicle and case study for my assertion that studying the pasts of individual programs can assist us in seeing important moments in our field's history; in this book, the moment under review is the political, curricular, and socioinstitutional intersection of composition and creative writing in mid-twentieth-century America, at one public postsecondary institution. I shift my spotlight on local history from the Ivy League to a far lesser-known college population: the postwar women's public college.

To explore this local institutional history is a mandate that goes beyond a personal desire to better understand my own position in my program, or the legacy of writing at my university. Without history, to borrow from Santayana, there is no check on the practices of the present; without acknowledging and sometimes rectifying our pasts, we cannot confidently advance into our futures, feeling certain about the truth of the *then* versus the *next*. Nowhere is this more true than in large institutional structures such as first-year writing programs. We continually and generationally define literacy in context, and in doing so define and redefine the critical first-year writing course, mindful of its "universal" requirement status that attempts to educate students in the acts of writing, reading, interpretation, criticism, and analysis with one wide swath of pedagogical practice, despite its complex institutional and cultural past.

In order to better understand the overriding ways in which institutions work and subsequently leave records of their workings for future generations—an important point of consideration for any archivist or archival scholar—and to lay a theoretical groundwork for my study, I have found significant value in the scholarship of Charlotte Linde.[1] In *Working the Past: Narrative and Institutional Memory,* Linde, a sociolinguist, argues that narrative is "the link between the way an institution represents its past, and the way its members use, alter, or contest that past, in order to understand the institution as a whole as well as their own place within or apart from that institution" (4). Linde believes that while institutions may "remember," the relevant question to ask when dissecting an institutional history, or memory, is, "is it the institutions that remember, or is it the people within them who do the remembering?" (8). Because Linde contends that "any historical account must be understood as being the history of someone, for someone, for some purpose," she resists the notion that either institutional documents, or official archives, *or* personal narratives/interviews can in isolation accurately provide us with a full institutional memory for future use (9). Instead, Linde believes that "remembering does not happen until these [aggregate] materials are used in ongoing interaction" (12), as checks against one another and as documents designed to make meaning actively rather than simply transcribe passively their past meanings, historically speaking.

Linde's definition of narrative—the core methodology upon which many institutional archives, and our readings of them, are built—comes from a wide variety of resources, including personal histories but also textual documents that tell the story of how the institution itself has narrated and preserved its historical legacy, through "meetings, speeches, conventions" as well as personal and shared artifacts (45, 67). Even class reunions, Linde argues, can serve as institutional narratives that "create the institution by remembering it" (53). This is due to Linde's twofold definition of *institution,* which can be "both formal and informal groupings of people and established recognizable practices" (7). In Linde's terms, the Woman's College would of course be deemed an institution, but so would its English department, as well as smaller groups within that department, such as the first-year writers who created and published the department's first-year composition magazine in the early 1950s, or the creative writing and literature faculty who sat on the English department composition committee and contributed to its curricular reform between 1954 and 1956. Keeping this fluid definition of institution in mind, Linde argues that the purpose of her study is to acknowledge that "institutions and people within institutions do not mechanically record and reproduce the past. Rather, they work the past, re-presenting it each time in new but related ways for a particular purpose, in a particular form that uses the past to create a particular desired present and future. These forms of representation of the past are not identical, but their differences themselves are important to study. There are important patterns in the way stories are reproduced and the ways they are changed" (14).

To apply Linde's core contention to composition studies is to re-envision its history as one of its people, those who "work" the past through competing narratives, some of which are heard and some silenced. Linde's claim that these representations create a "particular desired present and future" fits well with the politically charged history of composition and rhetoric, particularly the fraught first-year requirement that desires, in its field history, to be a course of continual progress and imminent theoretical realization—that is, a course that covers its tracks and learns from its historical mistakes in order to improve upon the progress of its inhabitants (student writers). Composition also desires to be a course that can be "universally" dropped into any institutional location with some expected degree of conformity—that is, a "one size fits all" model, regardless of that institution's history or local needs. As I argued in *Before Shaughnessy,* this blanket application of one course type or model to any and all settings is a troubling practice, and a historically fractured one at that.

Linde's theory of institutional narratives, however, reminds us that any universal, functional application of an institution—in this case, first-year composition—ignores the historical realities of its own meaning-making and competing narrative emphases. To translate to our current view of archival work in composition studies, Linde would likely argue that by focusing for many years on how prestigious private and large public institutions "do" composition, and by declaring that the histories of all-male (usually white male) colleges and universities represent the course into the future, across all other institutional types, we are turning a deaf ear to the voices struggling to make alternate meanings from that history. We are, in effect, ignoring the fact that the most important event in the life of the story of an institution is when it breaks from its origin stories and "moves to a new generation of tellers," since "if a story does not acquire new tellers, it can have no life beyond the life of the original person who experienced the events and first formulated them as a story" (Linde 73–74).

In his seminal archival work on the history of composition and rhetoric, Robert Connors states, "In a sense, the history of composition-rhetoric in America is a history of how this heretofore 'elementary' instruction took over a commanding place in most teachers' ideas of rhetoric" (*Composition-Rhetoric* 127–28). Following Connors's work, the narrative of composition studies' history has almost always centered on its movement from a perceived solution to student illiteracies at Harvard, to a widespread required course devoid of intellectual value and dreaded by faculty, but favored by institutions seeking "practical" training for growing first-year classes, to an uncomfortable ugly-cousin course of major (including graduate) study in the English department, despite its regular calls for independence from this (as it is argued) master-slave disciplinary relationship.

Connors's equation brought to the surface the importance of recovering the major trajectories of writing instruction, in the context of our cultural history, and spotlighting the waves of theory that have permeated our writing classrooms. But we continue to characterize composition studies at the institutional level—as a machinery rather than a field populated by specific individuals over time—largely due to Connors's spotlight on said machinery. Also in *Composition-Rhetoric,* Connors purports to cover "older and newer forms of composition-rhetoric, of school and university rhetorics, of women's rhetorics and men's. To do otherwise would be to reduce the formidable complexity of the situation" (7). Yet even as Connors devotes his first chapter to "Gender Influences," this discussion only attends to elite women's colleges and the admission of women to coeducational institutions in the late nineteenth and early twentieth centuries. Though Connors contends that 70 percent of all universities admitted women by 1900, he makes no mention of the vast number of normal schools or teachers colleges also educating primarily or only women during this pre–World War I era, noting instead the power of the feminization of the discipline due to the influence of women rhetors within these elite and coeducational institutional structures. Additionally—because to do so is not his particular historical project—Connors makes little mention of the position of creative writing as first-year composition's rival suitor for the funds, people-power, and social intellectual energies of the English department at large, particularly postwar. We find a similar lack of attention to women's education in other major field histories, such as James Berlin's *Rhetoric and Reality.*

I believe there can be a more intricate and nuanced definition and exploration of women's composing within composition studies' history than Connors tries to provide, one that is dependent upon local conditions and key individuals and one that highlights rather than glosses this history across institutional types. In the case of many colleges and universities, these local conditions revolve around conflicting student and faculty definitions of *literacy,* the value of the creative versus the expository in first-year writing, and the individuals who have been the decision makers versus the ones upon whom decisions were foisted. I argue we now should dislodge our historical analysis of writing instruction from a critique of the institution of composition studies and its politicized machinery and relocate it instead in a larger contextual analysis of the predilections and communal values of its people, famous, infamous, and unknown, or heretofore unnamed. This latter group encompasses the student writers as well as the faculty/teachers who inhabit the institution, those whose stories have not been told, who have not been "the tellers," in Linde's terms, including, in some cases, those who worked in and were influenced by the confluence of creative writing and composition studies in the midtwentieth century.

Linde also notes that "the highest ranked member of the institution" usually tells the story of that institution (203); in the case of composition studies, this member is often the external teacher/scholar who narrates the history of a program or programs, or prevalent pedagogy across programs, from the point of view of an outsider. But that teller is speaking from an external position, first, and is therefore unable to fully represent the local; this was my position in researching Yale and Harvard. Second, that teller is often re-presenting the story of the most dominant voices, whereas there are also "noisy silences" to be represented, or "silences in one situation about matters spoken loudly or in whispers in other situations" (Linde 197). These are what we commonly refer to, in our culture, as counternarratives; in composition studies, these include the voices of women students and faculty whose stories have not been fully represented in the history of first-year writing, and who were sometimes also the voices of teachers and students of creative writing within or beside composition curricula. Even though there has been measurable attention paid to the feminization of composition via the significant number of underpaid, overworked composition *teachers* (see Holbrook; S. Miller; and Schell), far less attention has been paid to women as viable, agentic *students,* or as student-writers, in any subgenre of English studies. Their "noisy silences" are what I aim to represent in this book through a case study of postwar writing instruction at the Woman's College.

Such a singular case study of women's writing as this book attempts is sorely needed, because despite the significant number of archival studies in rhetoric and composition over the past twenty-five years, taking many shapes and spotlighting myriad scholarly agendas, little has been documented that works toward a historical counternarrative of any kind of the institution that is composition studies, and few studies have as their author an individual with a personal role, past or present, in the institution being studied. Archival works have catalogued and interpreted key historical documents in the genesis and growth of the field (John Brereton's

The Origins of Composition Studies; Jean Ferguson Carr, Stephen Carr, and Lucille Schultz's *Archives of Instruction*), and have reviewed and classified key pedagogical movements in the field (James Berlin's aforementioned *Rhetoric and Reality* and his *Writing Instruction in Nineteenth Century American Colleges*). Archival work has also critically analyzed the politics of our field's history (Sharon Crowley's *Composition in the University;* Susan Miller's *Textual Carnivals;* Robert Connors's aforementioned *Composition-Rhetoric*), as well as turned a narrow lens on subgroups within composition and rhetoric (Barbara L'Eplattenier and Lisa Mastrangelo's *Historical Studies of Writing Program Administration;* Mary Soliday's *The Politics of Remediation;* Patricia McAlexander and Nicole Pepinster Greene's *Basic Writing in America*). In far fewer cases, scholars of the archives have studied specific programs, in isolation or in like groupings (Robin Varnum's *Fencing with Words;* Brent Henze, Jack Selzer, and Wendy Sharer's *1977: A Cultural Moment in Composition;* Thomas Masters's *Practicing Writing;* Patricia Donahue and Gretchen Fleischer Moon's *Local Histories*). In addition to these book-length studies, there have also been numerous archives-based articles and chapters by these authors and many others appearing in our journals' pages over the past several years.[2]

To index further the scope and professional reach of archival work, one can see its emphasis in the literature of composition studies in broader, more theoretical ways. For example, scholars such as Shirley Rose and Irwin Weiser have stressed the importance of archival work in locating and establishing the historical narratives of the administration of composition and rhetoric programs in "The WPA as Researcher and Archivist," and Robert Schwegler has compiled and catalogued a variety of primary documents, including first-year writing textbooks, that also narrate the field through the National Archives of Composition and Rhetoric at the University of Rhode Island. Susan Miller's *The Norton Book of Composition Studies* also privileges historical and archival work, including excerpts of some of the archival studies named above, in its aim to provide a comprehensive, quasi-chronological overview of the field for new scholars, particularly graduate students teaching first-year writing. One could additionally argue that the database Comppile (www.comppile.org), under the leadership of Richard Haswell and Glenn Blalock, is itself an archival repository of the scholarship of the field, particularly in its cataloguing of lesser-studied pieces from the early years of composition and rhetoric journals, aiding new and established scholars alike in navigating the field's history.

Yet even as this plethora of historical perspectives on rhetoric and composition points to a growing interest in developing a collective narrative about the history of writing instruction at the postsecondary level, scholars such as David Gold have pointed out that this narrative continues to be peppered with gaps, specifically those created and perpetuated by our own ignorance of how marginalized student voices in composition studies have shaped our collective history. As Gold argues in *Rhetoric at the Margins,* we do not know enough about lesser-studied corners of education, such as historically black colleges and universities and women's public colleges, and what we do know (or think we know) is too often driven by "an assumption that innovation begins at elite colleges" (ix). Gold believes that studying institutional types that seem "marginal" to historians of education allows us to "illuminat[e] the development of writing and rhetoric instruction in America as a whole" since "small-scale histories can illuminate, inform, challenge, and inspire larger histories" (7) of writing instruction. Gold's complaint is one that I also frequently hear from new teaching assistants and graduate students who wonder, as they read the large-scale histories of composition and rhetoric of Berlin and Connors, where the stories of our diverse, multifaceted students have been told. Where are the "real" women students and students of color whom they see in their first-year writing classes day after day, semester after semester? If these stories have not been told, these beginning instructors and scholars ask, why not?

Another noticeable oversight in this dominant archival history of composition studies is the absence of study regarding other types of writing as they have intersected with the development of first-year composition. While the infamous Tate-Lindemann debate has served as one public marker of the conflict between literature and composition, and while historical accounts of composition frequently emphasize the acquisition of literary "taste" and textual analysis as the backbone of early composition curricula, far less attention has been paid to the relationship of composition to creative writing.[3]

But such a relationship is important to explore. Creative writing is another comparatively "young" field within the university English department, and one that has a contested history told by dominant voices, especially those in graduate programs, and those teaching at historically prestigious institutions. Our larger histories of composition studies sometimes mention the intersection of creative writing and composition, and more rarely, the larger histories of creative writing as they nod to composition (see, for example, D. G. Myers's *The Elephants Teach*). But rarely do historians treat this intersection with any depth, certainly never breaking its history out into smaller pieces classified by multiethnic or gendered voices, or postsecondary institutions that have served those populations.

As such, the narratives of writing per se—those that detail the overlaps, conflicts, and juxtapositions that creative and expository writing have experienced in postsecondary English departments and writing programs—have been almost completely ignored by the archival scholars of our field.[4]

This book thus advances Gold's call in *Rhetoric at the Margins* for a spotlight on marginalized voice *types* in the history of composition studies by focusing on the inhabitants of a women's public college, but also takes that call one step further by complicating the pedagogical and institutional *content* of this history through a cross-examination of composition and creative writing as intertwined curricular activities and intellectual impulses in the Woman's College postwar. This focused dual analysis of writing at the Woman's College also clearly brings to bear my own cross-training in creative writing and composition, and casts it in an archival light—thus bringing my interests in history and writing full circle, but with good historical reasons. Too infrequently do we problematize the growth of allied fields until they suddenly are at war with each other—as creative writing and composition are in many English departments today. Understanding their shared histories through close examination of one sample institution—in this case the Woman's College/UNCG, an institution that is home to one of the oldest MFA programs in creative writing in the United States, proposed, developed, and refined during the postwar years—we can expand and improve our individual archival understandings of "writing studies" across these related fields, and take that expanded understanding into our own current writing programs for consideration or healthy debate.

Finally, it is important for me to note that the historical study in this book is designed, in large part, to celebrate underrepresented voices in their own right, rather than to use them as a vocal counterstatement to dominant histories of male voices in composition studies' archival histories. There is much to champion in studying women's writing for its own sake—its triumphs and progressive actions and actors—without setting it as the other voice that must speak against, or in opposition to, the male-centered, or more privileged, histories that have been highlighted before it. Similarly, this book does not aim to argue for a deeply hybrid notion of writing studies by virtue of its focus on the shared institutional history of creative writing and composition within this women's college setting.

Instead, I recognize that keeping our current pedagogical practices and ideologies responsible to our past is a continual challenge for those of us who direct first-year writing programs; at the same time, engaging new teachers in the narratives that have shaped who and what composition studies is at our own institutions seems a logical step in promoting and characterizing the current position and value of local enactments of first-year writing vis-à-vis the local past. Sometimes, these pasts were populated with strong creative writing influences, as in the case of the Woman's College/UNCG; in other cases, there were "creative" utterances that were less audible, but which bore a slow and steady influence on the politics and production of the first-year writing program. These influences, positive or negative, are worthy of our current attention.

As one newly minted teaching assistant recently posited during discussion in my pedagogy seminar last year, "it would be helpful if [the field's histories] focused on some of the more positive aspects of these [first-year] courses in addition to telling us what is so horrible about them." She raises a valid point. In our zeal to sometimes demonize the past and illustrate how far we have come in our theories and practices of writing instruction, we frequently forget that there are, in fact, enlightening and perhaps even progressive narratives of literacy instruction that have been elided in favor of the mass reconstruction of our misguided ways, and that some of these positive narratives may be found within our own institutional histories. To see the history of a community such as composition studies as a history of how its people interact with/in their institutional structures, we can begin to privilege the success stories—however small—and the less-studied voices of those success stories, as a critical part of our collective field history. For those who, like myself, serve as writing program administrators, noting this history of the positive alongside the negative is certainly as important as recognizing the history of the marginalized alongside the dominant in our archival work.

About This Book

To Know Her Own History is a sociohistorical study that focuses on the intertwined histories of first-year composition and creative writing at a public Southern women's college in the mid-twentieth century in order to examine how evolving definitions of literacy, as well as evolving views of women as writers, shaped American college writing instruction during the postwar era. I offer new historical insight into the historical happenings in women's writing postwar through an extended case study of the English department of the Woman's College of the University of North Carolina, and spotlight the national curricular trends and local institutional conditions that affected this college's students and faculty. These include the difficult economic conditions inherent to a Southern women's college during this financially precarious postwar period, wherein large, coeducational universities that served a variety of populations effectively grew to dominate the American educational landscape.

To Know Her Own History argues for the value of underrecognized narratives, such as those of women's public college students, that make up our collective history of rhetoric and composition studies. In reclaiming the literacy histories at work in this particular institution during the postwar era, and telling its heretofore untold stories, I mean to use the Woman's College as an archival vehicle with which to explore three central questions that add to existing archival perspectives on composition studies today. First, how was public education for women, particularly women's writing instruction, shaped by two influential movements in higher education—the general education movement and the surge in creative arts instruction—during these two decades of the twentieth century? Second, in what ways did the rise of the status of creative writing at the college level undermine or lessen the visibility and importance of rhetorical and/or expository instruction in first-year writing at the Woman's College, as just one institution among those so critical to postwar educational opportunities for women, the (evolving) teachers' college? And finally, what contested definitions of literacy and schooling arose during this critical era in writing instruction at the Woman's College that might provoke similar archival investigations into the histories of other English departments and writing programs across the country?

This book's investigation begins in 1943, as the postwar period of American education (and culture) begins to take shape, and ends in 1963, the year in which the Woman's College was compelled by state legislators to become a coeducational branch campus of the University of North Carolina. During these twenty years, the attitude toward writing and writing instruction at the Woman's College was atypical and progressive in comparison with its single-sex public college counterparts, and was influenced by a deep appreciation of the literary and the fine arts and a desire to grow its burgeoning program in creative writing. This progressive stance toward creativity in the curriculum emerged in part from the historical mantra of the college's founder, Charles McIver, who proclaimed the importance of women's postsecondary education in his decree that when "you educate the man, you educate an individual; when you educate the woman, you educate a family." This education, meant to extend to a woman's domestic and professional spheres of influence, emphasized a melding of vocational and intellectual training, which in writing and

English studies meant a creativity of mind and eloquence of expression, in addition to the more pedestrian grammatical correctness and clarity. To be well versed in English studies, in terms of literary history, speech communication, and writing, was one of the most important attributes that a woman should possess upon graduation; such a belief was demonstrated in the two-year program in English that was required of all Woman's College students, unique among peer institutions during this time.

The faculty at the Woman's College, many of whom were women as well as active scholars and writers themselves, shaped and encouraged the development of their students' literacy both inside and outside the classroom, through an extensive curriculum of expository, creative, and journalistic writing courses beyond the first year compulsory course; an annual departmental first-year magazine written, edited, and produced by composition students; and a university-wide literary magazine—also staffed and sponsored by the English department, in conjunction with regular literary festivals and campus readings. *To Know Her Own History* contextualizes these intertwined components of curricular choice and social and cultural training at the Woman's College during this twenty-year period. The book also demonstrates the often problematic interdependence of composition and creative writing that resulted from the department's whole-writer training agenda, as these two areas of study were in direct competition for both material and sociocultural resources in the English department, itself struggling to manage its programs during this era of limited resources. Such a tug-of-war over resources certainly resonates today, and was a reality at that time for the Woman's College as well, despite its status as the premier public institution for women in the South.

This legacy of the public, state-supported women's college, largely lost to the drastic economic turns in higher education occurring during the mid-1960s and to the absorption of normal schools into larger institutions, now deserves to be rediscovered for composition studies scholarship via a detailed, historical discussion of its little-known institutional literacy histories and their significance to Southern education specifically, as well as women's education generally. *To Know Her Own History* aims to fulfill this need, and as such is a continuation of the line of inquiry I began with *Before Shaughnessy,* in which I argued that the construction of writing programs should be local rather than global, and that it should utilize site-specific values and needs rather than slavishly follow a principle of universal curricular design. *To Know Her Own History* narrows the institutional subject of study from two colleges to one, but actually widens my scope of inquiry, as it more fully regards personal, archival narratives as the substance of our own programmatic futures. Unlike *Before Shaughnessy*, in which I was unable to represent the individual voices of students or faculty as part of my analysis, *To Know Her Own History* draws in part upon oral interviews with three surviving alumnae, as well as other personal documents and photographs of or about these students and faculty, including the composition and creative writing program directors themselves, so as to reinforce perhaps the most important argument underlying a project such as this: that the history of composition studies is, in fact, a history of its people.

Each chapter focuses on one integral part of the story of writing at the Woman's College postwar. Chapter 1 provides a brief overview of the history of the college, as well as a comparative history of its standing versus other contemporary women's institutions. It then situates the Woman's College in the context of normal schools in the early to mid-twentieth century and in the setting of the American South and its cultural traditions for women's education, using work by scholars of women's rhetoric and women's education. I make the argument in this chapter that the intellectual tradition of the Woman's College was certainly influenced by its teacher-training roots, but that it also heavily resembled the progressive curricular impulses of the elite northeastern schools. I also argue that, given the preponderance of current colleges and universities in the United States that are former teacher colleges or normal schools, the roots of women's education should perhaps be the true core of any archival study of twentieth-century writing outside the Ivy League. Despite its two strong institutional influences, the Woman's College, as an example of this legacy, occupied a separate position in the spectrum of women's education due to its mission to be a premier site for the education of (white) Southern women. This unique and progressive stance allowed for greater attention to women as not just students of writing, but also as future writers.

Chapter 2 examines the early part of the postwar era in the English department of the Woman's College via a study of the first-year writing magazine the *Yearling*. Proposed in 1944 by May Bush, director of first-year writing in the department of English, and put into print in 1948, it was led by a team of undergraduate student editors from the first-year composition sections. The *Yearling* was an annual publication between 1948 and 1951 that profiled creative as well as expository/argumentative pieces of writing produced by first-year students in the English department. The publication was a revival of the annual magazine published by the department's composition program in 1929 and 1930, the *Sample Case*. My analysis of this publication uncovers a blurring of the boundaries of "creative" and "expository" in the first-year writings spotlighted in this magazine, which complicates the traditional notions of writing pedagogy both in mid-century America in general and in public women's schools specifically. The alumnae interviews provide an added dimension to the archival analysis of the magazine, as well as the often contradictory position of Woman's College students as both "proper" ladies and sometimes radical prose writers. As such, the interviews alongside the textual analyses in this chapter collectively argue that the voices and narratives of the women of this college, and other colleges like it, are critical to our deeper understanding of this period of American women's literacy instruction—a period that is typically characterized as stagnant in its development of students as writers, and about which little has been said regarding *women* student-writers at all.

The third chapter of this book takes a larger administrative view of writing and literacy in its discussion of the year-long revision to the Woman's College first-year composition course, English 101, completed at the height of general education reform sweeping the nation. To give readers some additional historical context, I discuss the aims of the general education movement as articulated at Harvard University and in other elite and public institutions. I then detail the faculty work done at the Woman's College during this year of revision at both the university level and at the department level.

The impulses at work in these revisions included, at the university level, determining how general education could be revised to promote a more elite view of the college, and at the department level, settling on the question of whether or how much literature would be included in the curriculum, as well as attending to the curricular and financial resources that would shift to the burgeoning undergraduate track in creative writing. Importantly, at both university and departmental levels, the question of "What is an educated woman?" was at the forefront—a stark contrast to the discussions severely delineating women as separate-but-equal at Harvard, where modern concepts of general education were, arguably, born. Given also that these particular decades of the Woman's College ushered in both the first basic writing courses and the start of continual curricular proposals for a graduate concentration in creative writing, this chapter spotlights how the Woman's College curriculum was, in many ways, emblematic of the two ends of the spectrum of writing education emerging in this country, particularly at public colleges postwar. It aims to illustrate in large part what ways *writing* and *literacy* thus proved to be difficult terms for the members of the English department to define during this transitional and volatile period in the institution's history, and in the history of composition studies as it intersected with creative writing nationwide.

Chapter 4 telescopes to a more personal view of writing at the Woman's College, as it juxtaposes two faculty members at the school between 1947 and 1963: the poet Randall Jarrell, who elevated the visibility of the Woman's College both regionally and nationally through his advocacy for undergraduate and graduate creative writing instruction, and literature professor May Bush, who directed the first-year composition program for many years and whose institutional and financial status was continually limited both by her position as composition director and by the concomitant success of Randall Jarrell and the creative writing program. This chapter augments the positive ways that Jarrell and creative writing influenced composition and his unwitting negative influence, specifically the financial support his position and status required, financial support demanded to meet counteroffers from other institutions that was therefore unavailable for raises and promotions for Bush and other women faculty. I also profile Bush's extremely low and private profile through her thirty-four-year tenure at the Woman's College, and thereby spotlight her as an example of an early writing program administrator who embodied many of the longstanding complaints associated with composition-related work in the university today: minimal visibility, low pay, and secondary faculty status as compared to more high-profile faculty in other fields of English studies. Overall, this chapter turns a lens on some salient institutional politics of writing instruction and writing faculty present in the English department midcentury, using the Woman's College as a local case study.

Finally, in Chapter 5 I examine the arguments for and against the demise of the Woman's College as a single-sex institution in 1964, in the context of state politics and the expanding reach of the UNC system, in order to argue that other faculty, in particular fellow writing program administrators (WPAs), should conduct similar archival research and collect oral narratives on the histories of writing instruction and literacy at their own institutions, especially those WPAs who work at smaller public colleges and/or colleges targeted at particular populations whose narratives are fated to be lost to history, just as the Woman's College, as an institution valuing women's literacy, was itself lost. Such widespread work would help scholar WPAs to shape their own institutional futures by gaining a clear understanding of how the past continues to shape us as people (students, teachers, writers) and as inhabitants of writing programs nationwide. It would also call attention to the important histories that have been represented as singular or singularly voiced, as opposed to communally represented. This movement could ultimately lead to a new understanding of local archival research as not only cataloguing the past, but also troubling and resituating the present for writing programs within all institutional types.

1

Her History Matters

The United States Normal School and the
Roots of Women's Public Education

IF YOU ARE a faculty member or a student at a public university that is not the "flagship" institution of your state—for example, Eastern Michigan University as opposed to the University of Michigan, or Georgia State University as opposed to the University of Georgia—then your campus was originally a teachers college, or "normal school," in the parlance of nineteenth- and early-twentieth-century educational terminology. A significant number of our public universities in the United States today are former normal schools or state teachers colleges—189, to be exact.[1] These institutions were, in many cases, geographically situated to attract rural students who otherwise could not receive a college education, but who were in need of a useful and viable trade to practice in their home communities. In other cases, normal schools were situated in urban areas, near flagship (and all-male) campuses, to provide quasi-allied educational functions for those not allowed to attend these institutions, that is, women and African-American students. Many of these institutions that started as women's-only normal schools remained all-women's general colleges through the mid-twentieth century, including the Woman's College at the University of North Carolina, even after their original charters as teacher training institutions had been abandoned in the progressive era of higher education. But then the 1950s and 1960s ushered in financial and social pressures for both coeducational and demographically opportune campuses, and this led to the final demise of the all-women's public college or university as a known and respected institutional type in the United States.

Normal schools are therefore not only an important, if overlooked, part of the history of higher education in the United States; they are also critically important to understanding the position of women in American public colleges in the twentieth century, and particularly the postsecondary training of women as writers, since normal school students were charged, in large part, with shaping the literacies of their own primary and secondary pupils. Without this large number of normal schools providing a point of access to women where there otherwise were few avenues for learning, one may postulate that the legacy of women in higher education would be far more limited today—conscribed to the history of elite private schools and the slow integration of women into flagship state schools and Ivy League institutions, which in several cases did not occur until quite late in the twentieth century.[2]

To understand the fuller history of an institution such as the Woman's College of the University of North Carolina, therefore, one must understand its earlier past, including its origins as a normal school. Recovering and contextualizing this past also brings the Woman's College, as a local case study of the great number of women who sought a college education postwar and who were engaged in course work that sprung from a teachers college mission, into clearer and broader disciplinary focus for scholars of rhetoric and composition studies.

The students of the Woman's College, like their counterparts at other former normal schools, bore vestiges of the original institutional mission, even as the institution underwent sociocultural as well as curricular modifications throughout the twentieth century. At the Woman's College, archival records of curricular offerings and student written work show that despite its beginnings in the oft-conservative teachings of the normal school, its instructional aims in English—specifically composition and rhetoric—were more progressive than the contemporary norm for prior teachers colleges. In fact, the Woman's College curricular impulses that added creative writing to the curriculum as early as the 1930s exhibit a philosophy of writing education more commonly found at the elite private schools for women—the so-called "Seven Sisters" schools (Wellesley, Smith, Vassar, Radcliffe, Barnard, Bryn Mawr, and Mount Holyoke) founded between 1837 and 1889, concomitant with the founding period of American normal schools. Even though few women who attended the Woman's College and other similar southern single-sex institutions likely "viewed their entrance as a symbolic statement of sexual equality" (McCandless 103), and despite the regional conditions of the South which kept its admission of women to public flagship institutions at bay well into the 1960s, I posit that the college's stance on writing education did, in fact, set it apart from the typical teachers college, and put it more on a par with elite, private colleges for women.

Clearly there existed a visible class differential between the typical normal school and the more-often-studied elite northeastern colleges through the mid-twentieth century, when normal schools began to be swallowed up by state systems, such as the University of North Carolina system's appropriation of the Woman's College for its coeducational Greensboro campus in 1964. But as Kathryn Fitzgerald argues, the tradition of the normal school is unique and ripe for study, given that it was "grounded in a very different intellectual perspective from the rhetorical tradition of composition," namely the European system of education (231). Even as this divergent intellectual tradition unique to normal school training is highlighted, however—one which privileged sequencing and scaffolding lessons, "building associations between the old and the new" and "inductive-deductive" principles (Fitzgerald 233)—the social aim of these institutions to produce classroom teachers and to produce ladies of tact and intelligence who would handle themselves admirably in the classroom necessarily constricted their ability to be very revolutionary in scope, particularly in the subculture of the American South. Despite these constraints, the Woman's College, first named the State Normal and Industrial College, made significant inroads regarding individual approaches to literacy, and literacy instruction, as evident in its curriculum as well as its extracurricular, writing-focused activities.

In this chapter, I turn my attention to the institutional history of the normal school as it pertains to English composition and literacy education, and the Woman's College's specific pedagogical approach to writing education as part of, and sometimes in contrast to, that history. I employ archival records from the Woman's College, including samples of the short-lived literary magazine the *Sample Case,* produced by students in the first-year writing classes in the academic year 1929–30, to illustrate the curricular trends and writing emphases within the English department during the period 1913–31, covering the last eighteen years of its existence as a normal school and its transition to a general women's college.

I also discuss some prominent perspectives on women's education in the twentieth century, including the juxtaposition of the normal school versus the elite women's college, so as to foreground my discussion in later chapters of the ways in which women were educated as writers, postwar, at the Woman's College.

My purpose in providing this broader history is twofold. First, as noted above, I feel it is necessary to provide a larger historical context for the normal school and its typical positioning as inferior to contemporary elite women's colleges, or even other public coeducational colleges; and second, this broader history of women's education highlights some lingering questions about the intellectual and social position of the writer in his or her cultural milieu, and the sociocultural components of the teaching of writing that may be generalized to composition studies as a field, and thus deserve to be more prominent in our archival studies of writing instruction.

Normal Schools versus Elite Women's Colleges

During the twenty-year period of American prosperity following World War II, the social import of writing and communication at many women's colleges qua normal schools was still rooted in, if slowly emerging from, a specific socioeducational tradition that separated these schools culturally from the eastern elite women's colleges. As a normal school that was transformed into a general women's college in 1931,[3] the Woman's College of the University of North Carolina for its last decades of single-sex existence was heavily influenced by its original charter purpose and legacy, particularly in terms of its mission to provide a sound and challenging college education for southern women, and to provide them with the tools to be independent writers and thinkers in an American subculture that often did not privilege the professional capabilities of women's minds, or their valuable position in the larger workforce.

As historian Amy Thompson McCandless details, upon its merger with the University of North Carolina system in 1931 that followed many years as an independent women's public institution, the Woman's College "lost all programs of 'professional and specialized training' except those for teachers and secretaries" (90). The small secretarial (or "commercial") class, in particular, persisted well into the 1960s at the college. McCandless also asserts that though "never specifically stated, one object of the consolidation was the transfer of all undergraduate women to the Greensboro campus," as legislators saw women as inappropriate additions to the culture and mission of the men's campus in Chapel Hill (90). In chapter 5,

I support that assertion, through Chancellor Singletary's speaking notes about the campus "tariff" imposed to keep all (public) college women in North Carolina at one institution: the Woman's College.

Just one year prior to this first system merger, in 1930, elite Duke University—which had historically admitted women students with day (non-residential) status since the 1890s—opened a parallel institution, or "coordinate" college, also called the Woman's College, within its Trinity College of the liberal arts. This women's college remained in operation until 1972. Like its public (and identically named) counterpart in Greensboro, the Duke Woman's College perpetuated the notion that a single-sex college was not only appropriate, but optimal, for southern women, appealing to a certain segment of the population that believed in the possible rigor, and cultural importance, of sex-segregated education. At the same time, separating women students from the general Duke population communicated a similar message, in historical hindsight, to the paternalistic message being sent by the University of North Carolina system: that women were, in fact, neither desirable nor appropriate community members within these flagship public and prominent private institutions (considering Duke's shorthand moniker, the "Harvard of the South").[4] The prevalence of small colleges for women only—affiliated, incidentally, with the church—such as Peace and Meredith Colleges in Raleigh, North Carolina, reinforced and significantly enabled this perception, resituating women in a church-related, segregated venue for "proper" learning.

Indeed, the prevalence of single-sex education was widespread in the South as compared to other regions of the United States. Despite the fact that by 1900 more than 70 percent of institutions located west of the Mississippi admitted women (the percentage that Robert Connors also cites in his discussion of women in *Composition-Rhetoric*), a full 66 percent of the women's colleges in the United States were in the South, and only six of the southern region's (white) universities were coeducational (McCandless 84). The Woman's College was the only public women's college in North Carolina, and was more specifically the college for *white* women, as its original charter as the State Normal and Industrial College clearly states (in contrast to Bennett College, also in Greensboro, which was a private college for African-American women).[5] There were, comparatively, six other public colleges in the state for African-American students, and one other for Native American students. Four of these seven schools continue to operate today, each continuing its mission of primarily serving its originally targeted student population (Elizabeth City State University; Fayetteville State University; and Winston-Salem State University, for primarily African-American men and women—though Fayetteville was originally an African-American women's teachers college; and the University of North Carolina–Pembroke (UNCP), for Native American men and women).[6]

It is clear from an examination of the historical wave of coeducational admissions in the 1960s and 1970s that, on the one hand, southern women had a plethora of single-sex institutions from which to choose—including some with religious/sectarian missions—in their home region, and so were not as excluded from higher education as they otherwise might be. In addition to the Woman's College in Greensboro, for example, and the Woman's College at Duke, there were several freestanding private women's colleges of varying selectivity in North Carolina from the early twentieth century forward, including the aforementioned Bennett, Peace, and Meredith Colleges.

On the other hand, southern women were at a stark disadvantage if they were only able to pursue a degree in or near their home communities and wanted a *coeducational* experience. These students were limited first to normal schools—which almost without exception admitted women, and were in many cases women-only—and later, to these regional women's public and private colleges, which offered relatively low tuition (in the case of the Woman's College and other public men's colleges) and a "safe" environment for women whose families feared their foray into strange, new, male, urban environments—a fear reflected in the remembrances of my interview subjects in chapter 2. Only those who had the means to travel West for a public, coeducational experience, or North for a menu of elite private women's college experiences, would have a full complement of postsecondary educational choices. Thus, the normal school became, through subcultural and distinctively regional traditions, the root of the preponderance of women's higher education in the South.

The American normal school was "established in a completely different social and educational environment from the elite schools," these being most commonly the subject of study for scholars of women's education (Fitzgerald 225–26). As an institutional type, the normal school has been grossly overlooked in our collective histories of women's education specifically, and higher education generally, as Christine Ogren argues in her extensive study, *The American Normal School: "An Instrument of Great Good."* Ogren carefully details the origins of the normal school and its rise as a prominent choice for both men and women in the late nineteenth and early twentieth centuries in America. She notes that prior to the advent of the first normal school circa 1850, colleges had "produced teachers rather unintentionally, in the process of preparing graduates to be ministers, doctors, lawyers, and college professors" (16). Ogren contends that with the emergence of female seminaries, such as Mount Holyoke Seminary in Massachusetts, these founding institutions "articulated teacher education—alongside motherhood—as a primary mission" (17). What began as struggling departments for teacher education at some larger state schools quickly turned into specialized institutions of learning, starting in Connecticut and Michigan, and quickly spreading to New York, Pennsylvania, California, Maine, Kansas, Illinois, and Minnesota in the 1850s and 1860s (Ogren 24).

The legislation for the normal school was fairly similar from state to state, as Ogren notes, providing Michigan's legislation as an example: "That a Normal School be established, the exclusive purpose of which shall be the instruction of persons both male and female in the art of teaching, and in all the various branches that pertain to a good common school education" (24). Further, these legislative acts asked that applicants be "examined for good moral character and a proclivity for teaching" and that said applicants be asked to sign a declaration that they would "follow the business of teaching primary schools in this State," or pursue a career in public school teaching in their local communities as a condition of the degree (25).

What is interesting about these conditions put upon the early normal schools is their emphasis on the social and ethical standing of the candidates themselves. If we consider the stated dual importance of teaching and "mothering," or family life, for women candidates during this era, as well as the "good moral character" required of the applicants, it seems clear that schools were, in many ways, sites of cultural as well as intellectual training, especially given Ogren's contention that many of the normal school students were young women (and men) who had never left their home communities—often in rural areas—and thus had little knowledge of the ways of the larger culture. Ogren also notes that "normal school students were immersed in the language of consecration. Their instructors consistently placed teaching on a higher plane than other pursuits." She adds that David Perkins Page, an early principal of the Albany, New York, normal school who had a strong influence on nineteenth-century teacher education practices, wrote in his *Theory and Practice of Teaching* that the rewards of teaching included "intellectual and moral growth, the satisfaction of helping others to grow, the honor of joining the ranks of Confucius, Aristotle, and Plato, and the *approval of heaven*" (Ogren 44; emphasis in original).

This near-beatification of the teacher was surely made more possible with candidates of (arguably) pure moral character, who coincidentally were, in the case of all-female southern normal schools, "pure" young women of unmarried status, not in small part due to the so-called marriage bar commonly imposed upon women who sought work as teachers. As Claudia Goldin argues, this marriage bar kept married women from being hired in many school districts (and businesses), and gave cause for those who were allowed to marry while employed to be fired if and when they became pregnant (160).[7] As such, the majority of women who completed normal school training would find themselves actively working only if they remained single, in an idealized state for instructional purposes in which students would be neither distracted nor "confused" by the sexualization of women's bodies in the form and status of marriage and pregnancy (Goldin 160, 170).

The issue of marriage—and one's marriage prospects after entering the teaching profession—were clearly a cultural concern for women in the South midcentury. As published in the August 25, 1940, issue of *Science News Letter*, southern women schoolteachers were, paradoxically, both more and less likely to marry than their nonteaching counterparts:

> Prospects of women schoolteachers getting married have been reduced to cold statistics by Harold H. Punke, sociologist of Georgia State Women's College. While the marriage rate for school-ma'ams is highest at 22 to 24 years, as it is for other native white American women with whom he compared them, schoolteachers in their twenties who must resign to marry have a marriage rate only one-half to five-eighths as great as non-teaching contemporaries, he states (*American Sociological Review*, August). Beyond 40 years of age, however, schoolteachers marry at a greater rate than women of that age in general, he finds. Mr. Punke's study was made in a southern city of over 300,000, in which women teachers until very recently were not permitted to teach after marriage. ("School Ma'ams' Marriages Statistically Analyzed," 125)

An interesting comparative to the history of the normal school in the United States, and the marriage issue for southern American women teachers, may be found in Great Britain. As Elizabeth Edwards points out in her study of the "culture of femininity" at the teachers colleges of England from 1900 to 1960, its demise in the late 1950s through early 1960s—roughly the same era in which public women's colleges, many of which were former normal schools, were being eliminated in the United States—was less due to progressive ideals of education and democracy than to a realization that postwar, women were returning to their traditional domestic roles in earnest. They thus were, perhaps, in less need of equal education that would enable them to enter the workforce, specifically at teacher training institutions. Edwards notes that by 1961, 808 of every 1,000 British women were married, and that since World War II, women were marrying at ever younger ages, and those with teaching positions were leaving them upon marriage, despite the temporary alleviation of the marriage ban during wartime (140). As a result, Edwards argues, the position of the teachers college in Britain was in question; given "the rapid rise in the marriage rate for women, was it any longer appropriate for girls to receive the same education as boys, when, in contrast to the pre-war period, nearly all of them were destined to be wives and mothers?" (141). Edwards claims that the core feminized culture of the teachers college was now at risk—with the potential admission of men to these campuses to make up for the loss of women students; a relevant question was thus, "how could the culture of femininity be adapted, let alone maintained, under such circumstances?" (141).

Certainly through the strict social codes, rules for visiting men on campus, and general standards of dress[8] at the Woman's College postwar, one can see the legacy of this "purity" standard for women in southern single-sex higher education as well. In broad terms, the culture of southern women in the early to mid-twentieth century is described by scholars of the region as significantly religious in focus, prioritizing the family and mindful of the sanctity of certain gendered traditions. As Holly Mathews notes regarding southern culture in 1989, southerners continued to place high importance on the role of "the family [in] society and on the role of southern 'ladies' as the preservers of the family unit and of the traditional culture" (2). She notes that there is thus an implied difference in attitudes toward, and expectations of, the behaviors of women and the behaviors of men (2). Caroline Dillman similarly argues, "For generations, Southern women have been taught to revere and honor the past and treat Southern culture as sacred. The combination of Southernness and religion with patriarchy has been and remains a powerful force in the socialization of Southern females" (10). Given these sociological trends in the subculture, the implementation of marriage bans, as well as purity standards and other traditional regulations on femininity and teaching, were ripe for implementation in the American South during the first half of the twentieth century.

Not surprisingly, then, the states with all-female normal schools were almost exclusively located in the South: Of the 189 original normal schools in the United States, the 10 all-female schools were in the states of Alabama, Georgia, Massachusetts, North Carolina, South Carolina, and

Virginia (Ogren 213–35). In other areas of the country, normal schools were more commonly coeducational, though regularly enrolling a great number of women students. Writing for the *Peabody Journal of Education* in 1941, the dean of the all-women's Alabama College, T. H. Napier, illustrates the double-helix of preparatory needs—the personal and professional—for the normal school student in the southern United States when he asserts that, following the Reconstruction,

> Most of the schools open to women were provided largely for the daughters of the land-owning class. They had not been interested in training for commerce and industry but rather for homemaking and social leadership. Little provision had been made for the education of the daughter of the small farmer. The schools were entirely too expensive for the people of this large class who came into political power at this time and who set out to give their own daughters a chance in the world. The State Supported College for Women was the plan followed in some of the Southern states . . . [to provide] women with the opportunity of getting the kind of education they want and need in the positions they are going to fill. . . . They are entitled to the information, to the experiences and to the appreciations necessary for a comfortable position in a rapidly changing world; they should be able to get a broad and liberal education as a preparation for life's emergencies; [and] they must get a higher type of special training for professional and business opportunities. (269, 274–75)

Interestingly, in his historical overview, Napier makes no historical or linguistic distinction between the original normal schools and the current southern women's colleges, including his own, when he discusses the "State Supported College for Women" category, which, in fact, was the name for the evolved normal schools–turned–women's colleges in the southern region: Winthrop Normal and Industrial College of South Carolina became Winthrop College for Women in 1920, and then coeducational Winthrop College in 1974. The State Normal and Industrial College in Georgia became Georgia State College for Women in 1922 and Women's College of Georgia in 1961 before becoming coeducational in 1967. The Woman's College of the University of North Carolina was renamed the North Carolina College for Women from 1919 to 1931, then renamed the Woman's College from 1931 to 1963. The school then became a coeducational university branch of the UNC system in fall 1964. The semantic distinctions here are important, as the postnormal school incarnations of these three institutions are *not*, in fact, designed to give women "the kind of education they want and need in the positions they are going to fill" if those positions are still implicitly as *teachers*. Yet the combined (or unintentionally aggregated) histories of these state women's colleges were still implicitly dependent upon the notion that women were, in fact, primarily teachers—and teachers are, in turn, primarily *women*, at least in the view of higher education in the South at this time.

Nonetheless, perhaps due to their focus on teaching as a noble career, even a societal good, as opposed to a focus on the integration of intellectual traditions and liberal arts subject matter of the traditional public or private general college, the normal schools were commonly viewed as "professional rather than 'academic' institutions" (Fitzgerald 226), an extension that continued into the mid-twentieth century, as reflected in Napier's writing, above. Fitzgerald notes that today's vernacular would likely label normal schools as "vocational" in their design and purpose (226). Yet she also recognizes that normal schools, limited though their original charters may have been, "democratized and expanded educational and vocational opportunity far beyond any existing institution, in terms of class and gender," offering women from non-elite classes the opportunity to gain a college education where there otherwise were few options, particularly for nineteenth-century rural women seeking an alternative to marriage and isolated life on the family farm (228–29). In 1918, for example, there were 225 normal schools in operation in the United States, including those that housed two-year rather than four-year programs of study (Barnes et al. 30). The training of teachers was a nationwide mission, and one steeped in Ogren's theory of the "greater good" for the intellectual and moral advancement of children of this country.

This mission as it was enacted for these women normal school candidates—to carefully and plainly balance the domestic and vocational needs of the college female graduate in the space of the college writing course, and to assume the role of teacher as primary career aim—stood in clear contrast to the educational mission found at elite colleges for women in the Northeast. The most studied examples of these colleges are Vassar, Bryn Mawr, and Radcliffe, also founded in the nineteenth century, which "remained committed, for all intents and purposes, to providing their students with a liberal arts education that was divorced from vocational ends," as Betty Weneck argues (6). In fact, the training at these women's colleges was often explicitly political in nature, with an aim to produce "fully realized political persons"; such was the case in the early twentieth century, when Seven Sisters campuses were infused with suffrage clubs, which in conjunction with students' explicit rhetorical training produced volumes of leaders in the campaign for the vote (Conway 218–19, 221).[9]

The Seven Sisters colleges argued that the more pedestrian and limited training found at teachers colleges was antithetical to their mission, since "professional education was a poor use of the valuable period of undergraduate study; or that training, for example, in the domestic arts and sciences not only was intellectually unfulfilling, but served to reaffirm women's traditional female roles." In other words, "the exclusive status of the eastern women's colleges and their intellectual commitment to the liberal arts went hand in hand" (Weneck 6). One may argue that the Seven Sisters was thus, in every way, a direct response to the exclusion of women from the Ivy League institutions of the eastern United States.

A common research angle into the history of women's education, therefore, has been to highlight this value and rigor in single-sex women's institutions as compared to male institutions, using this seemingly superior, alternative educational mission as a starting point. Mary Dockray-Miller argues that typically English studies scholarship "has failed to acknowledge aspects of women's English education . . . that made [these colleges] not only different from but also, in some critical ways, educationally superior to and more progressive than their male counterparts" (139–40). Dockray-Miller, like David Gold, laments the lack of attention paid in English studies to the history of women's education, and also argues that scholars of women's rhetoric, such as Nan Johnson, "assum[e] that women students were doing the same things in the same way that men students did" (146). Yet as Dockray-Miller notes, the Seven Sisters colleges were in large part patterned, even deliberately so, after their all-male counterparts in the Ivy League. Consequently, these women also suffered the same slow evolution of writing instruction led, in English studies lore, by Yale and Harvard, namely what James Berlin terms "Current-Traditional rhetoric," or the "objective" valuing of particular knowledge and staid conventions of correctness that exist outside the composing act. The women of the Seven Sisters were thus "offered the same current traditional courses and methods that Harvard and Columbia did; in Cambridge and New York City, men and women learned to write in basically the same way . . . both Barnard and Radcliffe women took daily theme courses like those offered at Harvard in the 1890s. Barnard women had to take two years of writing courses to graduate. Wellesley and Smith relied on current-traditional rhetoric as well" (Dockray-Miller 142).

Positioning the Seven Sisters and similar elite northeastern women's colleges as implicitly or explicitly more enlightened than the normal schools, particularly those in the South, a region also historically regarded as "less" by citizens outside its boundaries, as well as in specific studies of American higher education, not only is unfair to the intellectual work that women were doing in these southern institutions, but also sidesteps the fact that women's education *nationwide* was characterized by common limitations that were products of a male-dominated higher educational system in the nineteenth and early to mid-twentieth centuries.

For a material example of this, consider a few sample themes from English A classes at Radcliffe between 1923 and 1924, which confirm that the instruction—and feedback—received at this elite women's college was certainly no more enlightened than the type of instruction given to male counterparts. In fact, the comments on these themes, archived at Harvard, show a complete lack of any attention to writing development. For Frances Hitchcock's "Summary Sentences" paper of December 11, 1922, consisting of three very short paragraphs on Milton, the instructor notes a grade of E (F equivalent), and his only comment is, "You fail to penetrate to the heart of Huxley's paragraphs. Careless reading and careless composition." In H. N. Finkelstein's short response to this same assignment, submitted on the same day as Miss Hitchcock's work and entitled "Milton's Hypothesis," the only margin comment is "Bad." The grade is also an E, and the end comment states that "Comment would be superfluous." Finally, the instructor for Julia Eisman's paper of December 10, 1923, notes that she has the "Total inability to grasp the thought of two paragraphs," and gives her an E for the paper

In outlining these sample papers and instructors' comments, I aim to make a point about the reliability of narratives about progressive instances of writing instruction in women's educational histories. As JoAnn Campbell demonstrates, regarding Radcliffe in particular, an elite institution does not necessarily make for elite instruction. She comments that in the themes that she read from Radcliffe women writing between 1883 and 1917, "again and again students asked to be allowed to express their ideas, to share important parts of their lives, to be heard. And invariably their writing instructors either ignored their ideas and commented on their writing performance or dismissed their thoughts and observations by labeling them 'feminine' and 'therefore nonacademic'" (473). Kathryn M. Conway has similarly noted that Radcliffe drew upon the all-male faculty from Harvard, resulting in students who "remained silent" in rhetoric courses, in stark contrast to their male counterparts elsewhere in the yard (211–12).

Lest readers think that only poor themes such as those I employ for illustration above received minimal or dismissive comments, Campbell herself notes that one Radcliffe student, upon receiving an A on a theme, received as an accompanying comment only this: "avoid personalities" (477). Campbell argues that the Harvard English A program "encouraged vigor with the public criticism of themes" as its central pedagogical response to writing, both at Harvard and Radcliffe (478). Yet even though the comments on these papers show a complete lack of empathy for the students and, in some cases, an oversight of the potential content of the papers themselves in favor of demonstrating the "rigor" of teacherly authority, these papers *are* somewhat superfluous responses to a superfluous assignment. At the end of the course term (December), English A students at Radcliffe, at least those represented in the archives, were still being asked to write simple summaries, whereas their male counterparts were more often writing full-fledged literary analyses. This is thus one example of current-traditional pedagogies enacted—to a methodological extreme—in an elite, all-women's instructional setting, in this case, one that attempts to parallel men's instruction but ends up being "lesser" simply on gendered grounds.

Despite these curricular overlaps and similarities in the sometimes shortcomings of teacher response and student development, Dockray-Miller contends that the Seven Sisters colleges were fundamentally "better" than the all-male Ivies, due to larger learning initiatives both inside and outside the classroom, and thus now stand as models for early women's literacy education. These included the prevalence of individual instructional conferences at Vassar; Bryn Mawr's early writing-across-the-curriculum (WAC) model (not labeled as such); Mount Holyoke's major in rhetoric in the early twentieth century; and the literary societies or clubs at Vassar, Holyoke, Barnard, and Bryn Mawr. She also argues that the Seven Sisters had "the tradition of female aestheticism" due to their lack of graduate programs, avoiding a split between the "fragmentation" of "the expectations of male-defined professional success: research and publishing" (150–51). Dockray-Miller argues that the "complementary courses in rhetoric and literature" in place at Vassar today offer a "plausible, immediately implementable solution to the composition/literature divide that so many colleges are facing today" as it calls for an "emphasis on teaching rather than research, and requires collaboration between faculty members" (153).

Yet this somewhat idealized notion of women's elite education—in addition to romanticizing the practice of teaching therein as being *opposed* to research, and implying that collaborative work is more plausible and common in teaching and learning than in scholarly research-centered settings—ignores a postgraduate professional reality for these women students, one also in the background of instructional politics at public women's institutions outside the Northeast, such as the Woman's College. As Sally Schwager argues, the Seven Sisters "produced an exceptional generation of women . . . nurtured by the collective female life of the women's college, [who] emerged with aspirations to use their educations outside the confines of women's domestic sphere as it was narrowly defined in marriage. But while this pioneering generation rejected conventional marriage (some 60–70 percent remained single), the professional roles they developed for themselves perpetuated and, in fact, institutionalized the ideology of gender difference" (362). In addition, faculty were also limited in certain ways by their intensely collaborative teaching practices at the elite colleges, and still beholden to the larger realities of academia in the United States, just like normal school faculty and students, since these elite school faculty

> were not at Wellesley by choice alone—they were locked out of the research universities. Though most Wellesley professors were highly productive scholars, they might have accomplished even more had heavy teaching loads and administrative duties not forced them often to set aside important research projects. A commitment to Wellesley and a desire to remain within its close community, moreover, discouraged some professors from accepting offers for advancement elsewhere. . . . Whether women's colleges other than Wellesley served faculty in the same way will remain difficult to evaluate until comparable research on other educational institutions is accomplished. (Schwager 368)

I point out such contradictions between these women's educational processes and their postgraduate (or faculty) career experiences only to highlight a flaw in the enlightened versus unenlightened comparisons that tend to be formed concerning the elite women's colleges and the normal schools, later women's public colleges, in the United States, particularly those in the often resource-poor and deeply gender-divided southern region of the country. The culture of (nascent) personalized pedagogies was not just at the Seven Sisters, but also at the Woman's College, as indicated in the course descriptions for their English composition courses starting in 1917.

Similarly, the tradition of literary magazines, as well as extracurricular literary societies, was also alive and well in other women's public colleges outside the Seven Sisters, as I will discuss in more depth in chapter 2. The Woman's College literary magazine began as the *State Normal Magazine* in 1897 and was later renamed *Coraddi* to represent the three literary societies on campus: the Cornelian, Adelphian, and Dikean. So while the Seven Sisters may have been progressive, they were not alone in some of their thinking about advancing writing instruction through classroom as well as extracurricular initiatives. And as scholars of Harvard and Radcliffe histories note, this progressivism at the elite women's schools in some locations came with a high social price: Andrew Mandel points out that Radcliffe was "Harvard's neglected, precocious, younger sister—mocked in the pages of the *Crimson* and *Lampoon* for unsightliness and mannishness" (216). When it came time to begin the integration of women students into Harvard, the students at Radcliffe "knew that access to Harvard Yard did not connote equal opportunity. Some women called themselves 'intruders' and they were known as such" (217).[10]

Championing the special opportunity of elite women's colleges in order to make them appear superior to men's institutions—whether as subjects of archival study, or as simply historical precedents for women's equalized educational experiences today—offers a limited binary and somewhat falsely comparative approach to the fuller history of women's literacy education, based on a certain regional grouping of schools attended by students of particularly privileged backgrounds who subsequently faced, in many cases, sociocultural limitations of their own. This approach also necessarily disadvantages the rich history of the normal school and its rhetorical and composing traditions, and subsequently the women's public college, for the "vocational" emphasis originally aimed for at these institutional types rarely matches up—on paper, at least—to the more elite men's-only institutions that its students were not allowed, and in many cases did not aspire, to attend. To interrogate this problem deeper still, the southern normal school—with its accompanying gender-specific divisions as relevant to its cultural values and mores—becomes an often-forgotten subset of the normal school seen as inferior on both sociointellectual and material terms, than these elite women's college histories.

Parsing out the curriculum of the late-era southern normal school, through a review of a course such as first-year composition, may uncover some of the intricate and often layered goals of writing and literary instruction both inside and outside the classroom at these public single-sex institutions. A look at the curriculum will also illuminate its similarities to the intellectual work of the elite northeastern women's colleges. This review, however, is somewhat complicated by how local conditions affected the curriculum of normal schools, just as local conditions affect the curriculum of the public coeducational colleges and universities that these schools have become today. The curricular content of the normal school, particularly the English curriculum, was ripe for debates over standardization, due to its end goal of educating future teachers—and thereby improving the literacy skills of primary and secondary students across the country.

As such, a brief overview of what was considered typical—if troubling—for rhetoric and writing instruction at the normal schools during the early twentieth century as compared to what was being offered at the Woman's College does present a somewhat more progressive aim for the latter in terms of how the college delineated courses of instruction for composition as well as creative writing, in broader relation to literary study. This contrast between local standards and practices at the Woman's College versus national trends for normal schools highlights the importance of individual archival research in uncovering similar local contradictions in previously sanctioned mass histories of writing instruction.

Writing and Rhetoric at the Normal School: Early Debates

Published reports in the early twentieth century illustrate just how contentious was the issue of writing instruction, and, more broadly, rhetorical education, in the preparation of future teachers. A particularly hot topic of debate between approximately 1900 and 1930 was whether teachers were, in fact, receiving the kind of education in English—specifically writing and rhetoric—that they would need to educate future generations of students, and whether this training meshed with the larger social and professional training necessary to produce "model" teachers whom students would emulate in their own learning and possible future teaching. This debate over professional (educational theory) coursework versus subject-specific content coursework (English literature and rhetoric) continued into the report of the Committee on General Education at Harvard between 1943 and 1945 (which I discuss at length in chapter 3) and certainly continues to a great extent between our colleges of education and departmentally based English education programs today. A central question of normal school administrators and faculty of that era was: if there is an "ideal" curriculum in writing and rhetoric (and, in some cases, speech/elocution), what was it, and which schools were employing it? A few local examples illustrate the points of this debate.

The first-year English curriculum in 1915 at the State Normal School of Lewiston, Idaho, was highly contingent upon local student populations that the school's teachers would someday encounter. As Herbert E. Fowler noted in *English Journal*, "The fact that the population of Idaho is 90 percent rural has been a controlling factor in shaping the professional English work of our school. Most of our students go into country schools. Hence it became necessary to consider the conditions these new teachers would have to meet" (244). These local conditions resulted in the implementation of four quarters of the course Written Composition, which was for "students who have not mastered the principles of correct and effective writing." In this course, "constant practice in writing" was the daily focus, with "subjects [that] are chiefly of a professional nature" (245). In addition, the Lewiston-based normal school offered a course called Sentence Structure, designed for "those whose understanding of English grammar is insufficient for teaching" (245). As a supplement to these basic-training courses, however, the general faculty at the Lewiston normal school—including those outside of English—were asked to note which students were lacking in "Training in the use of the voice and carriage of the body; Training in clear-cut, accurate, and forceful speech; 'straight-talking,' in short; Training in writing English; Training in grammar and sentence structure" (247). Clearly, the nineteenth- and early-twentieth-century ideals of literacy as a marker of taste—critically important in the elite co-educational universities—were in evidence in this institutional alignment between physical and linguistic eloquence for classroom teachers.

C. R. Rounds, inspector of English for the Wisconsin normal schools, similarly argued in 1914 for the local conditions of teachers and their pupils being the driving force of the normal school curriculum and structure:

> The first truth for a teacher of English in a normal school to accept as, in a measure, fixing his point of view is that his vision must not be bounded by the walls of his classroom or by the library of his institution; he must even look farther than to the immediate needs of the particular students under his instruction; his thought must go out to the children who may soon be students of his students; his sympathies and his knowledge must reach out to the schoolrooms in which these young people who are now his students will soon be teachers. This is the thing that makes teaching in a normal school unique. (553)

Like Fowler, Rounds attends to elocution, and the professional presentation of the English teacher when he asks, rhetorically, his normal school faculty, "Are you willing to have them talk anywhere near as much as you do? Or talk *as* you do? Are you careful about your speech habits?" Rounds makes a special point of noting that these concerns are as critical as the content of the English lessons themselves, as he queries whether students remember "that your students will teach very much as you do, if you are a teacher of personality and power." (554). Rounds's points illustrate the importance of training the teacher as both an expert in her field *and* as a model for professional conduct, for her pupils who will someday become teachers themselves. His description models a selfless and proactive individual whose primary purpose is to serve her students, and to model behavior and skills worthy of emulation. Such traits are not unlike those of "good" mothers of this era, who acted as models for their children, particularly their girls—even at the cost of their own personalities and predilections—in the ways of polite society and interpersonal behavior.

An editorial written by the College Committee of the National Council of Teachers of English, and published in *English Journal* in 1914, states these dual concerns in far more forthright terms, when the committee declared: "The English course in the normal school, and in the college of education in the university as well, must perform a double service. It must train the individual and at the same time orient him in educational processes. . . . So long as poor teaching is common in any part of our American system of public education poor teaching will be found in all parts. There is no escape from the vicious circle" ("Editorial: Supervisors of English," 661–62). Yet as agreeable as state and national officials seemed to be regarding this "double service" of English normal school training, these same officials, as represented by their local curricula, were much further apart in terms of what the best set of courses would be in order to deliver the subject-specific training required of the English teacher, including in the introductory writing and rhetoric courses.

Contrast this view of writing, rhetoric, and associated lessons in elocution at the normal school with an article from 1922 by Helen Said Hughes of Wellesley College. Arguing from the position of a faculty member at an elite women's college, Hughes poses a counterpoint on the issue of standardized curriculum in writing and rhetoric (and introductory literature) in public universities by arguing against this curricula altogether. She does not mention teachers colleges or normal schools per se in her piece, yet contends that

> Most of the colleges and universities of the country require students entering with three units of English to take in college in their Freshman year one three-hour course (or its equivalent) in English composition. A considerable number of institutions require a second course in English, an elementary course in literature, taken usually in the Sophomore year. . . . It is my belief that these two elementary courses are for the most part wastefully negative in function. They are given chiefly to prevent trouble. They are founded on the supposition (not always easy to disprove) that the high-school training in English is of little value; that the college must lay its own foundations before the student can be trusted to enter upon new and intensive work in English or in any other subject requiring competence in organizing material and

in stating facts. This distrust of the teaching a student has received in the preceding stages of his education is responsible for overlapping of curricula in the Freshman year in high school and in the Freshman year in college. (199–200)

Hughes's position illustrates a key contention between the normal school and the elite college: that writing and rhetoric, and the introductory literature course (still heavily embedded in normal school curricula as well) are "wasteful" courses that double back on a student's secondary education rather than advance his or her learning in the college setting. While Hughes's complaint echoes what some teachers and scholars now also contend about the liminal place of first-year writing within the English curriculum, and within the liberal arts—especially in contrast to the more attractive coursework in creative writing, as I will discuss in chapter 4—the complaint raises a historical problem for the normal school and teachers college faculty and students.

The first-year courses in the normal school setting were clearly imbued with other functions, such as training high school teachers to mimic the stance and position of the "model" normal school writing teacher. These courses were also designed to be bridges from the secondary to the postsecondary curriculum as part of an overall deep training in English studies. Even though the elite women's colleges may have put less public emphasis on first-semester or first-year writing and rhetoric in order to elevate the perceived literacy skills of their students, the normal schools—and those women's colleges emerging from the normal school tradition—were far more indebted to the legacy of rhetorical instruction, from both a social and an intellectual standpoint.

Hughes's contemporary position, therefore, further illustrates the conceptual curricular divide between the normal school and the general college (elite or otherwise, though a more viable position when arguing that one's students are "advanced" beyond said content), as well as the argument over women's education in general—as many normal school students were, of course, women, and Wellesley was an elite women's college.[11] In addition, the normal school faculty viewed these introductory courses as actually *improving* the education of high school students—by osmosis (better prepared teachers provide better writing courses, leading to less need for said courses in college). Thus, to eliminate them at the normal school would be tantamount to turning one's back on these secondary pupils. This disconnect between the elite and normal schools illustrates, again, the difference in mission that set these two institutional types in opposition to each other, but not necessarily in terms of material educational quality.

Despite the outside view of the value of introductory writing and rhetoric courses at the normal school and other public colleges, the problem of uniformity—and thus the greatest chance for widespread quality teacher training and pupil learning—was still a concern some years following Hughes's article, as the 1920s came to a close, and as normal schools as an institutional type had been in operation for nearly fifty years. Ida A. Jewett's 1930 nationwide survey of seventy-one teachers colleges uncovered a distinct lack of uniformity in English offerings, despite (or as a result of) examples of specific curricula based on local needs. Jewett notes: "One college gives 4 percent of its total program to rhetoric and composition, another gives 42 percent; one gives 3 percent to oral expression, another gives 42 percent; one gives 10 percent to literature, another gives 72 percent. When the emphases upon the various divisions and subdivisions of the subject are so diverse, one is forced to the conclusion that there are many times no controlling purposes more valid than the personal likes or dislikes or ambitions of influential members of the department" (323). Jewett goes on to note that "in 1925, the word 'rhetoric' is used alone as a title only six times and as a part of a title but eight times. . . . The common practice of basing compositions on literary topics has decreased and the study of technique has given way to opportunities for creative writing and to wide readings of masterpieces of literary art" (324). She voices her implicit approval of this shift in focus in the overall English curriculum when she points out that "The large number of literature courses in comparison with those in versification, creative writing, and the like is a favorable feature, for it indicates that the departments are distinguishing between the values of consumption and utilization and those of production and accomplishment, a principle stated by Inglis to be one of the measures for determining the values of studies" (324).

Jewett concludes by asserting that, based on her survey findings, "The tendency in the language courses is toward practical use and away from the memorizing of bodies of rules and principles," yet while "the academic ideal of specialists highly trained in a narrow field of scholarship does not prevail among these teachers colleges, there is ample support for the statement that the great mass of the work is broadly academic in character, and not at every stage 'scholarship *relevant* to the work of the teacher'" (326, 328). Furthermore, Jewett's report warns against the normal school English departments doing too much to "imitate the colleges" (325) and ignoring the fact that "the functional values of English must be stressed," especially for those preparing to teach primary-age students (326).

Again, one sees a valuation of the English subject courses here over other kinds of theoretical instruction beginning to take place in the coursework, and a desire to not only concentrate more heavily on the courses in literature and writing that make up the English department general curricula, but also to *expand* that notion of writing to include creative writing courses—again, within the departmental offerings and outside the school of educational theory. Conversely, one sees a reticence to stray too far from the "practical" traditions long-since practiced in the training of teachers, and a concern over blurring the boundaries between regular college English programs and those at the more specialized teachers colleges. Such aims need not necessarily be contradictory as much as politically savvy; while Jewett clearly recognizes the expansion of other kinds of writing and reading happening in the normal school English department, she rightly, in context, fears that what makes the normal school "special" is its *difference* from this "drift from disciplinary to social values in education" in the 1920s forward (325).

This question of what would be "standard" versus how to expand upon that standard was also at play when comparing various regions of the country and their approaches to educating teachers. Prior to Jewett's analysis, Walter Barnes et al.[12] had published in 1918 the survey results of faculty at 106 normal schools—just about 50 percent of the total normal schools in operation at this time—in order to make regional distinctions regarding the quality and focus of the curriculum at said schools. I present the findings of Barnes et al. out of chronological order here to illustrate how the desire for a uniform normal school curriculum, in fact, never materialized, even and especially when lamented in geographical terms.

In the New England region, Barnes and his colleagues note that "colleges and universities in this section of the country are old-fashioned in their entrance requirements and will not accept credit from normal schools," thus negatively affecting curriculum through disincentive, that is, nontransferability (31). In the South, Barnes et al. note that the conditions are more problematic on a fundamental level, in that,

> In the case of the Southern states, where the condition of normal school English is reported unsatisfactory, the trouble is that probably until very lately the normal-schools have not been much more than high schools in their courses of study and faculty standards. It is evident that the teachers of normal-school English—that is, English in the courses beyond the four-year high school—should be, generally speaking, the equal in scholarship and experience of the teachers doing Freshman and Sophomore work in colleges and universities. In the Southern states this is often not the case. (31)

Barnes et al. conclude, as did Jewett twelve years later, that "it is amazing, the utter lack of anything approaching uniformity or standardization. The English courses in normal schools of the United States are, with a few exceptions, the result of the individual notions of the teachers in charge, or of the presidents of the schools. . . . For the most part each normal school has been a law unto itself" (35–36). Barnes's findings are also unwittingly echoed in Hughes's 1922 piece where she expresses concern over the overlap between high school and college instruction in writing and rhetoric. Despite his committee's more negative findings, Barnes and his colleagues conclude that "the English in normal schools is a special and specific kind of English work—not advanced high school or elementary work" (32). In making this statement, he prefigures Jewett's later concerns over how, and where, the English curriculum is becoming less "special" in the normal schools as the 1930s begin.

But most important to note in Barnes's article is his obvious criticism of the education taking place in the southern states. While Barnes does not, of course, single out any institutions in his study, his strong implication is that northern normal schools are providing more "college-level" coursework than their southern counterparts. Combine this observation with the fact that many of the southern normal schools were all-women's institutions, as noted previously, and we have a troubling report that divides the country into halves—the "lesser" one being significantly populated by more women teachers-in-training. Yet Barnes does ultimately answer the question of what is the "ideal" course of study in English, particularly writing and rhetoric, even if he cannot claim, conclusively, that anyone is currently offering this course of study.

The study by Barnes et al. mostly emphasizes *lack,* as do many of the other studies of this kind and in this era. But his committee does put forth ten principles, which are, in sum:

1. the primary aim of the curriculum is to educate teachers, such that "English work specifically designed for this purpose is more important than general work in literature and composition";

2. such work should not "repeat the work of the high school nor parallel the work of the college";

3. at least half of the instructional time "should be devoted to 'professional English,'" i.e., children's literature and English methods;

4. literature taught should have "general cultural value" and be more modern in chronology than not, more American than English;

5. work in composition should serve two purposes: "the general purpose of Freshman college composition courses and also the specific purpose of preparing students to teach more effectively," which includes making the work throughout "extremely practical";

6. all students should take a proficiency test in the "practical English arts" in their junior year. Those who fail should take remedial work;

7. a brief course in grammar should be required for all except "those who will teach upper high school or upper grades of elementary school";

8. special courses per the school's environment should be offered—e.g., "English in rural schools" or "English for foreigners";

9. composition should be offered in the junior year and professional courses in the senior year;

10. "If *any* work is required (except that suggested in 5 and 6, above), then it should be: first, professional English; secondly, composition; thirdly, literature." (38)

Clearly few, if any, of these ten principles were at work—at least in any broad, identifiable fashion—some twelve years later in Jewett's study.

This latter historical marker—1930—is critically important to the Woman's College in particular, for just one year following this the teachers college transitioned to a general women's college, carrying with it the still-varied traditions of that normal school curriculum, which often resisted the "practicality" that Barnes's committee so desired. In particular, the Woman's College exercised an almost "antipracticality" in its stalwart offering of courses such as creative writing, and promoted the inherent value of the first two years of introductory study by offering extensive work in composition and rhetoric to freshmen and sophomores. In addition, Barnes's notion that the normal school be a site for primarily "professional" education seems to have been rarely enacted in the normal schools surveyed, given the preponderance of elective courses in literature and other "noncore" courses that Barnes claims dominated these various curricula (35).

Instead of the committee's desired uniform outcomes, it is evident from these various historical accounts that normal schools were instead struggling for identities that were commonly determined by three general issues: first, local concerns over preparation for specific community populations (beyond the "special" courses the committee suggests); second, local and national concerns over preparation in the subject matter of English versus general "how to teach" courses and educational theory coursework; and finally, personal concerns over the production of model teachers with a sense of taste and eloquence, who would serve as figures for emulation for their pupils (both within the normal school and in primary and secondary school settings). This quality was nearly ignored by the 1918 committee report in addition to concerns over regional differences in overall normal school "quality."

It is critical to examine the specific curricula of the Woman's College in the context of these national and regional concerns, and to highlight where and when its curricula both answered the call for rigorous teaching in the subject of English, and writing and rhetoric, and where it made more progressive, even countercultural, strides in other areas of writing (such as creative writing). In particular, as an all-women's southern institution, the Woman's College (or State Normal and Industrial College) should not be lumped into Barnes's survey categories of "lesser" southern institutions, at least not on the basis of the curriculum and other literacy initiatives clearly in place from 1913 to 1931, nor should it be seen as slavishly adhering to this committee's hopeful "normalizing" standards.

Writing and Rhetoric in Transition at the Woman's College, 1913–31

In the prefatory material for the 1913 *Bulletin of the State Normal and Industrial College,* the entrance requirements for English Grammar, Composition, and Rhetoric are stated: "To test the candidate's command of clear and accurate English, she will be required to write one or more compositions, developing a theme through several paragraphs. The subjects will be drawn from the books prescribed for study and from the student's personal knowledge and experience." To meet the requirements in composition,

1. There should be practice in writing equivalent to weekly or at least fortnightly themes throughout the High School course. The subjects for themes should be drawn partly from the literature read and partly from the students' daily experience and observation. The candidate should be well grounded in the essentials of English Grammar, and accuracy in spelling, capitalization, and punctuation should be rigorously exacted. Proper effort should also be made to enlarge the student's vocabulary.

2. The theory of rhetoric should be studied in connection with the work in composition. The pupil should study the structure of sentences, paragraphs, and whole compositions; should analyze and make outlines of essays with a view to understanding the orderly and progressive development of thought, and should be taught the principles of good writing as exemplified both in her own work and in the work of others. (24)

The corresponding required courses—Rhetoric and Composition I and II, a year-long sequence required for freshmen, Rhetoric and Advanced Composition, and Advanced Composition, a year-long sequence required for sophomores—were described in the bulletin as such:

Rhetoric and Composition I: Three hours a week—first term. Study of prose selections, descriptive and narrative. Theme writing and other exercises. Individual criticism and interviews. Required of freshmen.

Rhetoric and Composition II: Three hours a week—second term. Continuation of Course I. Specimens of exposition. Essays of Carlyle and Stevenson. Required of freshmen.

Rhetoric and Advanced Composition: Three hours a week—first term. Study of prose selections of considerable length. Book reviews and literary criticism. Theme writing, outlines, and other written exercises. Personal interviews. Required of sophomores.

Advanced Composition: Three hours a week—second term. Theme writing continued as in Course III. Study of modern English prose, particularly the essays of Newman and Arnold. Required of sophomores. (47–48)

A parsing of these requirements in relation to the desired outcomes for teacher education in the larger normal school community reveals the State Normal and Industrial College to be in step with, if not ahead of, the desire for rigorous instruction in language and introductory literature. For example, while Jewett's survey notes the small percentage of courses in normal schools that use "rhetoric" in their titles, three of the college's four courses include this label, and the fourth only drops the label in favor of the emphasis on "advanced composition," even if the values of "rhetoric" in these earlier decades were more about technical mastery than larger civic awareness and expression. Additionally, the overall description of the first course, Rhetoric and Composition I, includes "individual criticism and interviews" as part of its course requirements, indicating that students would not only receive individual feedback on their writing, but that they would also be required to meet in student-teacher conferences for the purpose of assessing their work and overall progress. Again, this contradicts the contention that the Seven Sisters' approach to conferencing was an anomaly among other postsecondary institutions at this time. Finally, the sheer requirement of four semesters of introductory writing, with the final two semesters providing instruction in writing vis-à-vis literary study, indicates a strong desire on the part of the college to provide a true "foundation" in this area of English studies, despite its rather strict admission requirements noting that students should *already* have had considerable high school instruction in grammar and rhetoric, as well as exposition and argument. One can see that the courses were designed to be continuations of this secondary school study, not replication of it, as Hughes claims in her 1922 argument.

But the overarching description of the curriculum also privileges equally textual analysis and more personal, or experience-based, writing—as noted by the description of the entrance examination, which asks students to write an essay based on both the "books prescribed for study" and "personal knowledge and experience." This seems both progressive in its enactment of a "daily themes," that is, Yale College's approach to expository writing (at least three decades prior, incidentally, to the widespread use of that pedagogical method at that college) as well as a precursor to the entrance of creative writing offerings into the curriculum. The emphasis on "description and narrative" rather than argument or research in the first semester (Rhetoric and Composition I) also more strongly resembles later composition curricula in both women's and coeducational colleges, wherein an individual approach to seeing the writer as observer of social phenomena, and recorder of reality, takes center stage.

Once the students arrive in Rhetoric and Composition II, the emphasis then shifts to "specimens of exposition" and the modeling (one may infer) of work based on that of Thomas Carlyle and Robert Louis Stevenson. The second year-long sequence more visibly aims to incorporate literary analysis in its design; however, there is still an emphasis on "English prose," including Matthew Arnold, implying that the course is not completely a writing-about-literature course, as might be found in other institutions of prestige at the time, notably Yale and Harvard. Finally, the rhetoric sequence aims for students to demonstrate "orderly and progressive development of thought," a possible nod toward the intellectually and morally ordered writer-as-teacher model that would best create the proper woman to teach children.

In the 1917 *Bulletin of the State Normal and Industrial College,* the prefatory material about English literature and writing goes even further toward an emphasis on the personal and experiential in instruction, as well as in preparation for coursework:

> The first object requires instruction in grammar and composition. English grammar should ordinarily be reviewed in the secondary school; and correct spelling and grammatical accuracy should be rigorously exacted in connection with all written work during the four years. The principles of English composition governing punctuation, the use of words, sentences, and paragraphs should be thoroughly mastered; and practices in composition, oral as well as written, should extend throughout the secondary-school period. Written exercises may well comprise letter-writing, narration, description, and essay exposition and argument. It is advisable that subjects for this work be taken from the student's personal experience, general knowledge, and studies other than English, as well as from the readings in literature. Finally, special instruction in language and composition should be accompanied by concerted effort of teachers in all branches to cultivate in the student the habit of using good English in the recitations and other exercises, whether oral or written. (26)

In this statement of preparation, the addition of various genres is notable: "letter-writing, narration, description, and essay exposition and argument." Also notable is the consideration of knowledge taken from "studies other than English," implying a more cross-curricular approach to writing instruction than had been previously encouraged, as well as a nod to the use of literature proper as a basis for knowledge in exposition. Finally, there is a pointed additional mention of "oral or written" exercises, providing a greater space for the training in elocution for these future teachers and young women within polite society.

In consort with this revised statement, we see a slight shift in the organization of the first two years of rhetoric and writing coursework since the 1913 curriculum, with new attending course descriptions for 1917:

> Rhetoric and Composition I and II: Three hours a week for the year. Study of prose selections, with emphasis on the organization of the material. Weekly themes and oral composition. Reports on assigned readings. Individual criticisms and interviews. Required of freshmen.

> Literature and Composition III and IV: Three hours a week for the year. A survey course in English literature. Careful reading of poetry and prose se-

lections, supplemented by discussions, illustrating the development of various poetic and prose types of English literature down to the beginning of the nineteenth century. Outlines, written themes, and oral reports. Personal conferences. Required of sophomores. (80)

These descriptions seem to bear out the new, more equal emphasis in the first two years of study on writing and literature. The notion of a "survey" course is first mentioned here, and that course is in English literature, rather than the American literature emphasis desired by Barnes's committee. The literature and composition courses for the sophomore year also emphasize supplemental "discussions," indicating some room for student participation in what was otherwise a recitation format for the course. The inclusion of "outlines, written themes, and oral reports" also implies a somewhat participatory structure, and an equivalent emphasis on written and oral compositions based on the literature. The course continues the tradition of "personal conferences" noted in the 1913 courses, and in doing so completes the "individual criticism and interviews" practice of the Rhetoric and Composition I and II courses for the freshman year, only slightly altered in emphases from 1913.

This curricular structure remains in place, interestingly, through the college's transition to becoming the North Carolina College for Women in 1919—all the way through the 1922–23 academic year. In 1922, although the descriptions for the rhetoric and composition and introductory literature courses stay essentially the same,[13] we see another curricular shift outside the first two years. A new elective course is introduced, English Composition 25 and 26, an elective for juniors and seniors that seems to be a new course in creative writing. The description for the class, which remains stable and on the books through 1932, reads: "English Composition 25 and 26: Advanced composition, including practice in the short story, the essay, and other literary forms. Lectures, readings from modern and contemporary literature in each of the forms studied. Not more than twelve students will be admitted to this course. Consult the instructor" (101–2).

Clearly the normal school auditors did not prioritize creative writing in the overarching normal school English curriculum, but the Woman's College, as it transitioned out of its normal school era and into an era of single-sex general college instruction (heavily modeled on the liberal arts institution) began to experiment with such offerings. This experimentation would eventually lead to multiple creative writing offerings in the Woman's College by the late 1940s, a decision that would deeply affect the politics and construction of the English department in the 1950s, as I will discuss in chapter 4. By 1954, a regular course called Advanced Composition would offer one section per semester devoted to creative writing, and another devoted to expository writing. This is a far cry from the version of Advanced Composition offered in 1913, which was a more traditional *composing* course, in the sense of composing as primarily a codified response to literature and other texts, and as a nonliterary (expository essay rather than fiction or poetry), or intellectually generative, act.

This evolution of course offerings in the Woman's College's history as a normal school turned general women's college is mainly represented through these catalogues, which are static representations that fail to tell a complete story of student writing. To supplement these catalogues, "A Manual of Instruction" survives from the academic year 1930–31. The directives in this manual, written for the teachers of freshman English, provide some additional insight into the import of the courses themselves. The opening paragraph of the manual, for example, makes clear that the course is "distinctly a composition course, and themes or other forms of written work will be required throughout the year. It does not aim, however, to make theme writing a laborious and unpleasant task. It seeks to develop the individual's latent powers and to guide each one in forming correct habits of expression" (1). This directive—that it is "distinctly a composition course"—eases fears (of accrediting bodies, perhaps) that the course is not sufficiently focused on writing, that it is not an appreciation of literature course, despite the fact that course will impart to students "appreciation of literary values" (1). This opening directive also distinctively speaks to the importance of the student *as* a writer and speaks of her "latent powers," which will help her to succeed in the course, even if an end goal is for "correct" expression.

It is possible to attribute this notion of "correctness" not just to the general methods of teaching composition in the early twentieth century, but also to the specific culture of this college—as a southern women's school emerging from normal school traditions. Certainly a significant portion (nearly two pages of the eleven-page manual) is concerned with the "proper" type of paper that students must use for themes, the proper way in which to fold themes and label them for the instructor, and the proper way to "correct" the themes before resubmitting them to the instructor, including whether to label the paper "corrected, revised, or rewritten," depending upon the level of work needed (2). But as much as the manual emphasizes correctness, it also emphasizes the need for individual attention to student work—echoing the "latent powers" notion—in its paragraph on student-teacher conferences:

In the course in Freshman English personal conferences between the instructor and the individual student are regarded as a most important part of the work. Attendance at all regular conferences is a strict requirement of the course; unexcused absences from conference are regarded as of equally serious nature as unexcused absence from regular classes, and grades will be lowered accordingly. . . . It is desired that these conferences should be as helpful as possible, by giving the instructor an opportunity to meet the individual needs of each student. In order that you may do your part, revise beforehand the papers you have for revision and all notes made since the previous conference, and jot down all questions that you would like to ask about your work. Always bring your notebook to the conference. (3)

What is especially interesting about this passage is not just its clear directive about conferences as being equivalent to regular classes—in terms of attendance, for one—and how this mimics many of our current practices in first-year writing instruction. What is more revealing about this passage is its emphasis on the student *as* writer, and its instructions to the student in terms of how she should prepare for conferences, right down to the requirement that she "always bring [her] notebook to the conference," in order to have notes and ideas ready, and also, implicitly, to be a more active writer taking part in her education.

This is a striking statement, since much of the historical lore of composition and creative writing states that composition "stole" the workshop and conferencing methodologies from creative writing, and much later in the twentieth century—that such impulses were, in sum, born in creative writing and thereafter adopted by compositionists. But the writer-as-writer implications here point to an early recognition on the part of the Woman's College composition faculty that, in fact, even in an otherwise "corrective" classroom pedagogy, the individual student writer was key. This also hearkens back to the general concern of the founders of the college that women be educated equally and rigorously, despite the societal limitations set forth for them in the South, and in the United States more generally, in the late nineteenth and early twentieth centuries.

These official university records provide part of the story of writing in the normal school years. The manual exposes an interest in student *writers,* certainly, in the latter years of the college's normal school era, and sufficiently augments the hypotheses about the first-year curriculum that one might make from a reading of the course bulletins. But examining an ancillary student product as extracurricular enactment of the work done in these composition courses can give us a more personalized dimension of the range of writing occurring during the latter years of this era. True to Linde's admonition about the archives of institutional narrative, as discussed in my introductory chapter, I also want to emphasize the need to see multiple dimensions of this or any time period within the college in order to gain a full picture of the community and its actual practices.

In chapter 2, I will discuss at length the freshman composition magazine the *Yearling*, published in the late 1940s and early 1950s at the Woman's College. But the *Yearling*'s precursor was a smaller publication called the *Sample Case*, published in two volumes—Fall 1929 and Spring 1930, when the college was known as the North Carolina College for Women, prior to its absorption by the University of North Carolina system and its official transition to a general women's college. A brief overview of the organization and contents of this early publication can provide readers both a better glimpse into the early post–normal school curricular impulses, as reflected in the published writing that was completed in the first-year rhetoric and composition courses, as well as provide a segue into chapter 2 and a fuller discussion of the importance of the student magazine to women's writing education in general.

The *Sample Case* was a modest publication of less than twenty pages, with no cover or external binding, duplicated on 8 ½ by 11 inch pages in simple typeset and produced by the first-year students at the then-named North Carolina College for Women. The magazine was supervised by a team of faculty advisers. In the fall semester, these supervisors were Dr. Leonard Hurley, longtime chair of the English department and faculty member from 1921 to 1961, and Jane Summerall (who also supervised the magazine the following spring), a new faculty member and North Carolina College for Women alumna who would go on to teach expository as well as creative writing in the 1940s and 1950s. Hurley would be a critical figure in curricular revisions and the general discussions over women's writing in the English department in the 1950s, as well as in the retention of poet and faculty member Randall Jarrell, as I will discuss in chapter 4. Hurley would also be an imposing paternal figure in the department as remembered by my alumnae interview subjects, as revealed in chapter 2

The *Sample Case* was established, according to the foreword for the first of the two issues, as "an experiment which we hope may lead to the establishment of a permanent publication by the Freshman English classes." Further, the editors note that "our object has been to select material representative of all Freshmen work. Since every section has contributed something to our magazine, we offer you a typical collection of themes written for regular class assignments" (1929, 1). In the second of the two issues, the foreword notes that "in choosing the materials we have striven to maintain quality as well as representation," and that "we hope that our efforts and those of the classes who succeed us will establish at North Carolina College a tradition for excellence in composition" (1930, 1).

Archival records do not explain why or how the *Sample Case* only persisted for one year, or just two issues. Perhaps the change from a normal college to a general women's college was part of the equation, as missions shifted with the student bodies. Regrettably, no correspondence regarding this early publication has survived to be catalogued in the archives, and any individuals who may have taken part in its construction are long since deceased. But the statements made in the forewords, above, certainly point to a *desire* to persist, and a strong proclivity for offering not only compelling and relevant magazine content, but also for using the magazine to showcase the work *of* the courses—and to promote the idea of "excellence in composition," an idea that seems revolutionary for its time and location, and additionally striking as a statement made by students in a required and relatively lengthy course sequence otherwise tamed by overt concerns of correctness in expression, as noted in the manual of instruction.

The content of the *Sample Case*, then, becomes a window into this "excellence" that the students wanted to promote, as writers and as editors. In each of the two issues, the range of work is far more expansive than one would expect to see after reading the course descriptions and manual of instruction, and after considering the local social and intellectual conditions present during these last few years of the normal school era. Far from being an exemplification of "practical" training in writing—as would be the desire of the governing boards of the normal schools, as illustrated in the Jewett and Barnes surveys—the work presented in the *Sample Case* ranges from editorials to memoirs to brief autobiographies, to more extensive research papers, poems, and various aphorisms (for example, "Jazz is the result of efforts of a too-civilized society to forget" [Cowan 10]).

The content of these pieces is more often than not quite socially pointed as opposed to being simply responsive to an assigned text, or inquiry-based in response to a research problem or comparative assignment (except for the research paper on Carlyle and Emerson—Carlyle being a noteworthy choice, as his work forms the basis of the earliest version of first-year composition noted in the course descriptions above). An example of this social reflection is Mildred Brunt's piece, "Aunt Emmaline," which muses about the mother of "the negro woman who came after our wash" at Brunt's home: "I was always sorry that people saw her black skin before they really saw her face, because her face was so nice. It was almost as nice as Mother's" (4). Social commentary on gender relations was also a frequent topic of concern in the essays, such as Hannah McCutchen's curious piece, "Early Ambitions": "A boy wants to be a football hero, or to go out for the team, even if he acquires only one black eye. A girl wants to be invited to all the Friday night dances, and be the football or baseball sponsor. By the time the boys and girls graduate from high school, their only ambition is to go to college—the kind they see in the movies—and after that, well, the future will take care of itself" (18). In other cases, the social observations turn inward, as in Lois Covington's essay, "On Being Plain," which concludes, "It is quite all right for me not to appear beautiful. No one expects me to. And anyway, I really feel that, like beauty, plainness is only skin deep" (10). In still other instances, the writing delves further into memoir, positing less a self-awareness than an acute awareness of the self as developed, externally, by one's readership, in the case of the concluding sentences of "Of Such Stuff," by Blanche Parcell: "What a past for a sophisticated college girl! No thrilling escapes from disaster, no heart-stirring romances—in fact, nothing to make me qualify as a movie heroine. . . . Fortunately, however, it is not of this that I think when I grow reminiscent. Instead, I relive—but why say more? The reader has already seen of what stuff my memory is made" (12). The aggregate contents of these two issues signal a clear and present appreciation of student writing in the form of narrative, memoir, and lyric (several poems dot the two issues), as well as more "traditional" genres such as the literary analysis or research paper—though these are far fewer in number overall.

Here begins the noteworthy contradiction between the progressive writing done by Woman's College English composition students and the still-conservative social setting of the school itself, owing largely to its position as a southern women's school emerging from the normal school tradition. The Woman's College becomes, in this way, a cautionary case study against reading the archives of women's writing with a singular lens, or with the agenda of keeping institutional type as a primary barometer for judging how and why women were educated as writers, readers, and hopefully, critical thinkers. Recognizing the normal school as a site for early progressive education—despite national calls for standardized "practical" efforts and uniform curricula—as well as the origin for the majority of public women's education and regional coeducational institutions in the United States—allows for a broader view into the position of the English composition course, and its early vestiges of the "creative." In the next chapter, I will explore this contradictory relationship between expository and creative writing, and between social conservatism and curricular liberalism, through the midcentury first-year composition magazine the *Yearling,* which picks up—albeit some twenty years later—where the *Sample Case* so abruptly leaves off.

2

In Her Own Words

The *Yearling* and First-Year Writing, 1948–51

THE SOCIAL AND intellectual traditions embedded in the Woman's College of the University of North Carolina as a former normal school quite clearly and deeply affected how and what its students were expected to do socially, versus what the somewhat progressive curriculum would ask them to do intellectually in the English writing classroom. Yet despite this contradictory earlier institutional and programmatic history, an enterprising and savvy student-led publication, the *Yearling*, emerged from the college midcentury, enacting the college's continued priority to educate the whole student and promote a deep intellectual engagement with the arts and humanities. To continue to follow the trajectory of extracurricular writing initiatives at the Woman's College as begun with the earliest publication, the *State Normal Magazine* in 1897, and taken up at the department level with the *Sample Case* in 1929–30, as examined briefly in chapter 1, in this chapter I focus on the history, content, and institutional importance of the *Sample Case*'s successor, the *Yearling*.

I consider this magazine, produced by women in the English 101 (first-year writing) sections at the Woman's College between 1948 and 1951, both as a local and national (disciplinary) artifact of women's literacy instruction, and of the curricular influence of creative writing and creative expression on English composition postwar. I also see the *Yearling* as yet another instantiation of David Gold's assertion that those voices often silenced by master narratives—in the case of composition studies, those of students, in particular women students—are ripe for reinvestigation through a broader conception of the role of archival research in representing a historical community of disciplinary importance.

On a local scale, the *Yearling* is an institutional artifact that illustrates and recovers the range of writing that the Woman's College students were being trained to do, and were capable of producing, within the otherwise regarded confines of the first-year writing course. On a national scale, the *Yearling* is a disciplinary artifact for composition studies that represents an early extant example of a first-year writing publication created by and for women students, and one that showcases the various blurring between creative and expository prose. Such histories are critical to situating the student publications within our institutions today, as well as the national promotion of student voices in newly formed field publications such as the contemporary undergraduate journal *Young Scholars in Writing*. The *Yearling* is one archival precursor to composition studies' methodological stance that writing is a public act rather than a private, prescriptive academic exercise; it also illuminates the forgotten history of the midcentury student magazine as a vehicle for publishing and promoting student writing. Finally, given its location, the *Yearling* illustrates how such first-year publications may provide a model archival story of literacy education in public women's colleges during this era, especially when set against other human and institutional narratives of women students being significantly conscripted by social norms.

Postwar Student Literary Magazines and First-Year Composition

While the Woman's College's open affection for molding the complete student and consummate woman scholar is clear, it is also evident that the college's approach to educating women was significantly influenced by its educational history and mission. To reiterate the popular quote by Charles Duncan McIver, founder of the Woman's College, "when you educate a man, you educate an individual; when you educate a woman, you educate a family." McIver's admonition, reprinted in the front of each year's course bulletin at the college, reaffirmed not only the importance of women in the social fabric of the family, ergo the larger community in which women were domestic pillars of morals and grace, but also the importance of grooming women to be knowledgeable workers, even leaders, within this community postgraduation.

This curricular and social mission for the college within the University of North Carolina system is best illustrated by a September 1934 address by the then-new dean of administration, Dr. Walter C. Jackson, to the Woman's College faculty council. Dr. Jackson declared,

> While this institution is undergoing a change we must remember that the whole subject of education is undergoing a searching re-examination. Those of us here now at the College may set our minds at rest with regard to the particular task that is ours. Our place in the Greater University has been clearly defined and accepted. It is understood by those interested that our place is very definitely that of a liberal arts college for women. [I have] had opportunity to know the mind of President Graham through frequent and frank discussions. A number of the trustees and a number of the faculty of the other institutions have expressed the enthusiastic hope that this college may have the opportunity to become the best liberal arts college in the South. Nowhere [have I] found any real difference of opinion in regard to this. These people are all interested that this college shall have the opportunity to become a great women's college. (Minutes of the Faculty Council, Sept. 10, 1934)

This aspiration to be the preeminent liberal arts institution of the South required that the college create and sustain a liberal-arts–minded curriculum that challenged rather than placated its women students. As such, the coursework at the Woman's College was not for the faint of heart, as it was intended to attract the best female minds in the region and, in its regional status aspirations, frequently beyond.[1] For example, all students were required to take two full years of English writing-focused courses, an anomaly among peer institutions in the South during this time. This work resisted the typical manifestations of women's writing taught in the early to mid-twentieth century, which was often an exercise in dilettante practices for society-minded ladies looking toward postgraduation, a secretarial service for male corporate authorities, or a prescriptive endeavor to be taught to pupils in future classrooms. Instead, the Woman's College offered a full complement of undergraduate courses in first-year composition, advanced composition, and creative writing, exhibiting an attractive range of writing-focused coursework not always available in the typical state college English department today.[2] Few students in other normal school or normal school–influenced settings were afforded such an opportunity to engage in these varied genres, even during the later era of general education reform.

These administrators at the Woman's College were clearly fighting against the prototypical profile of the women's college as a holding pen for those seeking an education on the path to society positions, and/or sequestered marriage and family life. Early writing textbooks for women college students, in contrast to the aims of the Woman's College writing courses, were attuned to these commonly intertwined goals of vocational and domestic achievement taught at many colleges following in the normal school tradition. For example, *English Composition for College Women,* published in 1914, argues that "there are certain demands made upon women in the home . . . that must be recognized in the training of women" (v). In particular, *English Composition* emphasized the need for training in oral delivery—such as public speaking in women's clubs and in other similar social settings—and appreciation of forms such as lyric poetry, as "the educated woman must have *an intelligent appreciation of the best* in all art forms" (Moore, Tompkins, and MacLean 195; emphasis in original). This textbook argued for the importance of mastering the "persuasive address," since "No matter where a woman's lot is cast, or whether she be a student, a wage earner, a wife, a mother, or an independent citizen, she faces the call to use her influence to improve surrounding conditions" (94). Such positioning cast the educated woman as a potential public orator, and member of a rhetorically savvy society, but also promoted the education of women *as* women per traditional domestic and social roles—for example, the need for a woman to be a skilled letter writer in order to accurately and politely "represent her when she is not present to speak for herself" (297), and to interpret works of art, given that such skill "*should be part of the equipment of every cultured mother and teacher,* for good pictures teach lessons of many kinds in a pleasant way" (201; emphasis in original).

While Charles McIver likely would have agreed with many of this textbook's socially attractive learning goals, he would not have consented to its larger, accompanying philosophy for educating women students enacted in many single-sex colleges, particularly those that began as normal schools: to view them as *pupils* writing for sometimes narrowly defined purposes, rather than seeing them as lifelong *writers*. Within the Woman's College, the emphasis on writing during this era was richer and more complex than the curricular and vocational opportunities found at other similarly structured single-sex institutions that built upon former teachers college traditions. Though its students often still graduated into traditional career roles such as nurses and educators, those enrolled at the Woman's College were also being encouraged to explore other career paths in art, philosophy, psychology, and, significantly, English, and were given the opportunity to study the craft and techniques of writing in a range of genres, both in classroom assignments and through a range of extracurricular, school-sponsored publications. As one of my interview subjects noted, far from being a limited, vocational training, the requirements at the Woman's College were, in fact, "known to be on par with the Seven Sisters' curriculum,"[3] a point interrogated in chapter 1 and reinforced through Jackson's inaugural address to the faculty.

By the end of World War II, the dean of women, Dr. Harriet Elliot, noted that the reputation and standing of the Woman's College was growing within the university system, and she expressed concern that should this reputation not be met with curricular rigor, the mission of the school would become obsolete. Elliott's report to the college faculty, as noted by the secretary of the faculty council, stated that, in sum,

> The type of student we are getting is improving. The trend is up. Students are better equipped. Fewer are failing. We are on the up-grade. . . . We will become more selective as our program of selection goes on and we improve. . . . We can meet these demands and maintain our place as a Liberal Arts college. We are in a very strategic position. People are urging students in the high schools to come here. The attitude about the college is high. We have an obligation to meet as part of the University. If we don't meet it—then Chapel Hill will." (Minutes of the Faculty Council, Apr. 17, 1944)

The Woman's College deliberately trained its students to be inquisitive, politically aware, and competitive as students within the University of North Carolina system and outside of it in the greater southern liberal arts college arena. The stakes for failure in this regard, or even mediocrity, were clearly too great: the threat of elimination through the domination of the men's university at Chapel Hill was one such consequence. This careful training, and desire for curricular and student excellence, bore significant weight upon the writing these women did both inside and outside the classroom setting. Such training is evident in the first-year magazine the *Yearling*, a publication that promoted the intellectual capabilities of Woman's College student writers and that followed a nationwide wave of making public first-year writing—as both pedagogical carrot and stick— already emerging midcentury.

The First-Year Writing Magazine: A (Historical) Nationwide Phenomenon

Many faculty today may consider the first-year magazine a recent phenomenon, born of the embrace of process pedagogy and the theoretical position that first-year composition may be a training ground for effective public discourse. In fact, student magazines were popular means for augmenting the first-year curriculum much earlier in the twentieth century. Between 1950 and 1963, *College English* and *College Composition and Communication* (*CCC*) ran a total of ten pieces either focusing on the student literary magazine in the first-year composition classroom or using the first-year student publication as evidence of successful pedagogy. This flurry of attention paid to the first-year publication evidenced some lingering truths about the published dissemination of student writing: that it encourages writers to see their work as public in scope, rather than limited to the classroom; that it promotes the value of revision; and that it provides a useful artifact of the capabilities and limitations of student writers, to be used to improve and amend future writing pedagogies.

Prior to this postwar era, featured journal pieces on student literary or writing magazines are comparatively few, even though it is clear that such publications existed on many campuses, including the Woman's College in its historical institutional formations.[4] One hypothesis for this phenomenon is to link the rise of the communications era and general education to the renewed interest in the first-year student publication. As institutions continued to revise their curricula to meet broadly defined goals across the curriculum, including those in speaking, writing, and fine arts, the first-year magazine would have been an attractive venue for showcasing those skills—an early assessment tool, perhaps. The collection of the best student work (often selected and/or juried by the students themselves) in a given composition class not only called attention to the successful acquisition of literacies among these students, but also served as a historical reference for how and where students were able (or not) to achieve the new general education goals. In addition, the increasing attention to fine arts and creative expression found in many curricula—including that of the Woman's College—was easily illustrated by the frequent short stories, poems, and other literary contributions found alongside more expository-type essays, reports, or transcribed oratories.

Finally, the importance of the faculty member in these student publications cannot be overlooked or minimized historically. Given the growing number of women teaching first-year writing during this decade—

women who otherwise may have been limited in their scholarly pursuits due to educations conscripted by teachers colleges' curricula and/or a lack of post-masters' studies—the literary magazine may have been a public statement of their intellectual capabilities as passed on to their equally capable students. Three of the pieces focusing on student literary magazines published during this thirteen-year period were, in fact, authored by women faculty who championed the value of promoting student writing outside the first-year classroom. Edith Wells's 1950 *CCC* survey of 186 colleges and universities, for example, showed that thirty-one institutions, including Barnard, Vassar, and Goucher, sponsored some sort of first-year student magazine. Wells's listings do not include the *Yearling,* but do include publications at several other state teachers colleges.[5] Wells also provides sample rationale from her questionnaire showing how these student publications were used. These include the University of Idaho's mailing of their publication to all high schools in the state (10), to provide sample themes and subtly promote expectations of incoming students, versus the use of the magazine at Vassar College, wherein the publication is "in the hands of all students . . . [and] examined closely and discussed in detail as part of class work," as a daily pedagogical tool (4).

Vassar College's magazine at the time had been in publication for forty years and was titled the *Sampler*—nearly identical to the first version of the *Sample Case,* the Woman's College first freshman writing magazine, discussed in chapter 1. These publication titles are quite similar in their root words, perhaps deliberately so; nevertheless, it is interesting to see the *Sample Case* as invoking a traveling salesman's wares—a masculine image—versus the *Sampler,* which invokes needlework—a feminine image. Even though the "sample case" conjures this image of a traveling salesman and his wares—in this case, the products of freshman writing at the college—as with the similar naming of the college in comparison to that of Duke's women's college in 1930–31, one can see echoes of the elite in the short-lived magazine's title. Overall, Wells's study provides a valuable snapshot of the prevalence of the freshman magazine postwar, and clearly argues for the continuation of such publications in its closing: "By giving prestige to freshman writing, the magazine can brighten the often dull composition classes. The magazine of freshman writing definitely has a place in the modern composition course" (11).

Another article, Ruth Davies's 1951 "A Defense of Freshmen," takes a more direct approach. It opens much like a friendly advice column, the readers of which are fellow writing teachers looking for support for their grading woes. Given her rhetorical positioning—invoking the figure of the best friend and using feminine-associated adjectives of the time such as "nervous"—it seems likely that Davies was speaking to fellow women faculty:

> Are you a reader of freshman themes? Do you find yourself nervous, run-down, and tired? Do you see red pencil-marks before your eyes, and are you haunted at night by dangling participles, split infinitives, disagreement between subject and verb, and comma splices? Do the freshmen and their papers give you palpitations and give you a pain? Have you, in fact, arrived at such a state that even your best friend can't tell you what to do? Then you need to take stock of yourself and your job, to find the root of your trouble; for your case is not hopeless! (440)

Davies's desire to stand up for the intellectual capabilities of first-year students otherwise dismissed or scolded by the academy is the basis for her overarching argument in this piece, comprised of roughly four parts. First, Davies argues that obsessing over grammar, or the "scrawny skin and brittle bones of composition," ignores the reality that all writing carries with it some measure of flaw (442), and draws vital attention away from the subject matter. Hence, her second point is that "No textbook will 'work' . . . no book will do the job [for the teacher]" (441); therefore, students should be asked to write and be inspired instead by "things in which they are interested" rather than the "charming topics to be found widely in use" in current textbooks of the early 1950s, with which the students have no connection or facility (443). Third, Davies argues that campus visitations by famous writers provide valuable and "real" material for writing. Finally, Davies encourages the revival of the literary magazine, which is "languishing on almost every college campus," noting that writing for publication motivates students to write well, since "there is no better medium for the development of critical perceptions than the chance to see one's work—or even the outpourings of print." She believes that students must be "serious . . . for the best of their work to achieve the dignity of print" (444).

I emphasize here the voice and audience of this brief essay because the link between student literary magazines and teacher ethos, particularly for women teachers of writing, is of critical importance in the development of these publications, historically speaking. These brief narratives served as local accounts of pedagogies and practices, but also—in the case of Davies's piece—as celebrations of teacherly success stories, or teacher-to-teacher encouragements. In the case of single-sex colleges such as the Woman's College, where women faculty taught first-year composition and directed first-year writing[6] (in financial circumstances far less desirable

than those of their male colleagues), the need for women to be both disciplinary cheerleaders and positive intellectual role models for their female
composition students was all the more critical.

The third woman-authored piece was published in 1963 and shows a
marked change in how the campus publication was viewed in relation to
first-year composition. In "The Campus Literary Magazine and Composition," Jacqueline Berke champions the campus publication on her campus
(Drew University) and narrates how she encourages freshmen to submit
to the publication, even though many pieces published therein are by students in the upper classes. Responding to a typical question from one of
her composition students—"will we ever get to do anything *creative?*"—
Burke responds, "If you like to write, if you think you can write, if you
actually do write, and want to have your work read and discussed, get in
touch with the editor of *Columns*" (10). Burke's piece also includes correspondence with faculty from more than thirty-five colleges and universities around the country (echoing Wells's 1950 survey), querying the
aims of their own campus literary magazines and describing "the benefits
I had observed from the interaction of the composition course and literary
magazine" (11). One respondent, the composition director from the University of Pennsylvania, noted that forty of his students submitted "manuscripts, poems, short stories, and plays," whereupon "twenty five of the
most promising writers [were] exempted from the second-semester composition course and placed in a regular creative writing course instead"
(13). No doubt this director's response was seen as allied with Burke's own
view, as her initial query included the following about her own campus
publication: "The magazine is an outlet for the bright and gifted student;
he represents the back-bone of the publication. For the average but restless student who feels confined by routine composition assignments, the
magazine offers opportunity for creative writing" (12). In Burke's piece,
she overtly encourages her students' *creative* writing impulses as an outlet
from the "confines" of the traditional composition classroom.

Clearly the secondary purpose of such magazines was, in fact, to make
these two explicit connections: between the freshman writing course
and its "required" limitations (implied to be felt strongly by the students
themselves) and between the composition course and the more desirable
creative writing courses—as evidenced in the comments from the director at the University of Pennsylvania. Burke's admonition that the literary magazine be used to "liberate" students from composition and ease
them into the more carefree creative writing is an interesting parallel to
the relationship between creative writing and composition at the Woman's
College during this era, particularly in the alumnae interviews, and in the

regular inclusion of student poems among the themes and essays within the pages of the *Yearling*.

Other pieces from this time period also encouraged teachers to push students toward publication of their writing in order to improve the quality of their class work. In Edgar Stanton's 1950 article, this work is at a fellow women's college (Converse College, South Carolina): "The overwhelming majority of freshmen in American colleges and universities write merely for one instructor to read and grade and return their papers, and they are not going to exert themselves to do their best work. . . . When the Converse freshmen write their themes, they know beforehand that they are performing for highly critical listeners, their own classmates. And they write accordingly. [As a result], if Converse girls are any criterion, the maturity, form, content, and general interest of the themes will improve geometrically" (42). Here, the first-year magazine serves to improve the quality of student writing, which in turn will help teachers, with both groups seeing the work as public writing rather than busywork exercises done in private spaces. When Stanton discusses prizes won by former contributors, however, he notes that such results would be notable "even for a creative writing class," again reminding readers of the relatively lowly status of the composition course, and the potential entree to "real" writing that comes from being published in the magazine.

In a similar vein, Donald Z. Woods of the University of Minnesota writes in 1954 that his department's magazine, *Samplings*, serves not only to make student writing public, but also to use student writing as a teaching tool in the classroom. His department—of rhetoric rather than English—produced the magazine, but in doing so it attempted to "give representation, through choice of subject matter, to the many departments within our college. For example, in any issue of *Samplings*, we may have a term paper on 'Nutrition in Geriatrics' by a home economics major . . . [and] a descriptive paper on 'Patrolling the Western Forests by Air' by a forestry major who has spent a summer doing just that; Creative writing, in the form of fiction, essays, reviews and criticism, and narratives of personal experience, balances the more utilitarian writing" (123).

These various uses of and arguments for the first-year magazine within the composition program, or as part of the larger English department during the postwar era, provide a context for what was happening at the Woman's College with the *Yearling*, wherein women were writing for all of the above reasons—to connect with a wider audience, to elevate the status of their composition coursework, and to make print alliances between various types of writing done within the first-year course. An analysis of the publication's origins reveals its purpose to be in line with the motivations above, but its content to be far more difficult to classify as "creative" versus "expository," thereby troubling the seemingly limited (and implicitly inferior) definition of first-year composition that pervaded other first-year magazines and courses of this era.

The *Yearling* and the Freshman Essay, Redefined

Unlike the public analyses and announcements of student publications discussed above, the beginnings of the *Yearling* were far less auspicious. Yet the magazine's conception was a direct response to similar work happening at other women's colleges and thus was a local embodiment of a national trend that the Woman's College clearly felt beneficial to the education of its own students. In addition, the magazine reflects the challenging and wide-ranging writing and reading that students were being asked to do in first-year composition, and thus augments the more staid archival documents that scholars might otherwise rely upon to characterize this or any program's history.

In the years following World War II, the English department at the Woman's College faced plights typical of many institutions today: a growing major that results in courses bursting at the seams; faculty being wooed by rival institutions; concomitant struggles to cover their vacated lines; and a first-year writing sequence questioned from within and without regarding its educational effectiveness, including its help for "remedial" students, all without any composition-rhetoric specialists on faculty. This was a transitional era for writing education: fighting against the communications emphasis offered by general education revisions, many liberal arts colleges were moving toward generalist literary instruction as the focus of the major, while struggling to accommodate the continuing expectations of the larger university community regarding the "traditional" areas of grammar and speech within the first-year course. In addition, these were the years prior to the emergence of rhetoric and composition as a distinct field of study, and the years witnessing a rise of creative writing within the English department, a key specialization that pushed and pulled against rhetoric and oratory in practical, intellectual, and artistic terms.

Such points of national and local contention were reflected in the detailed English department minutes archived for this time period, many of which include play-by-play arguments over the very items above. Among these discussions was the figure of May Bush, who served on the Woman's College faculty from 1934 to 1967, and as the director of composition from approximately 1940 through the mid-1950s. While I will more deeply profile the sociopolitical departmental position of Bush in chapter 4, here I want to illustrate how her small utterances in department minutes about composition as a required course and as a broader area of study, and student training, give us some insight into the origins of the *Yearling.*

In the May 19, 1944, minutes of the Woman's College English department, Bush proposed that "the department consider the possibility of giving freshmen some opportunity to publish, as they are given at [fellow women's colleges] Bryn Mawr College and at Converse College."[7] No mention is made of this proposal again for nearly four years, until the March 8, 1948, meeting, in which Bush announces that "the title is to be *The Yearling,* and that March 15 is the tentative deadline for the submission of material." Then, in the December 6, 1948, minutes, following an extended discussion of the English major, junior and senior major advising, and the need for "note-worthy" items from the department to be publicized in the school newspaper and elsewhere, there again appears a slightly longer paragraph on the status of the second volume of the publication, stating, "the various section representatives had elected the following seven girls to the editorial board of the *Yearling.* . . . This group will meet December 9, 1948, to elect an editor-in-chief for the publication." Finally, on December 13, 1950, during its fourth and final year of publication, Bush announces that all faculty who teach freshmen will receive a letter about the *Yearling.*

These brief, easily overlooked announcements sandwiched in department notes detail the beginnings of the *Yearling,* which would appear in the spring semesters of 1948, 1949, 1950, and 1951. In the January 10, 1949, department meeting minutes, again dropped in between news on book orders and the new speech testing program for the university (as elocution remained a central concern in the education of southern women at this time), Bush reports that, "From each freshman section [of composition] a committee which would be responsible for working with the instructor on the matter of selection of material to be submitted to the *Yearling* should be elected as soon as possible, and that February 14 is the deadline set for the submitting of material from first semester work." Only two more mentions are made of the *Yearling* in department minutes—in December 1950 and in April 1951. The first mention from Bush announces that "a letter about *The Yearling* had been sent to all staff members who teach freshmen"; the second, in 1951, notes, "an instance of plagiarism [has] been recently discovered in the 1950 *Yearling* and the Honor Board had already acted on the problem."

What was this magazine that garnered so little attention among departmental business, especially compared to the noteworthy items about other types of writing-related business in the department? In search of answers to these questions, I examined archival copies of each issue in light of the other visible politics and developments occurring in the English department and recorded in the archives during this period at the college. Undertaking a textual analysis of the magazine's contents necessitates an overview of what the students were being asked to do in the first-year course itself. According to the "Manual of Instructions" for English 101 and 102 in 1949–50,[8] the purpose of the English composition courses at the Woman's College, designed as a year-long sequence with this course numbering from 1941 forward, were still to "give the student the degree of literacy expected of an educated person in a modern democracy. The instructors hope to develop in each student the ability to think with clearness, to read with comprehension, and with appreciation of literary values, and to write with ease and effectiveness. Freshman English is distinctly a composition course, and themes or other forms of written work will be required throughout the year. The course seeks to develop the individual's latent powers and to guide her in forming correct habits of expression" (1). This description is a slight reworking of the description published in the 1930–31 "A Manual of Instruction." Note that the larger emphasis here, in this overview, is *not* on educating future teachers (though some of these students certainly went on to teach), nor is it on refining the social communicative skills of young southern women. Rather, the first sentence emphasizes a world in which Woman's College students are part of an *educated, literate democracy,* populated by citizens who write with "ease and effectiveness." There is an emphasis not only on "correct expression," but also a continued emphasis on those "latent powers" of (creative) women.

These goals were put to teachers (and students) in the form of a set lesson plan to be followed in both courses. English 101, the more traditional expository course, was made up of five units, or "blocks": Review of Grammar, Punctuation, Mechanics, Letter Writing; Diction, Word Study, and Definition; The Paragraph, Summary, and Précis; Organization and Outlining; and Sentence Structure and Style (Department of English, "A Manual of Instructions," 1949–50, 6–7). Within these units, students would go over the relevant items in the handbook (at the time, *The MacMillan Handbook of English*) and also read several pieces per block, such as "Culture and Anarchy," by Matthew Arnold; "The Idea of Progress," by Charles A. Beard; and "Why Liberalism Is Bankrupt," by Nathaniel Peffer. Students were asked to write a minimum of the following, in this listed order: "one short impromptu theme and one short prepared theme; short definitions of concrete nature, and two or more short essays of definition,

concerned with ideas; summary sentences and précis of assigned paragraphs; an essay several paragraphs in length; an outline for a long paper
(1,000–1,400 words) and develop the paper from the outline; and one or
more impromptu themes and one slightly longer essay" (6–7).

English 102 was, in contrast, the writing-about-literature course, as
had been the case earlier in the institution's normal school curricula, and
as was common for English composition sequences of the era, particularly
as the concept of composition and rhetoric as a subdiscipline was yet to
be fully articulated in English studies. English 102 was divided into five
blocks: Continued Study of Exposition, the Informal Essay; the Research
Paper; Narration and Description, the Short Story; Narration Continued, the Novel, and Drama ("A Manual of Instructions," 1949–50, 8–9).
Within these blocks, students were asked to write, again in the following
order, "two informal or familiar essays; outline and develop a research
paper of from 1,200 to 1,800 words; write two or more narrative or descriptive themes, one of which is to be written in class; write at least one
impromptu critical essay; write either one long critical paper or a long
narrative; write three critical short themes" (8–9). Sample readings within
the blocks include literary standards such as *The Scarlet Letter,* excerpts
from *The Importance of Being Earnest,* the short stories "The Killers" and
"The Lottery Ticket," as well as other stories such as "The Gentleman from
San Francisco," by Ivan Bunin, and essays such as "Of the Resemblance
of Children," by Michel de Montaigne, and "The Chill of Enthusiasm," by
Agnes Repplier. In addition, English 102 classes were to cover "parallel
readings" from the "Bible (four weeks), Biography (four weeks), and Mythology (four weeks)" (10). A helpful list of "The Olympic Council," "Other
Important Gods," "Demigods or Heroes and Heroines of Famous Stories,"
and "Groups of Deities" is included in the handbook for instructor reference, as is an extensive list of biographies, novels, and "familiar essays" for
possible instructor inclusion within the set course structure (13–15).

As is evident from this course sequence of English 101–102 that existed in the late 1940s and early 1950s at the Woman's College, students
were expected to write a considerable number of pages each semester and
to demonstrate clear ability to write in a variety of subgenres, or modes,
such as the research paper, the narrative, the critical essay, and the reflective essay, as well as write in-class and out-of-class themes on a variety
of subjects. Also evident are instructors' emphasis on and explication of
classical narratives as well as modern philosophical arguments in their
writing pedagogies, which ask students to engage not only in a variety
of expository pieces, but also in some degree of emulation next to these

literary and essayistic models. Such a combination of strict adherence to a two-semester sequence culminating in literary study and an overriding emphasis on being an educated and literate citizen of a democracy sets the stage for an interesting variety of materials profiled in the *Yearling*.

Each volume of the magazine opened with an introduction by the student editors, which curiously evolved (or more accurately, devolved, in terms of length and depth) over the four annual issues. In the forward to the inaugural (Spring 1948) issue of the *Yearling*, which contains six poems, one research paper, and twenty-one themes completed for the first-year writing course, many of which are actually observational narratives, social commentary, and/or memoirs of childhood, the editors write:

> *The Yearling* is a revival of the literary magazine, *The Sample Case*, which was published by the Freshman English classes of 1929 and 1930, when it was discontinued. It is our hope that the freshman classes to follow will make this magazine a permanent publication at Woman's College. The Board of Editors, in selecting the themes printed here, has tried to choose the best writing representative of that produced in the classes this year. We have all worked hard—you, the class representatives and contributors, the faculty advisory committee, and we, the student editors. Thus, as David McCord says in his anthology, *What Cheer:* "Now that the labor of gathering, sifting, admiring, accepting, rejecting, regretting, arranging, rearranging, and re-admiring these many items is definitely over," we have energy but to say, "This is it!"

The subsequent (1949) issue includes four poems, two book reviews, one research paper, two short stories/dialogues, and ten essays, chiefly variations on creative nonfiction such as travel narratives and imagined historical narratives, plus a modified foreword to its contents that declares: "Our freshman magazine is a limited anthology of writing by the students in the twenty-nine sections of Freshman English which offers a limitless opportunity for creative writing and self-expression of various types. We, the Board of Editors, feel that these attempts, failures, and successes represent the best compositions of the average freshman student. By the continuation of *The Yearling*, freshmen maintain a higher goal in their English work . . . to see their writing published." In the third edition, published in 1950, contents include only two poems, one research paper, and no book reviews; the twenty-one remaining pieces are memoirs or observational narrative/imagined dialogue. Also included in this issue for the first time are seven items labeled "trivia," or aphorisms, scattered throughout. The issue's foreword is rooted in literary allusion: "As spake the scepter when she won the Ancient Mariner, so speaks the staff of *The Yearling,* as the youngest publication of Woman's College shows its face for the third consecutive year." And continues: "This year, a writing club, *Fifty-Three,*⁹ designed for members of the class of '53, was organized as an outgrowth of *The Yearling.* It is the goal of this club, like *The Yearling,* to maintain a higher standard in the individual's work in English." The final issue, published in spring 1951, includes several aphorisms, as in the 1950 issue, as well as three poems, one research-based paper, and twenty-six essays, and opens with only a single brief paragraph: "In this, the 1951 *Yearling,* we present to you the best of the freshman writing of this year. The subject horizon was unlimited, and pen and ink took over from there. This is our best, and we very proudly present it to you!"

The evolution of these introductions, as well as the associated content of each of the four issues, is perhaps a window into the evolution of the magazine itself. By the fourth year, the introduction is brief and less personalized; literary allusions are absent, as are mentions of specific individuals. In the first year, the editors seem keen on situating the magazine historically, and on alluding to the difficulty of their selection and editorial processes; they also include a nice play on language with "limited" space versus "limitless" showcasing of student work. In the second year, the editors specifically note the opportunity for "creative writing" included in the issue; indeed, this year's volume contains six specifically "creative" pieces, more than in other years. By the third year, the editors largely leave the introduction to literary allusion, save their self-labeling of the magazine as a kind of "club." By the fourth year, the introduction is perfunctory and does little more than, in fact, open the issue for readers. Of course, the true amount of motivation behind these introductions is unknown, and other considerations, such as space limitations, may have been in play. But clearly the magazine becomes more focused on content and less on editorial commentary by the final issue, as the content itself becomes more focused on essayistic prose as opposed to literary or poetic forms.

When we examine the sometimes surprising content of the magazine, we can also see some clear trends in what types of items were being selected for publication, and what types of writing were being valued as publication-worthy, among and between these first-year student writers. Although each issue contains a small number of labeled genres—poetry, research papers, book reviews, noted in the table of contents as such—what is striking about the aggregate contents of the *Yearling* is the wide range of the remainder of each issue's content, considered "freshman themes," or more precisely, work falling under the moniker of "essay."

Far from the polar divisions of the theme that we might expect from a midcentury first-year course—for example, text-based literary analyses or dry, research-driven paper or reports, especially given the formulaic requirements laid out in the "Manual"—the *Yearling* profiles a number of works written in the belles lettres tradition, as well as pieces that are more difficult to classify or categorize, except to call them a kind of literary reportage, even early examples of creative nonfiction. Given the wide and perhaps atypical variety of writing the women were actually doing, however, in English 101 and 102 (compared to, for example, an institution such as Yale, where the required content of "Daily Themes" during this time rarely diverged from that which emulated the course title—daily essays of limited length on specific topics within a traditional "theme" subgenre), it is not surprising that students were submitting writing in a range of genres. What is more surprising is that the chosen content was often quite compelling and current, especially for women who otherwise were socially trained to be "proper" in their behavior.

These pieces are on topics such as spirituality, social mores (for example, the joys and ills of smoking), and the plight of living in a women's dormitory. But a greater number of these pieces are social observations about southern culture or the life of a southern woman, or some critical aspect of it, told from the position of a quizzical, sometimes cautiously judgmental narrator who paints a rich picture of the issue at hand. Some are partly fictionalized, while others are from a deeply personal perspective, all with an authoritative narrator at the helm.

Consider this from "Make Mine Southern Style," by Pat Thomas, in the 1951 issue: "By the time I had discovered that plantations are practically obsolete today and that all southern gentlemen are not exact replicas of Clark Gable—or even, necessarily, gentlemen—I had, nevertheless, determined that my four years of college would take me South. Against the protests of intellectually-minded individuals who praised to the skies the merits of Wellesley, Vassar, and Smith, I named Woman's College as my future abode, without a great deal more purpose than my curiosity about the land of the flourishing hospitality" (4) Thomas's essay illustrates a popular subgenre of writing—about the South, or about southern life—in the *Yearling,* but also unintentionally serves as a narrative of one woman's choice to attend the Woman's College as a nonsoutherner, versus attending one of the named elite institutions of the Northeast.[10]

Her essay, aligning itself somewhat with anthropological concerns, later describes the juxtapositions she encountered when engaging more intimately with life in North Carolina:

I found that southern girls dress much more casually for a date; that southern boys are much more courteous (my one illusion which remained undaunted) and seem to delight in making their dates feel helpless and protected . . . [but] Rose-Colored [as] my new-found spectacles were, they presented a slightly darker picture when I investigated groups instead of individuals. . . . I felt, rather than saw, a certain disdain of the Negro race, evidence of the Jim Crow laws in practice. . . . Certainly I was slightly shocked at the willingness of southern gentile girls to date Jewish boys, and made two very close Jewish friends. My Yankee head by this time was a whirl of checks and balances on these strange people who were fast affirming their normality as ordinary human beings. (4–5)

We can read Thomas's essay using a few different frames: First, it is a sample of what kind of work the women students were being asked, or encouraged, to write in their composition classes, so we may view her essay as a literacy narrative of sorts—in this case, becoming literate in the ways of the South. Second, it is a historical document that shines light on the perspectives of these women as they began their postsecondary work at Woman's College, particularly the visible population of northern girls who saw the college as equivalent in stature to elite northeastern schools, as Thomas's narrative relates. Finally, it is a cultural artifact showcasing the ways in which racial politics entered the lives of these women and intersected with their writing educations, in turn clearly influencing the kind of writing they produced in the first-year courses. Using any of these readings, Thomas's piece is unexpectedly insightful in its examination of what passes for "acceptable" social practices in the South versus the North—and how these traditions are often working at cross-purposes.

Another example of the "living in the South" subgenre is visible in Shirley Berger's "An Approach to Segregation," published in the inaugural 1948 issue of the *Yearling*. This piece takes the form of an (imagined) dialogue between a "mysterious stranger" and two other individuals, a southern storekeeper and a northern banker, as interpreted by a third-person narrator. The piece opens with the mysterious stranger, who "had come from nowhere and [whose] only destination was 'the answer to racial segregation in the south'" (22). Berger's dialogue goes on to detail the conversations about segregation between the mysterious stranger and a southern storekeeper, who declares, "'I certainly wouldn't have no nigger eat at my table or sit next to me on a bus,' the southerner proclaimed dogmatically. Then seeing a glint in his companion's eye that denoted his feeling were not in complete harmony with his own, the storekeeper added,

'And I wouldn't marry one either. Would you?' The stranger was perplexed at this question, for the segregation problem was not one of intermarriage to him. It was rather an issue involving human dignity" (22). The next conversation takes the mysterious stranger to New York, since "he realized his answer to segregation was not in Andrew Jackson's General Store" (22). In this section, he dialogues with a "rich banker" whom he hopes "might solve the enigma":

> "I believe," [the banker] said in a stock-holders' committee tone, "that old Uncle Sam should pass a law forbidding segregation in all forms—on the buses, in the movies, and especially in the schools. Then once the children started going to schools together all racial problems would automatically dissolve." This statement surprised the mysterious young man. "Don't you feel that suddenly thrusting white children who have been bred in the jaws of intolerance all their lives with colored children would cause friction? Don't you think that gradual, progressive steps forward which would finally lead to assimilation of white and colored schools would be better?"

The mysterious stranger thinks aloud (via the narrator) in the closing of the piece, remarking that "he had learned that the solution did not lie in extreme conservatism, a doctrine advocated by some southerners who liked the present status of the Negro in the south and desired no change, nor did the answer lie in extreme radicalism, a doctrine advocated by some northerners who wanted to mow down tradition and prejudice without first pulling up the roots" (23).

The clever structuring of this piece as first a dialogue—positioning the views held therein far outside the writer, or even the writer-as-narrator—and second, as a *historical* dialogue (set in, presumably, 1928), allows Berger to both fictionalize and hypothesize the kind of arguments for both sides in the debate over segregation without naming her own personal views.[11] Berger's piece proposes that *neither* side has the "right" answer, which is a bold statement to come from a first-year college student living in the South. Berger's piece, unlike Thomas's, more directly addresses the politics of racial harmony, yet also exposes the contradictions found in life in the South. Whereas Thomas is puzzled by southern women who discriminate against blacks yet date Jewish men,[12] Berger expresses these contradictions as greater shades of gray, wherein "instant" integration is neither possible nor necessarily desirable in the South she observes.

For those who now view the twenty-first-century college writing course as overly fraught with politics or current events, rather than the grammar-based drills that prevailed in previous decades and are romanticized to be the true "teaching of writing," Berger's piece is an interesting challenge to that mythology. Berger may have indeed learned about mechanics in her English 101 course (my interviews with alumnae, and the above material from the English 101 and 102 course guides indicate that grammar was, indeed, a key course component), but she was using that knowledge to engage with the politics of the day, as writers often do. Sometimes the local observation narrative was more lighthearted, but still with a keen eye toward the unique regionalism that the women students felt. In Jean Hollinger's 1950 *Yearling* piece, "Carolina Moan," she waxes nostalgic (with a sharp, satirical wit) about a "failed" songwriter, and how he could have improved his fortunes simply by writing lyrics about her home state: "Everybody writes songs about North Carolina, even those who think they are writing about Rhode Island or South Carolina. Of course, I refer in part to such obvious illustrations of mass affection for my home state as 'Carolina Moon' and 'Carolina in the Mor-or-or-orning.' But natives of North Carolina . . . who moan about the only moon this old earth has as if it were their private nutshell, or who insist upon rhyming 'Carolina' with 'finer' are not the only ones who realize the unique position of North Carolina as the only state worthy of notice" (16).

Hollinger's satire—while also representing a fascination with the local that permeates the issues of the journal, and consequently must have had some prominence in the writing done in the first-year courses, as these pieces were selected from that aggregate work—illustrates yet another dimension of the writing published in the *Yearling*: humor and self-deprecation, often directed at the culture in which the women were living, or at the women themselves. These were not dour, stereotypically proper ladies who dared not engage in satire or sarcasm in their writing in order to sometimes make a larger point about the values of their communities. These were women who exercised their wit in order to advance their social observations within a classroom setting—and then in a more public forum, when chosen for publication in the *Yearling*. Take as another example Sally Beaver's 1950 essay, "Of Baby Brothers and Modern Art." Beaver laments her father's insistence that her toddler-aged brother go into sports as a career, based on her father's continual (and obviously somewhat facetious) observation, "Two and a half years old, and look at that pitch, will you?" (8). Beaver also observes that her mother wants "Jerry" to go into law or medicine—based on his interest in having books read to him. Instead, she offers her own somewhat satirical take on her brother's future career possibilities: "As for me, however, I agree with neither Dad nor Mother as to Jerry's future career. I have seen him wield a pencil or crayon and make wild arcs and lines resembling nothing under the sun; so I have decided that he should be a modern artist. Usually, my parents win all the family discussions by reason of seniority. However, this time I think my logic will overwhelm theirs, and I shall be able to win them over by reasoning such as this" (8).

Beaver's argument takes her through Jerry's possible futures—as a baseball player, in which he will "be remembered only in newspaper stories and newsreels, not by any lasting work which he himself produced" or as a doctor, which leads him to die "from arthritis, overwork, and ulcers, [whereupon] only a few antiquated patients and some records in the civil books will testify that he ever existed" (9). Instead, Beaver argues that her brother should "pursue the career of a modern artist," since, "given a free hand with the materials in the house, a little encouragement, and a few days' free time, he should turn out enough masses of atrocity to insure him of a place in the Metropolitan Museum of Art between Picasso and Matisse" (9).

On the surface, this is keen satire on modern art—and the author's distaste for it. But what else does this piece evidence, in historical context? A woman writer of visible facility, no more than eighteen or nineteen years old, who recognizes two "typical" career roles assigned to men of stature (athlete, doctor) as well as the reality of art being a male-dominated field, and who likely sees her own career prospects less scrutinized and planned than those of her brother. Beaver's piece also shows the pointed jabs that authors in the *Yearling* were not only taking in their first-year writing assignments, but also the kinds of perspectives, arguments, and positions that the magazine saw as the "best" of what the freshman writers had to offer across the twenty-nine sections of English 101, few if any of which were rooted in the analysis of literary texts, a subgenre we know did dominate the reading list of English 102, and many other first-year courses like it around the country during this era.

This is not to say that there was a complete absence of traditional pieces featured in the magazine's issues. Works such as "The Ocean" (1950), "Summer Evening" and "Diving at Acapulco" (1951), and "The Candle" (1948) are definitely in the introspective, nature-as-beauty trend of observational writing, harkening back to nineteenth-century literary traditions and representative of the more stereotypical work expected from young southern ladies of the time. There were also poems published in each issue, as mentioned previously, some short and observational in nature, others more traditional verse. For example, Glenn Harden's poem in the 1948 issue, "Burning a Letter," reads, in full:

The sudden-kindled flames leap up
Like hungry birdlings,
Mouths gaping for a morsel held in their mother's beak.
They die down to sparks,
Like soon-shut eyes
Peering from beneath the dead bird's breast. (7)

In the 1950 issue, in contrast, Mary Alice Ballew's poem "No More" begins, "The cherry tree has never bloomed / Since childhood's day before, / Or is it that I just don't watch / Beside the back porch door?" (15).

The proportion of poetry to other types of writing in the *Yearling*, however, should not lead readers to believe that literary works were not valued in the Woman's College English department. Instead, this proportion is due to the prestige of the college's institution-wide literary magazine *Coraddi,* a publication originating in the State Normal and Industrial College era, in which students from the Woman's College, as well as other single-sex and coed institutions around the country, published their poetry and fiction and took part in yearly literary festivals featuring writers such as Robert Penn Warren. In fact, two of the editors of the 1949 *Yearling* were also on staff of the *Coraddi* in their junior and/or senior years at the Woman's College.

In its four years of publication, the *Yearling* included poetry on a regular basis, but the more prominent venue for this type of work would have been *Coraddi,* a collegewide endeavor with a national reputation—yet another site of extracurricular writing in which students could participate. Given the diversity of the published pieces in the *Yearling,* including the wide range within the essay/themes category, it is fair to say that the magazine did not fit the typical, or expected, characterization of current-traditional, standard-format teachings so often lamented as being the result of early to midcentury composition teachings. These women's work highlights a great range of subject matter and style, as well as an affection for a variety of subgenres within the expository to creative writing spectrum. The positions put forth in the expository pieces, and some of the creative work, were far from what one might expect from students at a former normal school in the South—wherein conservative social values and gendered expectations still controlled many nonclassroom aspects of life—and in some cases belie the purported traditions of first-year writing midcentury, especially for women. This is a central contradiction I explored when interviewing alumnae who worked on the magazine during its brief existence.

Speaking for Themselves: The Women of The *Yearling*

In the spring 1949 issue of the *Yearling*, twenty-six students from the college's English 101 and 102 classes would see their work appear in print. These included Elizabeth Poplin (Stanfield-Maddox), a member of the magazine's editorial team, who published "Same Time, Same Station, Same Everything," an extended and pointed critique of radio "soap opera" programming; Jacqueline Jernigan (Ammons), the editor in chief, who published "Prayer," a short essay on the value of spirituality and faith; and Lucy Page (Wagner), an English major who did not serve on the magazine's editorial board, but who published "They Also Serve," a brief narrative account of her visit to her father, a patient at the Veterans Administration hospital. These three diverse pieces of writing nestled among the other work published in the 1949 issue—three poems, two book reviews, one research paper, and sixteen essays—would be emblematic of the work these three women would produce in their postgraduate writing lives.

I interviewed Elizabeth, Jacqueline, and Lucy via phone and face-to-face interviews.[13] Each woman generously shared her time and memories of life at the Woman's College, as well as artifacts from her own college and professional writing.[14] These conversations led me to understand that the legacy of intellectual and social instruction that intersected with the writing classroom at the Woman's College reached far into these women's personal and professional futures and affected their valuations of literacy education to this day. It also led me to conclusions about the magazine and about writing instruction at the Woman's College that I did not anticipate upon starting this research—namely, that *creative* writing, in its various manifestations, was what these students remembered best about their writing at the Woman's College, and is the image of writing most often conjured when they discuss their college writing experiences today. This trend indicated that while the *Yearling* may have been a springboard for building confidence in students' own writing, and experience with seeing their writing in print, the first-year course, which served as the material for the magazine, was only one of several literacy-related events at the Woman's College that would shape who these women became as writers, readers, and teachers.[15]

Elizabeth, Jacqueline, and Lucy's backgrounds are in some ways similar: each married shortly after college and had children, each became a teacher, and each spent the majority of her life residing in North Carolina. But their specific career and life trajectories were quite diverse: Elizabeth majored in Spanish at the Woman's College and received her master's and doctoral degrees in the subject. She then worked as a tenured professor of Spanish literature at Georgia State University and as a freelance writer of southern history. After receiving her undergraduate degree in home economics, Jacqueline went to Europe for a short time, where she taught high school diploma–level English and math to servicemen in Germany. Upon returning to the states, Jacqueline wrote regular columns for both her church and a local newspaper. After receiving her undergraduate degree in English, Lucy taught eighth grade for many years, then received her provisional and master's degree in library science while teaching in a primary school library. She became town historian for the city of Hudson, North Carolina, and coauthored a book on the history of Hudson, in addition to producing a DVD on the Hudson Methodist Church for the town library, of which she is currently the librarian.

Despite these different emphases, for Elizabeth, Jacqueline, and Lucy, the foundational instruction that they received at the Woman's College bore a common and significant weight on each woman's postgraduate livelihood. When they speak of their experiences with writing as undergraduates, similar adjectives recur in the descriptions: "encouraging," "motivating," "supportive," and "high quality." All agree that the English department was one of, if not the, top departments in the Woman's College, and all similarly agree that the writing they were required to do in the department was varied, challenging, and beneficial to their future lives as teachers, and as writers outside their primary career fields. Each woman speaks of her college experience fondly, and each also narrates a somewhat complex relationship between the desire for the college to produce independent, thinking women writers and the social constraints of attending an all-women's college postwar.

It is relatively easy to see Elizabeth, Jacqueline, and Lucy's recollections as in some ways in conversation with one another, both then and now. Each recalls a positive educational experience that bore upon her future career; each emphasizes the importance of personal choice and personal responsibility within her narrative of the past, both personally and educationally speaking. But these interview recollections also remind us that any segment of history—whether it concern an institution or a larger community that stemmed from that institutional space—is filled with individual perspectives. Elizabeth's view of the Woman's College as beneficial but perhaps socially limiting bears witness to Lucy's view of these limitations as necessary to a young woman's slow self-discovery. Jacqueline's remembrance of a largely interdisciplinary team of women working on literacy initiatives that were defined, for the most part, by creative writing (yearbook, first-year magazine) contrast somewhat with Lucy's memories of being drawn to English—as the only major among these three women—through one teacher's interest in her work, separating herself from the more preprofessional training desired by her family upon enrolling in college. Finally, each woman's approach to preserving her own literacy history is similarly varied—from Lucy's meticulous archiving of her own writing, to Elizabeth's emphasis on archiving the work of herself *and* her regional community (the South), to Jacqueline's sharper recollections of the editorial over the written, the inner relationships over the finished products of her literacy endeavors.

These interviews, set against the material published within the *Yearling,* evidence a paradox between social and literacy education at the Woman's College postwar: this was a strict and high-mannered college that exercised considerable control over its students' moral and ethical constructions, yet also published a politically savvy and thought-provoking first-year writing publication demonstrating the wit, insight, and political awareness of these same students. Opining that this paradox may be present within the histories of other institutions, especially women's public colleges, I question whether the larger narratives (and accepted myths) of first-year writing in the United States are wholly representative of all sites of instruction, or in individual sites represented by just one kind of narrative artifact. In the case of the Woman's College, an examination of the *Manual of Instruction* would yield one kind of perspective on literacy; an examination of the *Yearling* on its own might elicit a competing assumption; and an isolated discussion with alumnae would elicit yet other conclusions. Ultimately, no one of these remembrances stands as *the* history of the Woman's College during this era, nor can it represent the complexities of social and educational norms being reinforced, and sometimes contradicted, within the college itself.

Elizabeth Poplin Stanfield-Maddox: Professor, Writer, Historian

Elizabeth studied English and Spanish during her time at the Woman's College. She had originally planned to do two years' worth of coursework at the college and then transfer to Duke; at the time, this was the only path for women who wanted to attend that university.[16] However, by her junior year, she realized that she "was serious, and if [she] wanted Phi Beta Kappa, [she] had better stay at Woman's College." Elizabeth's first aspiration was the University of Chicago, which admitted women, but she remembers that her parents "were not about to turn me loose in Chicago." Elizabeth notes that the Woman's College had a "fantastic reputation" and that her freshman year was the first time she and many of her friends—including the "large contingent" from her hometown of Wilmington, North Carolina—"had met any Yankee girls." Woman's College, for Elizabeth, was the logical choice; its position as a public, nonsectarian school drew "serious" students such as herself from the Carolinas. It also was a lower-cost alternative to the Seven Sisters schools of the Northeast. Elizabeth asserts, "my career as a professor was really built more on what I learned at the Woman's College, more than graduate school. When I was in the classroom at Georgia State, I was always drawing on what I learned at the Woman's College."

In terms of intellectual standards intersecting with social mores—a paradoxical intersection at best during these years at the college—Elizabeth remembers the English department at the Woman's College as one led by the imposing figure of Leonard Hurley, one of the longest-serving faculty members of the institution overall, and a professor whom Elizabeth characterizes as "right out of a Dickens novel." His stringent intellectual and moral supervision of the women students in the department's courses is evident in Elizabeth's story of an interlibrary loan request that she made—but was denied—due to Hurley's intervention. Elizabeth remembers:

> He [Hurley] gave lectures on Mark Twain. He mentioned a scurrilous piece that Twain had written—I don't even know why he cared to mention it. It took place in the court of Elizabeth I, and it was about an ambassador there who had an unfortunate experience with flatulence. So some of my friends and I got the idea, it's a very rare piece, they put me up to go to the Walter Jackson library and try to get it (laughs). Well, of course 2–3 days later after I filled out all the forms, I was called into Dr. Hurley's office. They of course had consulted Dr. Hurley first before sending off for the piece. He told me it would really not affect your knowledge of literature not to have this piece of writing . . . and that was the end of it!

Interestingly, Elizabeth does not remember these kind of sanctions being generally imposed in her coursework, which led first to art, then to English, and finally to a degree in Spanish. Rather, these sanctions were a daily quality of her social and residential life. Elizabeth remembers that a hallmark of the Woman's College was its aim to make a girl into a young lady, "even if [she] didn't want to be one." She describes the traditions of closed study, lights out at 11:30 p.m., strict policies against men in the dormitories, and the standard dress code of a skirt and the "class jacket," a blazer with a color combination specific to each year's class (hers was orchid and white). Elizabeth also recalls that meals were served "family style" with an appointed hostess for each table who enforced proper table manners and was responsible for "keeping the conversation going" within each table of diners. This oversight of manners and morals was reinforced in coed situations, but the women students were aware even then of the sometimes ridiculous rhetoric associated with these traditions. Elizabeth remembers a friend coming home to the dormitory with a date one night, rather innocently holding hands. The house mother pointedly asked her, "Young lady, what are you saving for marriage?" Her friend then cleverly replied, "The other hand!"

Despite these witty exchanges—illustrating the inherent social savvy of Woman's College students, despite strict campus rules—Elizabeth remembers the overall training at the college as positive, in that Charles McIver's theory, to Elizabeth, was that "an educated woman is a nurturer in the true sense of the word. If she has children, she is going to instill that." Elizabeth notes that her own two sons were encouraged to read from an early age and that their household was characterized by a desire for lifelong literacy. Indeed, Elizabeth notes that at the Woman's College she became a Spanish major by placing very high on the language entrance exam, by being "too dumb to put down the wrong answer" in order to enroll in lower-level courses and "start over" with language, as many of her Georgia State students would do in subsequent years.[17] Instead, Elizabeth completed a double major in English and Spanish, graduating with honors. She took this high level of achievement nurtured at the Woman's College into her own home, passing on that intellectual nurturing to her sons, and then on to her own students at Georgia State.

The roots of that intellectual training were certainly in place in the Woman's College English department, which Elizabeth remembers as a rigorous and relatively formal site for learning. She notes that every major was required to take an advanced grammar course, taught by a professor trained at Oxford and using a textbook that still conjugated "to be" as "I am, thou art." She also remembers a heavy emphasis on memorization and the use of the Bible as a core text in the introductory literature courses—which match the archival information found in course manuals of the time. This combination of memorizing passages and reading Scripture as literature, however, served Elizabeth very well, since she was active in the Baptist church throughout her life and in that setting learned the value of memorization. As a result, she found the approach to English at the Woman's College to be quite logical. This approach also fits neatly with the college's philosophy of educating women—as domestic teachers and storytellers, and as harbingers of an oral tradition passed through generations.

Elizabeth's continued engagement with language and literature throughout her professional career reflects her training as an undergraduate. In addition to her career as a professor of Spanish literature, she has published books on southern history and architecture, in part due to her status as the granddaughter of a plantation owner in Georgia and her connections to historical organizations such as the Daughters of the Confederacy. Elizabeth notes that she is always "publishing out of [her] field," including a book on the history of Atlanta, briefly on the bestseller list, and numerous articles on the Civil War. But long before her time as a professional writer and Spanish professor, Elizabeth was engaged in writing. She recalls the pivotal point at which her "writing career began":

> A boy I was dating in high school gave me a charter subscription to *Seventeen* Magazine, when it had just started, for Christmas. So I sent them a short story that I had written in an English class when I was a sophomore. It was called "Purpose in a Potato Vine." It was published in the magazine. Then, they called me—the thrill of my life—to write an article for an issue which was going to be devoted to all sections of the United States—they wanted me to do the Southeast. I was a senior in high school. They paid me for that article. On Honors day, they sent this beautiful engraved medal, for the principal to present to me.

Given this early and notable foray into authorship, and her continued commitment to writing and particularly publication, I asked Elizabeth to give some general thoughts about writing, especially for young women who might read this account of her life and life's work. She readily offered some points of advice, and perspective:

> It's really hard when you are so close to a subject—what you have written is your baby, you love it, you can't see anything wrong. So one of the difficult things is to find someone that you know has the right to edit, critique, what you have written, and then to tell you that no, this absolutely doesn't work, and you need to change that. It's like somebody telling you your child's shoes are crooked. . . . The ugliest word to a writer is "rewrite." And I think the way a lot of people today talk about writing, [they] get the idea it's sort

of a breeze, or something you do off-handedly. But it's not—it's really hard work. It's really different from what a lot of people think. It's really you in your office or some cubbyhole, you and your pencil and pad or you and your computer, and that's it. But when you are done . . . it's like when you bake a cake and it comes out of the oven, and there is this beautiful-looking cake that everyone is going to enjoy, and you put various and sundry things in it and it comes together in its final form, it's something that either informs or pleases or amuses, and it's something that you have created and it gives you satisfaction.

Jacqueline Jernigan Ammons: Teacher, Writer, Editor

Jacqueline entered the Woman's College after attending a series of high schools in North Carolina due to her father's career. Because she had two excellent women teachers in high school who influenced her to enter the teaching profession, and because she had several friends who were attending Woman's College, Jacqueline also enrolled in fall 1948. She reports that her teachers in high school were "just above and beyond—in teaching grammar, literature, and creative writing. I was looking at them and seeing . . . if I could be like her, to influence children." After enrolling at Woman's College, Jacqueline found that her time there influenced her ability to "become a leader"—a common thread that crosses each of these three women's observations about their college experiences and a sentiment that would seem to contradict the typical, limited personal and career goals set forth at other non-elite, former normal schools of the time. Jacqueline remembers that, for example, the dean of students, Katherine Taylor, was "definitely a leader and she could reach out to all kinds of girls and make them feel like they were worth something." Elizabeth and Lucy also noted particular leadership figures in their interviews—men (Warren Ashby in philosophy, for example) and women. Jacqueline notes that being attentive to leadership opportunities was (and is) especially important for women, however, as she comments, "Trying to stay out of little tiny groups—you got to blend your talents with everybody, not just the few you go around with. I think all through life that's so important, to learn to live with everyone. They might not be—excuse me—your kind of people, but you have to get to know them, where they come from." Jacqueline's other primary memory of how the Woman's College influenced her outside the classroom was her belief that a woman's college is "a good way to send girls to school," another common theme for these women. Jacqueline notes that she is "proud to be a person who graduated from [Woman's College]. They gave me a good background so that I could have a good life." Her belief in the women's college as an institution led her to send her only daughter, Jackie, to Peace College for women in Raleigh, North Carolina, and after her daughter's untimely death prior to her college graduation, to found a scholarship in her name. Jacqueline's memories of the *Yearling* are slightly more specific than either Elizabeth's or Lucy's, perhaps because she was editor in chief of the publication during her first year of college. Jacqueline would also go on to become editor in chief of the school yearbook, *Pine Needles,* in her senior year, and was also crowned "Sweetheart of Sigma Chi" in the senior issue. Jacqueline was thus the kind of student who would stand out in archival materials as a leader, but who in her interview demurred in recollections of her own achievements. She notes that her major was home economics and that she still somehow became involved in publications such as the *Yearling* and *Pine Needles,* though she is quick to add that "all kinds of majors" were involved in the yearbook, and in other campus publications—a sign that literacy activities outside the classroom were not limited to English majors at the college, a factor not always present on other college campuses today, where students tend to specialize as part of a career-minded trajectory.

Jacqueline's recollections of the Woman's College also include her memory of the English department being a place where "we did more creative writing and literary writing than we did grammar and that type of work." She notes that, in working as the lead editor for the *Yearling,* her self-appointed mission was to try to "get a balance of different types of writing." Yet she also now looks back at the issue for which she was editor in 1949, and says, "The thing just amazed me, when I read all those things—it doesn't even sound like me! I thought good grief, I read all those things I wrote in the whole year. The idea of life, or the idea of whatever—I think so much of it is the type of writing or word use is so flowery and . . . we just tried to be so *creative.*" Jacqueline's current view of the magazine contrasts in many ways with my own, though as a new reader of a text, and as someone outside the writing and editing process that resulted in that text, I am at both advantage and disadvantage. Still, her insight into the desire for balance of genres and subgenres at the time, as well as her current view of the work as perhaps overly "creative," presents a different perspective than my own as a scholar of field history. Where Jacqueline sees flowery prose, I see progressive ideas; where Jacqueline sees balance, I see also clear themes in content and purpose across the writings. But Jacqueline remarks that the *Yearling* may have been the result of the faculty's attempt to "make us a little more creative in writing," which would not be surprising, given the strong presence of creative writing faculty and courses within the department at the time. She also points out that this "creative" influence was widespread beyond just English majors, since *Pine Needles* included majors from "art, phys ed, chemistry, and home economics," indicating to her that "the English department must have been doing something right!"

Jacqueline's early experiences with both writing and editing allowed her to later work in Germany, teaching English and math to "the sergeants who were going to have their stripes taken if they didn't do their high school diploma." She considers this work to have been "mostly in grammar" for the English component. When I asked her what it was like to teach servicemen—especially coming from a women's college, where she would not have had experience with men as classmates—Jacqueline noted that the men looked upon their schooling as "a command performance—they had to come!" and that the flip to a single-sex classroom of men did not "bother [her]." After teaching for two years in Germany, Jacqueline returned to North Carolina with her husband and "wrote some articles for church, things like that. I didn't stop." She also worked with high school students to "get them up to the right grade level," as part of a local learning initiative. When I asked how she became involved in writing for her church and how this related to her needs and interests after leaving the Woman's College, she provided some thoughts that helped to justify this archival project for me, but she specifically aimed her comments at young aspiring women writers today: "Sometimes you just want to write, you just have a feeling you want to put something down on paper. The only thing I regret in my life, to tell the girls in the English department, would be to get a journal notebook and keep it, because it would be so interesting to look back at those years. If I had a journal, I could see how things have changed over these years. I think it would be nice if the English department could tell the girls about that."

Lucy Page Wagner: Teacher, Librarian, Archivist

Lucy began our interview session with the pointed question, "what is the purpose of this study?" This question would prove to be emblematic of Lucy's keen interest in documenting and preserving the history of her own education, as well as the history of her community of Hudson, North Carolina. Lucy is a meticulous and prolific writer and archivist who has concentrated the fruits of her literacy education in both educating young men and women in the classroom and in the library, and in educating her fellow townspeople about the history of Hudson. In this capacity, Lucy serves as a community leader—one who is well known at the town hall building where we met for our interview.

Lucy's memories of the Woman's College echo Jacqueline's in one key respect: Lucy remembers the college as a place where leadership and academic as well as personal success were clearly considered and calculated by the faculty and administration, so as to produce women graduates who excelled on their own terms and who did not engage in overt competition for resources. Lucy remembers that there was a limitation on how many clubs or organizations to which a girl could belong. Because she was heavily invested in her work with the church, and with the student Episcopal group, St. Mary's House, Lucy had to make choices about her leadership roles. She recalls the "points system" that kept one or a small group of girls from holding all of the leadership positions on campus, and how this affected her:

> We had a points system, and you couldn't have too many points. To be Editor in Chief of *Coraddi* I could not also be president of St. Mary's. Very wisely, I chose St. Mary's—I was much better suited there. Because I was still not very confident in the writing circles, and I knew that my quality of writing was not up to some of these other girls. That was good [the points system]. I would not have felt comfortable saying, "this goes, and this doesn't" [for submissions]. But I *could* say, "it's time to have a cookout!" instead.

Lucy characterizes her experience at the Woman's College, at least her first two years, as significantly affected by this lack of confidence, as well as her father's continuing belief that she "should not teach school. He definitely thought that I ought to do better." Lucy thus initially concentrated her studies in business, until she received encouragement from Mary Jarrell (the first of Randall Jarrell's two wives, who both taught as contingent faculty in the English department). Lucy recalls, "I got back a couple of papers from her and she said I ought to be writing, so that encouraged me. . . . She was very good to me in recognizing and encouraging me, which was nice because I didn't feel very confident as a freshman."[18] Lucy explained that her background, as a young woman who was raised by relatives from time to time, due to her mother being deceased and her father's poor health,[19] stood in contrast to some of the other young women who had enrolled at Woman's College:

A lot of them came from middle-class families. The Woman's College had a reputation then that it does not have now [after becoming coed and being absorbed by the UNC system]. The Woman's College had a lot of northern girls who came because the quality was great, and the price was right. So we had a lot of influence on northern girls. I felt totally insecure at first, for a good long time. [I went to the Woman's College] partly due to the tuition—Daddy was in the hospital and I could go there less expensively than Lenoir-Rhyne with a scholarship, here in Hickory. It was just a coincidence that it was a women's school. Certainly the Woman's College improved my self-confidence. I'm portraying myself as a little mouse, and I was, in many ways. . . . I was smart enough, but not aggressive [like some other students].

Certainly Lucy's postgraduate experiences allowed her to exhibit her increased confidence, developed at the Woman's College. While her husband, Carl, served in the army, Lucy's geographical choices for employment were limited to her immediate hometown area. So she took a position, perhaps ironically—given the shift in emphasis and training at the Woman's College from explicitly a normal school to a liberal arts curriculum—in which she thought she would be teaching at the high school level, but which quickly became a position teaching eighth grade. She remembers that "the night before school started, the principal and the superintendent arrived at my door and said, the state won't let [you] do that. You've got to teach the eighth grade." With one night's notice, Lucy began teaching thirty-six students math, science, English, and health. After several years of doing this level of teaching on and off, often with limited supplies and lacking administrative support and an explicit teaching degree in these subjects, Lucy went back to school for her provisional library science degree, which eventually led to a master's in library science from Appalachian State University. She contends that her background in English and her strong training at the Woman's College helped her as a librarian since she "had a much better foundation" in the literature than she might otherwise, and because she got to "choose books, and read books . . . and have [the students] for thirty minutes and then they go!" Lucy's experience would thus belie the fears raised in chapter 1—that the normal school traditions in English departments were not preparing students for the various challenges of secondary school teaching.

One striking artifact that emerged from my interview with Lucy was her presentation to me of her sophomore year writing project, "Page's Pages," written for Jane Summerall in a section of the Advanced Composition course offered at the college for English majors as well as nonmajors.[20] In addition to the witty title that she gives this project, Lucy crafts the project as a magazine of its own—an interesting companion to the "real" magazine in which her work would appear, the *Yearling,* as well as her other publications in *Coraddi.* Lucy, then a sophomore, created a masthead for the magazine, which indicated that she was the editor, managing editor, editorial staff, business staff, letters staff, circulation person, cover person, and "sole subscriber." She also lists Jane Summerall as a member of the literary staff, and two other students as responsible for cover art. Lucy organized her collection with a table of contents that listed the categories of short story, editorial, profiles, articles, and review, all but three of which were written by Lucy herself (Elizabeth Poplin contributed one article, as did two other fellow students). In sum, "Page's Pages" is forty-one pages of student writing, mostly Lucy's own, and is a clever collection of subgenres assigned in the writing. Of the project, Lucy remembers only that this is just one example of the type of writing she has kept from her years at the Woman's College—that she has "a stack about *this high* of things I did then." Given her reticence to take leadership editorial roles, I find her self-edited publication for this course to be especially interesting, in context. Additionally, as an archival document, "Page's Pages" is a fascinating example of the kind of extended, sequenced, and made-public writing that students were doing at the college during this postwar era.

Lucy and I ended our discussion of her memories of the Woman's College with some general thoughts about women's education, both then and now. Lucy feels strongly about the importance of education and the ways in which students, particularly women students, view their own abilities and limitations. Lucy asserts, with a view likely amenable to Charles McIver, the college's revered founder:

> I think that education is a key to a lot of things—whether it's a woman's college or a community college or a regular four-year institution. And I think that not keeping that education so narrow that it is just a mechanical thing, as some of the technical things sometimes tend to be, but a broad situation would be much easier, better thing to do. I think that women today have so much more that they have offered to them, but much more responsibility too. The choices they get to make—are much more pressing upon them. Living in the dorm, while I didn't meet the outside influence—Elizabeth says, "this is just keeping us from growing up! I'm still wearing bobby socks and my friends who are working are wearing hose!" But I felt like while we did have that shepherding, we also had the influence of society a little longer on us to implant on us, to bring into our families and homes.

Reconciling Historiographies of Literacy

Elizabeth, Jacqueline, and Lucy's recollections stand as a check against simple readings of archival materials such as the *Yearling*. While the magazine itself highlights a range of student writing, and a variety of samples of rhetorical awareness among these young writers, the memories of the social circumstances surrounding their literacy instruction, as well as their own material souvenirs of their writing, both in school and in their professional lives, provide a much fuller picture of what it meant to be educated in, and later influenced by, the English curriculum at the Woman's College. Bringing forward voices to complement material artifacts is critical in recovering these lost histories of lesser-known instruction, insofar as we can rapidly collect such voices in our scholarship before these subjects are no longer present to speak.

How, then, can contradictions such as these be subsequently employed by scholars within the larger field of composition and rhetoric, and how can this employment live beside the field's own accepted disciplinary master narratives? As just one example, can women's education be historicized both progressive and conservative at the same time—and if so, how does that paradox bear upon our need to cleanly categorize certain historical periods of writing instruction, as James Berlin does in *Rhetoric and Reality,* or even the assertions that the "feminization" of composition studies was primarily negative, as made by Susan Miller? Certainly the postwar literacy endeavors at the Woman's College owed something to the emergence of efficiency-based pedagogies put in play with the surge of enrollments funded by the GI Bill. However, the Woman's College—as a single-sex, if public, institution—bore little effect of that surge, given its protected status as a woman's college. This status afforded it a significant autonomy from nationwide trends, and the option of picking and choosing curricular and extracurricular initiatives more suited to its specialized student population.

Indeed, the students at the Woman's College engaged far more reflective and genre-bending writing in the first-year composition courses than Berlin would characterize was the "norm" between 1940 and 1960, or the decades of the "Communications Emphasis," in his field taxonomy. The college was, in fact, ahead of its time in anticipating the emphasis on creativity and the arts in general education, a wave that would most fully engulf college campuses in the mid-1960s, with the proliferation of the MFA degree in creative writing and the rise of heavy process-based pedagogies in first-year writing. At the same time, the campus culture of the Woman's College—as recalled by my interview subjects, and as documented in other records, for example, the college yearbook—paints a picture of a conservative, mannered community wherein women were inculcated in the ways of society and were supervised in their social interactions to a fault.

A comparative tension between disciplinary expectations and student writing production also existed at the University of New Hampshire between 1928 and 1942, just prior to the era of the *Yearling,* as profiled by Thomas Newkirk in his 2004 article, "The Dogma of Transformation." Newkirk's study of the publication the *New Hampshire Student Writer* is an appropriate theoretical parallel to the arguments I seek to make here. In his essay, Newkirk offers the prewar personal essay as a challenge to the conception of the mid-twentieth century as a "pedagogical wasteland" for composition. Newkirk instead contends that the aggregated essays in the *Student Writer* evidence a "self-confident writing program in good health" that produced reflective work more meaningful than the prevalent pedagogy of daily themes (252, 254).

Describing a sample student theme, for example, Newkirk observes that what the student is *not* trying to do in her work is "draw conclusions: she doesn't directly comment. . . . This form of 'meaning making' would, I suspect, be viewed as heavy-handed and inartistic moralizing" (256). Such an assertion recalls the sample *Yearling* piece by Shirley Berger profiled earlier, in which the student author does not take a personal stand on desegregation, but instead calls attention to the inherent contradictions in the social practices of the modern South. Newkirk's interpretation of this selection, and others like it, in the context of social mores on and off campus but most importantly promoted in the writing program itself, bears striking resemblance to the contradictions present at the Woman's College, where "moralizing" was far less an explicit element of production as it was an element of *instruction,* both socially and pedagogically speaking. Certainly the agency afforded to Dr. Hurley that allowed him to keep "inappropriate" literature out of the hands of students such as Elizabeth was not personally afforded to her in kind. Rather, she and her colleagues were being trained as ladies *and* intellectuals, but not necessarily as moral arbiters for the larger culture where more heady subjects were concerned.

Newkirk also characterizes the bulk of the New Hampshire essays under analysis as containing "more sight than insight," given that "as students moved to longer nonfiction essays in the 1930s, many of these same qualities dominated; they were outward looking, intensely descriptive, and rarely revealing of any personal crisis or transformation" (256).

Newkirk argues that this stance was imitative of the work being published in literary magazines and other publications during this era, noting that, "A number of New Hampshire selections are clearly in [the genre of] genial commentaries, written at the depths of the Depression, about the smaller daily pleasures and irritations" (259). Again, I find striking echoes in the publications of the *Yearling,* but with one small caveat: whereas the New Hampshire students rarely revealed work of any "personal crisis or transformation," certain pieces profiled here—such as Sally Beaver's essay on gender roles and expectations, and Pat Thomas's essay on interracial dating—do, in fact, evidence some implicit elements of both personal crisis (why are males destined for certain roles; why am I, being a young woman, less scrutinized?) and transformation (why do I see the hypocrisies that others do not; why are my principles being challenged?). Perhaps because the Woman's College was a discrete, specialized social and educational space, the issue of "transformation" was indeed more likely, or possible, and the event of personal crisis more easily vocalized.

But what may be most interesting to a study of the *Yearling* alongside these recollections from its student writers and editors—and to its implications for how we view the history of composition studies as an unbroken narrative of ascension to staid pedagogical traditions and social movements—is the way in which Newkirk grounds his reading of the New Hampshire essays in the context of contemporary writing pedagogy and its sometimes zealous desire to "transform" students. He asserts,

> the expectation for transformation [is a goal] that is, ironically, shared by both the expressivist and socio-epistemic cultural studies "camps" in composition studies—though the means of transformation is different. Both, it seems to me, share a sense of developmental urgency that is not felt by 1930's instructors. This sense of developmental urgency comes from a sense that students today exist in a global media culture in which corporations, government spokesmen, and popular culture outlets (and it's sometimes hard to distinguish one from the other) actively seek to construct them, to name their pleasures, to define the "normal." There is an urgency for students to name, to question, and to actively resist these friendly-seeming attempts to shape them. (263–64)

Newkirk chooses to read the impetus of these prewar students' instructors as rooted in the danger of "inattention, the dulling of sensation and perception, the trap of routine, the unwillingness or inability to appreciate particularity" (266). He argues that, "Viewed from this relentlessly progressive historical perspective, the pedagogy at the University of New Hampshire in the 1930s and '40s would seem an antiquarian curiosity. It will have little appeal for compositionists who set out to rescue students from the mystifications of global capitalism" (268).

While I do not share Newkirk's implicit championing of the genre of the personal essay, I do agree with his noteworthy characterization of the history of composition studies prior to the 1970s as, essentially, pre-enlightened. This broadly convenient view of the pedagogy in first-year classrooms (and in New Hampshire's case, advanced composition classrooms) as uniformly primitive opens up a view of archival research as a methodology defined by what it can *trouble,* rather than what it can reinforce. Newkirk's assertion that today's writing pedagogy is highly rhetorical—in its desire to change students, chiefly into politicized beings—is, to me, reasonably accurate. I would argue, however, that the desire to be vocal, rhetorically aware citizens, if within certain acceptable social boundaries, also characterizes both the reason behind the advent of the *Yearling* and the essay pieces profiled therein. Certainly the creation of a magazine such as the *Yearling* at a site such as the Woman's College points to an impulse to make the private public, as well as to bring these women writers into the national arena wherein new and emerging extracurricular literacy endeavors were rapidly taking shape. And as represented in my interviews with Elizabeth, Jacqueline, and Lucy, such efforts led these three women to value and practice writing throughout their adult lives—surely an implicit, if not explicit, goal in college writing instruction today.

Even as I do not share Newkirk's interpretive motives, I nonetheless believe that as we look at individual local histories such as that of New Hampshire or that of the Woman's College in North Carolina, we must keep this link between the past and the present in mind and provide a clear social and material context for what we include and exclude within our disciplinary narratives so we can accurately represent the voices that are not often afforded opportunities to speak—in this case, students at women's public colleges. Our narrative of composition as a universal course that persists in its instructional values across geographical and historical spaces does not allow for these archival paradoxes at the Woman's College to exist. To make them visible, therefore, we must reconceive our predilections when reading, interpreting, and reaffirming our field histories, and recognize dissonance as a welcome addition to these histories. We must allow for conflicting narratives between material and human sources, for example, as Linde argues is symptomatic of good archival work. We also must interrogate our own local histories as represented by institutionally produced documents only, and instead re-create these histories with an eye toward upsetting dominant discourses and challenging accepted narratives. The Woman's College is but one institution in a chain of disappeared public women's colleges deserving of a voice for their complex histories. Let us begin to allow for those voices to be heard, as careful "tellers," in Linde's terms, attuned to gaps as well as uncomfortable silences.

3

Revisionist History

General Education Reform from Harvard University to the Woman's College, 1943–56

The two sides of the problem thus stand forth clearly: on the one, a need for diversity, an even greater diversity than exists at present in the still largely bookish curriculum, since nothing else will match the actual range of intelligence and background among students; and on the other, a need for some principle of unity, since without it the curriculum flies into pieces and even the studies of any one student are atomic or unbalanced or both.

> Harvard University Committee
> *General Education in a Free Society*, 1945

Our admissions are selective only as our accredited public schools are selective in whom they graduate. . . . Our major problem, therefore, is to devise the best that we can for the gifted (and we have an encouragingly large number of good minds among our undergraduates) and for those who, by comparison, are the academically halt, lame, and blind.

> Woman's College of the University of North Carolina
> Chancellor Edward Kidder Graham Jr.

The discussion centered chiefly around a statement of objectives in teaching English as proposed by Dr. Bridgers: namely, (1) Skill in reading and writing, (2) Knowledge of literature, (3) Appreciation of literature. "Achievement" and "Competence" were both suggested as substitutes for "Skill," but no one of the three words met with unanimous approval.

> Committee to Examine Freshman and Sophomore English Course
> February 15, 1954

AT THE CORE of the modern liberal arts college or university is the shared curricular principle of general education. It informs every department in which first- and second-year core subject courses are offered. As the three juxtaposed statements opening this chapter suggest, the "general" component of the educational reform that constitutes this core has been articulated as a historically contested definition, attempting to cover a wide range of student preparations and abilities, and to simultaneously meet a wide range of departmental and institutional values regarding the nature of a liberal arts education, particularly in the writing and reading-intensive curriculum of the humanities.

In 1945, per the directive of university president James B. Conant, the Harvard University Committee on the Objectives of General Education in a Free Society published the results of its two-year study, titled *General Education in a Free Society,* later to be known in circulation by the short-hand term "the Redbook." This all-male committee included the Harvard dean of arts and sciences, the president of Radcliffe College, and eight other Harvard faculty and fellows, some of whom were also department heads. In this report, Harvard University set out a plan for the future of the liberal arts in the secondary schools and the postwar university, the latter of which was evolving under new pressure to offer increasingly prac-tical and career-focused curricula to new types of students, such as GI Bill recipients and traditional-age as well as adult working women, even on elite campuses. The Harvard plan would represent a permanent reconsid-eration of undergraduate education in the United States, and would go on to characterize the ways in which colleges and universities would define the "educated" individual, even as the plan proved limiting in its broader curricular implications.

At the same time as the Harvard committee was beginning its work, in spring 1943, the Woman's College of the University of North Carolina was producing a report of its own concerning collegewide curricular revi-sion. Several years later, in 1951, the Woman's College again took up the issue of general education reform, launching a two-year study led by its then-chancellor, the controversial figure Edward Kidder Graham Jr. Un-like the 1943 curricular revisions, which were organically grown from lo-cally specific postwar concerns, the 1951–53 general education proposal, ultimately unrealized in the curriculum, represented Graham's efforts to employ the Harvard model, as outlined in the Redbook, at the Woman's College. Following this attempt at larger curricular reform, between 1954 and 1956 the English department of the Woman's College conducted its own subsequent, department-level inquiry into the first- and second-year required courses in writing and literature. The discussions contained in these department meetings focused on how to best teach writing, as well as what a woman writer (and reader) should be able to achieve, and subsequently exemplify, upon completion of this general education coursework. The department's effort and recommendations were an indirect response to the college's previous general education revisions; its prior rejection of much of the Harvard plan; and the college's increasingly fevered pursuits to remain competitive with, but distinct from, fellow institutions such as the University of North Carolina–Chapel Hill and North Carolina State University, whose larger and more powerful male-centered campuses encroached on the all-women's social and intellectual ideals that the Woman's College sought to protect.

I contend in this chapter that the Woman's College rejected the general intellectual wishes and claims of the Harvard study because they were, in fact, drafted in ignorance of the special needs of institutions such as the Woman's College. The gendered nature of the study itself ultimately did not employ the available data where women's postsecondary educational futures were concerned, not even the responses culled from hundreds of surveys completed by Radcliffe alumnae and commissioned to infuse the Harvard study with a perspective on women's education. What was acclaimed by Harvard as a proposal for nationwide implementation was a report authored by few, but purporting to speak for many. The report ultimately fell short on many campuses that were founded upon special educational missions and/or were created to serve student populations in non-elite venues. Such institutions necessarily instead subscribed to the notion that curricular reform, including the examination of the values upon which that curriculum is founded, must be a local endeavor.

Studying these failures of enactment of the Redbook's plan at the Woman's College in comparison with the college's own more viable local curricular planning thus allows one to understand the real limitations of "general" education for young women college students—particularly those studying at non-elite, public institutions—across the nation during this postwar era. It also raises the critical question of what *postwar* meant for women's education more generally in a society whose thinking was dominated by the immediate needs of postwar *men,* specifically returning soldiers henceforth guaranteed an education by the federal government. This examination of general education reform and its storied origins illustrates the widespread desire of the postwar American educational populace to blindly mimic theories and practices of notable, elite institutions (such as Harvard) rather than develop their own, locally feasible approaches to educational reform. Such a desire is replicated in the field of composition studies today, as it searches for widely applicable and universally "true" histories of its discipline by often limiting its archival research to a select group of institutions, including Harvard itself. It is that desire that I wish to challenge, by local historical example, in this chapter.

To foreground the study of general education at the Woman's College from an archival perspective, I explore first the importance of the creation of the Redbook, and some of the responses to it, as represented in published contemporary reviews in disciplinary journals as well as in Harvard's own précis of the publication. I then examine the archival data available at Harvard and Radcliffe from the construction of *General Education in a Free Society,* alongside an inquiry into the very limited role of Theodore Morrison, head of English A at Harvard at the time of the Redbook report.[1] Interrogating these archival records allows for historical connections between what the Harvard group tried to set forth as ideals for students in universities nationwide, and the necessary reinterpretation of these idealized principles at the Woman's College in curricular discussions during this same postwar era. I highlight how data was collected from Woman's College students, how writing and literacy were regarded—and, at the department level, the relationship between writing and *literature*—and ultimately, how a collaborative and primary concern for overall excellence in women's education dominated all other intellectual and philosophical divisions within and among these groups in charge of making curricular recommendations.

In beginning this chapter with a fairly extensive look at curricular issues at Harvard, and then a comparative look into those of the Woman's College, finally telescoping into its English department, I highlight two major areas of concern as relevant to a study of women's public literacy education postwar: the Harvard study's recommendations regarding the content and delivery of writing instruction, including its relationship to first-year writing curricula and introductory literary study; and the study's relative omission of educational goals and directives regarding women on postwar American college campuses. I analyze how the local concerns regarding writing instruction and women's education at the Woman's College were, in fact, an enacted response to Harvard's desire to address the "practicality" of postwar student consumers, while still maintaining, in some viable way, the prior intellectual and more genteel traditions housed within the disciplinary units of the traditional university. At the same time, the inability to completely resolve these concerns at the Woman's College, chiefly due to its struggle over ability levels and the relationship between writing and literary study, provided an opening for the surge of "alternate" curricula in creative writing, and specific departmental/faculty energies backing this surge, starting in 1947 and stretching through the end of the college's life as a women's-only institution.

To Whom Are We Speaking? The Framework and Reception of *General Education in a Free Society*

In terms of marking an era in postsecondary education in the United States, it is hard to find a more widely appropriated, or variously lauded, document than *General Education in a Free Society*. Following the accepted practice of viewing the Ivy League, particularly Harvard and Yale, as the leaders in postsecondary educational thought, this relatively compact book (267 pages) gained a significant amount of attention from colleges and universities nationwide. The idea of foregrounding a four-year college education on broad areas of instruction; developing a common two-year liberal arts core; and unifying the curriculum, subtly, by institutionally defined morals and ethics, is still pervasive in most American postsecondary institutions. Even as general education undergoes regular and seemingly rigorous reform and local assessments on any number of college campuses in the twenty-first century, it still bears the vestiges of the carefully, if loftily, constructed aims within the Harvard report, and still purports to serve the "common" student in its universally minded design.

Yet the roots of the Harvard study likely owed more to its participants being positioned within an elite institution, and having insider knowledge of the prior practices of other elite institutions. When constructing their report, the Harvard committee had access to the other general education–inspired plans of fellow elite institutions, including Amherst College, Williams College, Yale University, and Columbia University, and one non-elite institution, the University of Minnesota. Perhaps this is why Columbia continues today to cite the Harvard report as being entirely derivative of its own curricular impulses, which were in place well before World War II. In chapter 4 of the 1995 Columbia publication *An Oasis of Order: The Core Curriculum at Columbia College*, Timothy Jacobs asserts,

> Columbia College graduates would see little new in the renewal proposed in the Harvard Redbook. Its authors [had] much the same concerns that had given life to general education courses at Columbia twenty-five years earlier. In order to combat a lack of cohesiveness and commonality in collegiate education, the Redbook advocated the creation of required undergraduate courses in the humanities, social sciences, and natural sciences that would

emphasize the heritage of Western civilization and endow all students with a common intellectual background. The content of the Redbook's proposed humanities course (Great Texts of Literature) and of the social sciences course (Western Thought and Institutions) only heightens the sense of *déjà vu*. Both proposed courses cover the same ground as Humanities and [Core Curriculum]. . . . the Redbook was curiously reticent in acknowledging its debts to Columbia or Chicago, though both these schools had promoted general education for years. (Jacobs, *An Oasis of Order*)

Anne Stevens similarly notes that the scope and influence of the Redbook was partially due to prior curricular revisions at Columbia—as well as at the University of Chicago—and partially due to the temporality of its argument.[2] She argues that while the Redbook had a "tremendous" influence nationwide, its influence

cannot be attributed solely to the ideas elaborated [at Harvard], since [others at the University of Chicago and Columbia] had been making similar pronouncements for twenty years. Instead, the Redbook gained national attention because its timing was right. As its title suggests, educators felt a need to assert Western culture and democratic values in the aftermath of the threat of fascism and the developing culture of the Cold War. Equally important to the Redbook's influence was the massive influx of students after the war, particularly returning soldiers on the G. I. Bill. (Stevens 184)

There is no doubt that the timeliness of the Redbook weighed heavily on its mass reception and following; were it not for the influx of young men returning from military service to enroll at colleges where they previously would not have had standing—such as Harvard—under the terms of the GI Bill, the need for "general" education would have been less apparent, and its immediacy, especially at more selective institutions, perceived to be less dire. As Conant openly admitted in a 1943 meeting of the Harvard committee, such student influx would be challenging, but ultimately profitable, given the support provided by the federal government to cover these students' tuition costs and, implicitly, institutional costs in accommodating said students:

One of the things I think is going to be interesting in the post-war period is the period in which the returning veterans are going to dominate the scene. . . . It seems to be that if the current legislation passes, and if it will be implemented by generous appropriations—both of which I hope—we are going to have a period when the great majority of students in our schools will be returned veterans, all publicly financed. It is estimated that this period will last three to five years, it taking at least two years to bring the veterans back. It is a favorable opportunity for Harvard. (Harvard Committee on General Education, meeting minutes, Nov. 18, 1943)[3]

The governmental support to which Conant is referring is outlined in Senate Bill 1509, drafted "to provide for the education and training of members of the armed forces and merchant marine after their discharge or conclusion of service, and for other purposes," and put forward on November 3, 1943. Bill S1509 provides that

> Persons eligible for training under this Act shall be selected, in accordance with such rules and regulations as the President may prescribe, on the basis of their intelligence, aptitude, skill, interest, prior training, education, and experience. Any person so selected shall be entitled to receiving training at any approved educational or training institution in any one of the fields or branches of knowledge for which he shall have been determined to be qualified and in which the number of trained personnel is or is likely to be inadequate under conditions of full utilization of manpower. Persons selected under this Act shall be entitled to training at an approved educational or training institution for a period of one year, or for such lesser time as may be required to complete the course of instruction chosen by them. A further period of instruction not exceeding three additional years may be provided for persons of exceptional ability and skill. . . . The President shall provide for the payment by the United States of customary tuition, laboratory, library, and other similar fees and charges to the educational or training institutions furnishing instruction to persons selected under this Act. . . . If the established tuition fees at any publicly supported institution shall be found by the President to be inadequate compensation to such institution . . . he is authorized to provide for the payment of such additional compensation as may be fair and reasonable. ("Senate Bill 1509," 1–3)

A personal message from President Roosevelt, sent from the U.S. Government Printing Office in 1943 and archived within the committee's records, reinforces the importance of this bill for returning soldiers, and for the future of the American population as a whole: "Vocational and educational opportunities for veterans should be of the widest range. There will be those of limited education who now appreciate, perhaps for

the first time, the importance of general education, and who would welcome a year in school or college. . . . Lack of money should not prevent any
veteran of this war from equipping himself for the most useful employment for which his aptitudes and willingness qualify him. The money invested in this training and schooling program will reap rich dividends in
higher productivity, more intelligent leadership, and greater human happiness" (3).

Certainly Roosevelt's words are echoed in the committee's report,
chiefly his idea of the "importance of a general education." His notion that
the government's investment will increase intelligence and *happiness* within the greater U.S. society is perhaps a lofty one, but a principle also voiced
in the Redbook in several places. For example, regarding fine arts education (defined as such), the report argues that "The happiness of many, perhaps of nearly all, people will be enhanced or diminished by the presence
or absence of aesthetic sensitivity to music and the fine arts, as well as to
literature" (127). In another case, the report notes that communication (in
this case an understanding of rhetoric) "is that unrestricted exchange of
ideas within the body politic by which a prosperous intellectual economy
is secured" (68). Upon being presented with this legislative paradigm and
personal executive office appeal, an institution such as Harvard would be
generally bound to take any worthwhile applicant, and would be wise, in
fact, to do so. In an era characterized by the proliferation of junior colleges
and other state and regional universities close to any prospective student's
home, the idea of going "East" to Harvard and other elite schools was less
appealing financially, and geographically, to a good many students. Certainly Harvard still benefited from its prestige within its core target audience—eastern seaboard applicants, private school/academy graduates,
and "legacy" admits from longstanding Harvard families, in sum—but
it also most certainly felt its own mortality in the face of this government
directive that allowed a (partially) free education for all and a widening of
the entrance gates of the university as a communally centered institution.

Given that an applicant's tuition and fees would be covered in full by
the government, and any "additional compensation" necessary for instructing that student would also be covered, it was surely wise of Harvard
to step up to the challenge of constructing a true "general education" for
the students who might choose to attend. After the one-year time limit
proposed in the bill, the student might continue at Harvard—or not. This
system allowed for guaranteed student income via filled seats for each
first-year class, and additionally did not yoke Harvard (or any institution)
to that serviceman after his required year of study. When Harvard's gen-

eral education reform is viewed using these lenses—as a response to the drawbacks and benefits of postwar student enrollments—it becomes less of a philosophical good designed to level the educational playing field and empower students of all socioeconomic backgrounds, and more of a calculated response to an economic reality. As such, one may view the applicability of a report such as the Redbook to be far less for institutions such as the Woman's College—who, by institutional design, had no mandate to admit returning service*men*, even as it did provide for service*women*; who already had secure operational funding from the state of North Carolina; and who served a special, largely local populace in a manner decidedly unique when compared to other sites of women's education of the time.

Despite these issues of perfect social and economic timing on the part of the Redbook, and the less timely repetition of values set forth at other fellow elite schools under less dire socioeconomic circumstances, the applicability of the report—in terms of less selective institutions being able to take its advice wholesale and implement its curricular recommendations locally—was still problematic on a micro and macro scale. From the position of Harvard itself, as outlined in the Harvard publication "A Précis of General Education in a Free Society," there are extended moments of praise for the report's content and approach within the section "The Objective Report" from professors at elite Stanford University and the University of Pennsylvania, and from the headmaster of Phillips Academy (Andover). But when turning to a student's view of the Redbook, the praise is qualified; instead, Thomas S. Kuhn—a 1944 Harvard graduate and former editor of the Harvard *Crimson*, well known to readers for his many later intellectual accomplishments[4]—reflects on the true novelty versus the immediate viability of the report's recommendations. His comments are labeled "The Subjective View":

> Liberal education is no longer a probable end-product of conventional teaching methods. No better reforms than the Report's have yet been proposed, and educational experiments testify impressively to the soundness of the Committee's plans. Successful general education, however, requires great teachers. Scholars without enthusiasm or enthusiasts whose vigorous perception is not infectious cannot cause students to discern meaning and value. Without such men the reading in general education courses might better be done over the summer, as recommended at Yale, for the student's net gain from the course would reduce to unaided apperception of the reading plus some unassimilated criticism which might well be harmful. Teachers who cannot kindle enthusiasm ought to be restricted to instruction

in facts. Teachers of this caliber are not now to be found at Harvard in sufficient number to support a truly general education program . . . [and] the
Committee fails to consider where the proper balance between scholarship
and teaching ability lies. ("A Précis," 9)

Here, Kuhn makes pointed assertions about the division between "general" education and specialized training as found in academia, a division
found to be unacceptable in the idealized view of general education that
Harvard was promoting. He also characterizes the average Harvard faculty as being less than qualified to teach highly generalized subject matter. To be "specialized" means offering more narrow training than the
postwar student can use. Short of calling for outwardly vocational work
(though championing its value, especially for the student in community
adult education programs), the Redbook did, in fact, call for professors
to teach in broad areas that crossed subdisciplinary boundaries, in some
cases, and resisted specialized knowledge, in order to provide the widest,
most humane education available for underclassmen.

Delineating the needs of special, vocational, and general education,
the Redbook argues for a return to the values of the liberal arts—and asserts that said values need not belong only to the elite class, nor to a wide
range of otherwise negligible coursework:

Special education comprises a wider field than vocationalism; and corre-
spondingly, general education extends beyond the limits of merely literary
preoccupation. . . . [Today] there is implied a more serious contempt for the
liberal arts, harking back to the fallacy which identifies liberal education
with the aristocratic ideal. The implication is that liberal education is something only genteel. A similar error is evident in the student's attitude toward
his required courses outside his major field as something to "get over with"
so that he may engage in the business of serious education, identified in his
mind with the field of concentration. (54)

Such a statement allows Harvard's plan to be viewed within the ideal
paradigm of the U.S. government's (and President Roosevelt's) proposal: a
general education for all, promoting the growth of an intellectual core of
citizenry. Such a statement also allows Harvard to become a leader, rather
than a follower, in the GI Bill's implementation while still preserving the
core values of its existing curriculum—simply labeling it as one now appropriate for all, rather than for a select few.

For its very specific recommendations regarding Harvard—or, as it was called, the "Prescription for Cambridge" (meant to include Radcliffe College)—and thus for the faculty whose teaching skills Kuhn found so limited, the committee recommended the following plan, which resembles a great many templates for general education today: "In the Humanities: Great Texts of Literature; a study of six or eight of the greatest books in world literature; In the Social Sciences: Western Thought and Institutions; an examination of certain institutional and theoretical aspects of the Western Heritage; In the Sciences: either a course in Principles of Physical Science or one in Biological Science; a study of basic physical principles and concepts and the methods by which these have been developed." In addition, the committee recommended "three additional general education courses," not one of which should be in "the students' field of concentration, and only one of which should be in his area of study." Finally, the committee recommended that there should be a tutorial system for juniors and seniors, to supplement faculty instruction in upper-level subjects, and that "English A, the required composition course, should be altered to make it increasingly 'functional to the curriculum,'" and be parsed into two hours of instruction per week for one semester, on "techniques and skills essential to composition" and another semester in which "frequent themes will be required on the material in the basic general education courses." In other words, English A would become a servant counterpart to the larger general education curriculum, as opposed to a course of its own—or, in fact, a course in English studies, a proposal not supported by Theodore Morrison, which I will discuss later in this chapter.[5]

Kuhn's point of view as a student—that the Harvard faculty would be even less suited to the general education plan than its students—provides some local insight into the problems of implementing this (or any) large-scale curricular change on a campus. Several contemporary reviews of the book, appearing in the immediate months after it was published, also evidence the study's immediate impact upon, and reflection of, the thinking about curricular reform at other universities in postwar historical context. These reviews, authored by faculty at public institutions in various geographical areas,[6] also indicate some dissatisfaction with Harvard's attempt to create a new approach to undergraduate studies for their own students that would be highly relevant to other non–Ivy League institutions and their student populations.

For example, in the October 1945 *South Atlantic Bulletin,* George Coffman of the University of North Carolina provides a Southern states' perspective with a laudatory overview of James Conant's credentials, noting that "President Conant combines to a high degree in his activities and his spoken or written word intellectual zeal and a social conscience. No college or university president, with one possible exception, has given himself so completely and devotedly to the winning of the war as he" (1). Yet further into the review, Coffman takes issue with the makeup of the committee authoring the report, specifically its "notable . . . absence of any representative of the modern languages" and for having "as its only representatives in English, Professor Richards, known most widely as the sponsor for what many regard as the esoteric program for Basic English" (4). One might note, as a contextual issue beside Coffman's complaints, that in the committee's list of consultants for the study, not one representative was from the southern United States. Instead, committee minutes evidence significant concern that the Midwest and West be represented in the sources consulted for the report, but no such concerns were raised about the southern United States—which, when referred to, is typically represented as being poor or economically disadvantaged, behind in public school educational opportunities for students, and less progressive in educational theory than its northern counterparts.[7] This limited national framework is important to keep in mind when reading the report, and considering its applicability to institutions of all emphases located below the Mason-Dixon Line.

As much as Coffman criticizes the report's lack of perspective on English studies and other matters, M. H. Willing's review in the *Journal of Educational Research* in October 1946 is even less charitable. In addition to his dissatisfaction with the lack of transparency in the committee's methods, Willing, on the faculty at the University of Wisconsin, also raises questions about the homogeneity of the committee—the twelve distinguished Harvard men and their relatively uniform views of the world, and, importantly, their neglect of women's educational issues: "That this committee would agree . . . was made doubly sure by excluding from representation on it such educational interests as health and physical education, the fine arts, the practical arts, education for women, religion, and social welfare. The committee was essentially unanimous to start with and nothing in the traditional letters and science curriculum had the least cause for anxiety about the result of two years of interviewing, conferring, and verbal gymnastics" (149). In fact, committee records do show evidence of discussion of areas such as physical fitness and related topics (such as sex education), but little in the final report emphasizes these areas. As I will detail further, women's education was also almost entirely glossed in both the intellectual considerations explicitly framing the report, and the quasi-concrete curricular recommendations that conclude the study.

It is apparent from these sample responses that some individual in-

stitutions found subsequent difficulty embracing the goals and requirements of the Harvard study, as well as intellectual dissonance with the
study's methodology. But how *was* the report formulated, and what did
it ultimately hope to achieve? What were its aims and how immediately
applicable were they intended to be, especially for institutions such as the
Woman's College? A perusal of archival records at Harvard informing
the published report allows for some insight, particularly as relevant to
the evidence upon which the report was based, and what evidence ultimately made it into the report explicitly, implicitly, or not at all. Knowing
this fuller story allows us to better understand the objections raised over
the study at the Woman's College, and how these relate to the position of
women postwar, particularly in the humanities.

Constructing Freedom: Archival Evidence of Lost Opportunities

General Education in a Free Society aims to promote an overall philosophy of education and of ideal youth training more so than a specific
educational plan or blueprint. Published after two years of intense study
by the Harvard committee, the book includes a "Letter of Transmittal"
to Conant. This letter notes that the study was at times arduous, but deliberately collaborative, taking into account that the group was "advised
[by Conant] that the educational process falls short of its ideal unless it
includes at each stage of maturity some continuing contact with liberal
and humane studies" and that the group was "directed not so much to
make recommendations for general education in Harvard College as to
venture into the vast field of American educational experience in quest of
a concept of general education that would have validity for the free society
which we cherish" (xiii). The committee noted that

> Whatever else the report may be, it is the result of joint effort. It is the
> product of twelve men living in close association for two years, grappling
> cooperatively with a complex and stubborn plan of major importance. The
> committee regularly met as a whole once a week, frequently more often,
> and periodically secluded itself for sessions of several days' duration.[8] We
> maintained a central office into which memoranda poured and where daily
> groups smaller than the whole committee met informally to discuss our
> problems. We sought advice from both our colleagues in the university and
> from persons from various walks of life and sections of the country.... All
> in all, we tapped so far as was our power the rich and varied thinking and
> experience of American education. (xiv)

In fact, the acknowledgments do evidence a great number of individuals outside Harvard who were cited as consultants. These individuals represented, in sum, seventeen colleges and universities, thirty high schools and academies, two state boards of education, and seven businesses, corporations, or professional organizations. Of these institutions, only one (Minnesota) was public, and only Stanford was located outside the eastern seaboard. None, notably, were from the southern United States, where women's public education was thriving. The higher emphasis on secondary schools in the report's final construction (at least half of the book concerns itself with education of public school children) was due to Conant's admonition that "the general education of the great majority of each generation in the high schools was vastly more important than that of the comparatively small minority who attend our four year colleges" (xiii).

Despite these numerous consultants from outside Harvard, in addition to Theodore Morrison, whose recommendations were ignored by the committee, only one other faculty member from the Harvard English department was consulted for the report. This was literary theorist and rhetorician I. A. Richards. Richards is listed as a committee member in the Redbook itself, and his photo is even featured in a Harvard précis regarding the committee's report. But on a read-through of the meeting minutes for the committee from 1943 and 1944, Richards appears to have been physically absent from all meetings, and was not assigned any particular role within the governance structure. He does contribute a report, however, that is considered to be "supplemental" to the committee's deliberations, and also took limited part in one subcommittee meeting.

Richards's views of "communication" as a metaphor (a view akin to those in his well-known *The Philosophy of Rhetoric*) are the basis of his book *Basic English*, which was designed to be: "(1) An international secondary language for world use in general communication, science, and commerce; (2) an introduction to English, rationally simplified and complete in itself, for the foreign learner; (3) a remedial discipline promoting clarity and precision of thought and expression, for English-speaking peoples at higher levels of proficiency" ("Basic English," 306a). Richards's plan—coauthored by C. K. Ogden—involved a list of just 850 words that "would do the work of 20,000 words," and were selected by "the systematic elimination of (1) all words which can be defined in not more than 10 other words in the Basic vocabulary; (2) of words which, whether susceptible of definition within the vocabulary limit or not, are primarily emotive rather than referential; (3) of words which though not susceptible of definition within the vocabulary limit have chiefly a literary or stylistic value; (4) of words which, whether susceptible of such definition or not, are so limited by the context in which they may be used as to be uncommon in general communication" ("Basic English," 306a).

None of Richards's work appears in the Redbook, as it was likely considered fringe to the broader purpose of general education, particularly in its implicitly vocational aims. In general, the report does not deal in theoretical understandings of educational practices beyond John Dewey, and certainly does not explore linguistics as relevant to writing and literacy. Yet even as Richards's ideas were disregarded by the Redbook group,[9] they were apparently adopted in many foreign countries as a mode of learning and were the basis for at least three books on the subject published in 1930, 1934, and 1943. In addition, the British government purchased the copyright for Basic English and "decided in 1944 to develop Basic English as an auxiliary and administrative language" ("Basic English Worth $108 a Word"). Short instructional films titled Basic English I and Basic English II also appeared in 1952; these illustrate the employment of Richards's principles through tedious staged dialogues that use varying combinations of the 850 words Richards promotes, presumably to teach nonnative speakers the principles of conversational exchange on these specific terms.[10]

Despite this lack of participation by faculty in English studies within Harvard, and the great number of secondary schools and officials consulted, which resulted in a rather incomplete interrogation of the key subject of college writing for the report's recommendations, the Redbook's legacy still remains most visibly at the postsecondary rather than secondary school level, wherein courses such as first-year composition hold down the foundation of general education curricula. Additionally, a great number of the secondary schools represented in the report were preparatory academies rather than public high schools, thus slightly skewing the notion of "great majority" within the schools consulted. Finally, adding to these acknowledgments, and clear limitations on perspective, the committee recognized the external subcommittee on Special Problems in the Higher Education of Women at Radcliffe College, a group that contributed a significant report to the Redbook's data collection, but did not employ its data with any prominence or deep consideration in the Redbook report itself. This neglected consideration of women's education in general, as well as the position and value of first-year composition, is significant to an analysis of how the Redbook was, ultimately, inapplicable to curricular revision efforts at less-studied institutions of higher education such as the Woman's College.

Women's Education and the Redbook: "Accepting the Feminine Role"

While the Redbook may not evidence an attention to women's education per se, the group did commission a special study by Radcliffe faculty
in order to add such a dimension to their report. As Radcliffe president
W. K. Jordan proudly noted in a 1944 issue of the *Radcliffe Quarterly,* the
Committee on the Education of Women was, at that time, "carrying out
an extensive program of research which, it is hoped, will analyze carefully
many important topics of a general nature and interest." Jordan additionally noted that "Since the higher education of women, in a strictly academic sense, is not more than a century old, it is felt that a full estimate of its
present strength, special problems, and future possibilities is badly needed" (7). The research reviewed by the committee was an alumnae questionnaire—surveying Radcliffe graduates of the past sixteen years—plus a
separate questionnaire on the tutorial system at Radcliffe sent to selected
graduates; a comparative study of the Radcliffe curriculum against other
colleges; and the geographical distribution, graduate and professional
training, and marriage and personal achievements of Radcliffe alumnae
(7–8).

While the Radcliffe committee appeared to undertake a fairly broad
cross section of materials, the ultimate conclusions of the committee were
far less broad. In fact, they were extremely modest, given the scope of
the data collected. As noted in the committee's official final report, titled
"General Education at Radcliffe College," the curriculum itself was not
something the group sought to alter in any significant way apart from
Harvard's: "the Radcliffe curriculum, save for unimportant differences,
is precisely the same as that offered in Harvard College . . . this fact must
be regarded as the prime asset of Radcliffe College. . . . In other words,
Radcliffe's more than five thousand graduates have been educated within
the frame of this conception, which alone gives Radcliffe meaning, and
it would generally be agreed that the product so trained has been sound,
well-adjusted, and has attained many peaks of high distinction" (4). On
the contrary, the Radcliffe committee recognized that within their curriculum, Radcliffe students were fortunate to have training not found, in
their view, at other women's colleges:

> We feel rather sure that few colleges for women have imbued their gradu-
> ates with as keen a sense of civic and cultural responsibility [as at Radcliffe]
> and it seems essential that these interests should be at once sharpened and

strengthened by the programs that we are planning in general education. It seems probable that educated women in a free society must carry an ever heavier burden of responsibility in these immensely important activities and interests which have very direct bearing not only on the richness but on the stability of our culture. These manifold activities of our graduates are for the most part non-professional, they are in a true sense the cultural dividend with which Radcliffe women repay society for their education. (11)

Despite the Radcliffe's group apparent ignorance and lack of data regarding the kind of "civic and cultural responsibility" being taught at other single-sex institutions, including the Woman's College and other public women's institutions, as none of these college-types were consulted, the report asserts that its unique curriculum results in not only well-educated and "well-rounded" women who would participate fully in civic action, but also women who were interested in the arts. This minor perceived flaw in the Radcliffe curriculum—the lack of offerings in fine arts—was singularly noted in the report. As cited above, the Redbook report does promote education in the fine arts, though not for women in general, nor as requested by Radcliffe students in particular. The Radcliffe report, in contrast, observes a need for such courses—which were already in place in great earnest at the Woman's College at this time:

> In view of the very strong interest of Radcliffe students in the fine arts, both with respect to concentrations and elections, it would seem to the committee that the general education course in humanities as planned fails to meet an obvious and important need at Radcliffe, if not a probable need at Harvard. Hence it is submitted that an elective course in general education should be designed in this seriously neglected area of the humanities. Such a course should deal broadly with the arts, and should include materials, standards of criticism, and training in values from the fields of Fine Arts, Music, Aesthetics, and Design. (15)

Perhaps due to these rather minor and arguably tepid recommendations put forth to the Committee on General Education at Harvard, no explicit recommendations for Radcliffe College women, or college women in general, appear in the Redbook.

Nor does the report mention whether single-sex education is a tradition that should be continued (inside or outside the Ivy League). Instead, the issue of gender differences is completely elided in the report, which instead focuses on class and social (significantly, economic) differences among youth and the issue of opportunity—assuming that education for men was, and had always been, delivered and received in the same manner as education for women. Ironically, the report does not recognize or identify the separate-but-equal approach that the Harvard College/Radcliffe College organizational split enforced in this regard.[11] The report circumvents the practice of Ivy League men's education by using Harvard as a baseline that implies an ability to apply the report's findings to a cross section of a population outside Harvard, with modifications, regardless of the gender of that population.

In what ways did these survey findings represent lost opportunities for a fuller accounting of women's education in the Harvard study? Another way of parsing out this question would be to ask, what considerations *were* made in the Redbook report for women students, as well as their future career paths postgraduation, considerations that might be applied to institutions such as the Woman's College—and to others whose primary mission was to educate women, either as future teachers or as recipients themselves of a "general education"?

While the mention of women students in the report itself is barely traceable, the archives of the Harvard Committee on General Education do contain a few minor discussions about women, education, and the public sphere—though not the kind of material that would make it as presented into the report (nor of the nature that the committee would likely want to be shared). In its September 28, 1943, meeting—only the second gathering of the group—the committee articulated eighteen areas in U.S. education and society that they "ought to consider" in drafting their report. Among these were income level; vocational training in college; the college to secondary school relationship; distribution of illiteracy in the United States; catholic education;[12] the "human pool from which the teaching staff will be drawn"; the effects of movies, comics, and radio; analysis of book consumption; and the possibilities for "improvement in the methods of selection and preparation of teachers." The committee's areas only covered gender or women's education in one spot, and that was "the place of women teachers and the relation of women teachers to the problem of discipline in the schools, teacher preparation, etc." (2). In other words, women were to be considered, at least explicitly in the background data collection, chiefly as teachers, and within that subset of study, as related to "discipline in the schools" and their pupils' preparation. Such a singular view of women within the larger subject of general education led to some very narrow discussions in the committee.

For example, in a discussion on November 18, 1943, attended by Conant and focusing on the preparation of secondary school students, the committee discussed in what ways teachers—specifically female teachers—contributed to a young person's education in primary through secondary schooling, as the following exchange illustrates regarding the document, "The Development of Ideals and Values" and its propositions. Those cited are Robert Ulich, professor of the history of education at Harvard; R. J. Havinghurst, a committee consultant from the University of Chicago and the General Education Board of the Rockefeller Foundation, and author of the document under discussion; and Alfred D. Simpson, another Harvard professor of education:

> Ulich: I am sure some of us remember teachers who exercised great influence and who were not particularly neat or physically attractive. They were so identified with their subject that the neatness and attractiveness did not play any particular part. Generally speaking, and under normal conditions, it may be all right to select neat and attractive teachers, but it may lead school superintendents to overlook other necessary attributes of teachers.

> Havinghurst: Yes, to make a complete picture of the good teacher, I had intended to point out here what I thought were the shortcomings of teachers in terms of inculcations of values. I think women teachers of grades 5 to 8 are especially short here and tend to do a lot of damage. They tend to be intolerant, unattractive in appearance, and the girls in their classes especially lose a lot.

> Simpson: I agree, and I think the reason for it is the practice of putting teachers into those grades who are strong disciplinarians. They have been disciplinarians at the expense of other things. (Harvard Committee on General Education, meeting minutes, Nov. 18, 1943)

This brief exchange—in which the dichotomy of teachers as either mother/ nurturer or spinster/disciplinarian seems to be a baseline assumption— refers to the following propositions for attributes that every teacher should "embody" from preschool through college, per age and grade levels specified, as produced by the committee and archived in its meeting minutes:

> a. For nursery school, kindergarten, and primary grades, teachers who are affectionate and motherly in their attitudes.

> b. For intermediate and junior high school grades, more male teachers to serve as examples for the boys.

> Next, physically attractive women teachers, whose social attitudes are tolerant, especially on matters of religion, race, and social class.

c. For the age-range 12–16, a group of teachers of both sexes who are selected for simple sturdiness of character and broad human sympathy. Those teachers should be responsible for the common core of non-academic activities—sports, arts and crafts, music, civic work, dramatics, etc.

d. For the age-range 16–18, if the community supports a youth-serving program for out-of-school youth, a corps of attractive young men and women trained for work with non-bookish youth, and trained to understand the normal emotional development of adolescent boys and girls.

e. For the age-range 18–20, as teachers in the regular high schools and colleges:

> 1. Attractive young teachers who are trained to understand developing adolescents and to take the responsibility of serving as objects of imitation,
>
> 2. Teachers who are so enthusiastic about their subjects that students catch their interest and enthusiasm,
>
> 3. Teachers who are morally sincere and who are interested in the moral convictions of their students. (Harvard Committee on General Education, "Revised Timing Schedule," 6)

Connected to the issue of girls' appearances and education, the committee records include an ancillary document entitled "Accepting One's Physique and Accepting a Masculine or Feminine Role." It is recommended that the upper grades of high school and initial years of college take several steps "to help boys and girls with this task," including:

Help girls to think through the problem of accepting the feminine role.

In senior high school and college there should be opportunity for girls, individually or in groups, to discuss the problem of accepting a feminine role. Courses in psychology and literature are probably best for this purpose. A woman's college could deal with this problem through the study of literature. Free class discussion with a skillful teacher would meet the problem for most girls. Women should be available to lead such discussions who have been outstandingly successful in the usual feminine role of wife and mother, as well as women who have been successful in other accepted feminine roles. (8)

How do these discussions of appearance—and appearances—and ancillary recommendations relate to the application of the Redbook's directives to the Woman's College, and other like institutions? First, it is important to reiterate that these highly gender-biased recommendations do not make their way per se into the final Harvard report. Though half of the report relies on extensive discussion of the morals and values that should be imparted to impressionable youth, or our "boys and girls," it does not explicitly advocate for education in traditional gender roles. In fact, it avoids such discussions of sexual or physical education, as mentioned earlier in the published reviews of the Redbook. Instead, we can read these committee documents as both informing the conversation, limited though it was, about women's education and women's educational roles (that is, as teachers) and as representative of the limited attention to women students *as* women, evident in the final report.

What is striking, certainly, about these minutes and archival documents in this regard—as background and confidential data shared by the committee—is the amount of attention paid to the ways in which women look and how "feminine" they are, *in the school setting;* and how teachers, particularly attractive versus nonattractive female teachers, ultimately affect student behavior and academic success. Given that in 1945 the teachers college or normal school, as I discussed in chapter 1, was a significant institutional type in the United States, it is doubly striking that despite these fevered claims about the potentially positive relationship between a pretty (not necessarily intelligent) teacher and her students, there are no consultants on the committee from teachers colleges, public women's colleges, nor any other institution whose primary or significant mission was to *train teachers.* It is further surprising that these three male committee members conversing about women's teacherly appearances were themselves either professors of education or consultants for prominent educational foundations. This kind of discussion certainly would stand in stark contrast to the conversations about women's educational roles—as teachers or otherwise—that were shaping the Woman's College, an institutional type whose voice was not heard on this committee, during this same era.

Additionally, the focus on the appearance and placement of teachers—and their implicit roles in developing boys and girls into appropriate masculine and feminine identities—reduces the position of the teacher to little more than a well-groomed model. Since the vast majority of teachers in the secondary schools were women, this is akin to saying these women were in need of a personal makeover. Since the majority of teachers in colleges (certainly at Harvard) were men, this is also akin to recommending a peppering of well-placed women in the classroom for "discussions" of proper roles. As literature is deemed the "logical" place for such discussions, we again have the *English* teacher being drawn as (ideally) a sympathetic woman, with access to other sympathetic women who are not "career girls," as they are, but who are wives and mothers. Such a stereotypical notion of where a woman teacher is most "appropriate" pervades the historical teaching of English, and particularly first-year composition.

This focus on acceptable roles for women in and out of college is also present in the summary of the Radcliffe surveys. An overview of 72 of these 372 received surveys was submitted to the committee by Byron S. Hollinshead, a visiting Harvard fellow and president of Scranton-Keystone Junior College (Pennsylvania).[13] Hollinshead begins his report by sorting Radcliffe "girls" into three categories, quoting a survey respondent: "(1) A small group of career girls; (2) A small group who want a husband, children, and a domestic life; (3) A large group which does not know whether it will have one or the other, and ought to be prepared for both" (1). Hollinshead notes that this respondent claims "Radcliffe puts all girls in the first group . . . therefore [it has] failed the majority." He continues, "of the surveys I read, the career girls seem quite satisfied with the curriculum; the girls who later married were least satisfied" (2). This despite his additional finding that, "Most of the respondents seemed to feel that it was unfortunate not to be able to get sufficient vocational training at Radcliffe to be able to get a first job" (2). Another end of the response scale—and perhaps socioeconomic populace at Radcliffe—is evident in Hollinshead's quote from another survey respondent who wanted, among other things, training in "Household management—how to clean, do laundry, etc., or see that someone else does it" (2).

Indeed, the Radcliffe survey contains a great number of questions about not just educational life, but also about future family and career plans, as the committee is focused on determining the type of "vocational" training that Radcliffe graduates might want (and which the survey determines is a vocal desire among alumnae). The first assumption of the survey is that many of the graduates would be married—given the questions about anniversary date, husband's occupation, and ages of children at the start of the survey. The survey also includes, on page 2, questions about the "type of activity" that alumnae have been engaging in since graduation. The sample activities, interestingly enough, are "homemaking," "writing," and "teaching." This is a significant window into, perhaps, some of the either acceptable or common, or both, vocations that graduates were undertaking postcollege—or those that the committee imagined were being undertaken. Of course, at the Woman's College, the vocations of writing and teaching were, in fact, common, as discussed previously in this book. Finally, the survey asks, under the category of "Personal Equation," "from your experience, do you advise combining work with marriage?" This question again assumes many Radcliffe graduates will have married, or that those who have not married or have divorced will have an opinion on this, since there is no space for skipping this question if it is inapplicable to the respondent. While in general the survey thus pays a good deal of attention to women's lives pre- and postgraduation, at no point does it ask the respondents to comment on a *woman's* education explicitly, except insofar as it asks gendered questions about marriage and family, questions unlikely to appear on a survey of male Harvard graduates.[14]

This slant toward the personal/gendered aspects of graduates' lives was, however, less of analytical interest to the committee than the responses to questions 9, 10, 11, and 22 regarding the curriculum and the faculty. Mirroring Thomas Kuhn's student-based concern that Harvard faculty were, perhaps, not up to the challenge of general education instruction, the committee's summary report of these questions, including the alumnae respondents' views of Radcliffe faculty, found similar lack:

> The faculty come in for their share of attention, their chief fault being, apparently, their remoteness and inaccessibility. "More personal contact with the faculty" appeared in many answers, and reflects a need which is still felt and admitted by the present student body. The lack of inspiring teachers was mentioned by some; the inadequacy of the graduate student instructor or tutor feelingly commented upon. Pleas for a more careful fitting together of tutor and tutee were made, as well as suggestions that more women tutors be employed. . . . Quite a few (principally [respondents who graduated in] the late 20s and 30s) complain bitterly of their lack of maturity as students, suggesting that sympathetic advisers, who knew the students as individuals, could have helped them develop more. (3–4)[15]

Yet despite internal recommendations regarding an increased attention to residential college support staff and first-year student counseling on academic as well as personal issues, the proposed outline for the official Radcliffe general education report does not concern itself with this aspect of a college education. While the Redbook is laden with discussions of morals and ethics, and longstanding educational and societal values that contribute to the "well-rounded student," as it were, the Radcliffe report also offers no such recommendations as specific to the education of women. Instead, the outline drawn up by the committee suggests the opposite: item 3.1 notes that there are "Limitations, which we think fortunate, imposed on Radcliffe College by traditional and contractual arrangement with Harvard (use data from questionnaire on reasons for entering Radcliffe)" and that there should be a "discussion of the theoretical case for sexual differentiation in general education at the college level" (Hollinshead, "Memorandum," 1). Because 69.8 percent of women cited their reason for selecting Radcliffe as the fact that "they would receive from the Harvard faculty instruction normally offered at Harvard," ("General Education at Radcliffe," 5), apparently the committee interpreted this as a positive and ongoing reason for sex-segregated education— and did not consider whether such instruction could be either made coeducational, or could be found at a freestanding women's college—public or private—led by equally outstanding faculty as those found at Harvard.

One of the other data-gathering methods of the Radcliffe committee was the Women's College Conference held in Williamstown, Massachusetts, on November 4–5, 1944, attended by representatives of two coeducational universities (Cornell and Minnesota) and by deans and presidents of like-minded women's institutions: Mount Holyoke, Smith, Bennington, Bryn Mawr, and Vassar. The question of "curricular differentiation in colleges for women" came up during this conference, with five main points attached to this discussion. One of these was, "In courses designed for general education, are there differences in content or emphasis that might profitably be introduced when they are offered by colleges for women? Would it, for example, be desirable to lend greater emphasis to Fine Arts and Music than in similar colleges for men?" Another question raised asked whether "it can be argued that thorough training in 'general education' is even more valuable for young women than for young men?" Neither of these questions, or the undoubtedly fascinating responses to these questions (not recorded in archives of the committee), are explicitly or implicitly addressed in the Redbook. Instead, the report reads as if it were directed to a generalized, nonsegregated populace of students—a populace that did not exist as of yet at Harvard and Radcliffe (despite the slow migration of small numbers of Radcliffe students to occupy seats in Harvard courses, those vacated by enlisted men, in the early 1940s).

In sum, it appears that this apparently thoughtful attempt at investigating the specific issues in women's education was met with scant coverage in the final Redbook report. Such a lack would prove difficult for institutions such as the Woman's College to address, if they wanted to adopt Harvard's model as the one that is "good for all," in both an educational and, implicitly, a patriotic sense, given President Roosevelt's directive and its immediate response by Harvard as a self-selected leader in such matters. But what was perhaps equally lacking in the report, as applicable to the Woman's College and to any other public institution wherein writing served as an important and prominent facet of the existing curriculum, was the conflicting attention to first-year composition, even as this course sat at the heart of general education itself.

English Composition and the Redbook: "Everyone's Responsibility Is No One's Responsibility"

Much as the Redbook failed to offer a full consideration of women's education, even with considerable aggregate data on its own women's college at its disposal, so, too, did the study fail to discuss in any depth the position of first-year writing within a liberal education. Because institutions such as the Woman's College deeply valued communication and written expression both in its curriculum and in its extracurricular activities—and promoted a solid culture of writing among its women students—such an oversight in this regard in the Redbook would make the report even less palatable. As discussed previously, writing thrived at the first-year level at the Woman's College and supported for several years a first-year magazine written and produced by its students. It is within this framework that one can see how the approach to first-year writing in the Redbook not only ignored feedback from its disciplinary committee consultants, but also aimed to overturn the autonomy of first-year writing as an academic and intellectually promising course, as represented within many public university curricula.

David Russell's snapshot of the Harvard report in his book *Writing in the Academic Disciplines* observes that the Redbook was "disarmingly vague" regarding the elements that would make up this "ideological common ground" of general education; Russell notes that while "humanities, social sciences, and natural sciences were recommended . . . there was no effort to find common ground among the three perspectives" (252). Additionally, in terms of literacy education, the Redbook "never considered what kinds of writing students would do or how that writing would be taught and evaluated," even as it called for writing to be integrated across the curriculum, and for composition instructors to have an "intimate relation" with the other general education courses (253). A second-semester focus on individual conferences was proposed, but not enacted in the Harvard curriculum, after the Redbook's publication (253).[16] The general import of the report, according to Russell, was to remake the curriculum from a "Great Books" into a "Great Man" endeavor, with exposure to a "great mind at work" (a faculty member of prestigious reputation/standing) in the classes, with the grading of writing left to teaching assistants (254).

It is surprising that such an influential report failed on this significant educational count, since, as previously mentioned, one figure positioned to be at the center of the writing and composition component of the Redbook, Theodore Morrison, was highly experienced in first-year writing instruction. Morrison advocated for a more traditional, autonomous approach to composition—the distinct English A as a writing course, and as an introduction to writing in higher-level courses. His approach was ultimately discounted in the final report. Instead, the new vision of English A was proposed as a two-credit-hour course that would be followed by an additional semester of general education writing, wherein essay or "theme" topics would be directly connected to the other general education courses that students were taking that semester. This system is what Russell means when he critiques the notion of professors farming out the teaching of writing beyond their subject-based courses. This system also positions English composition as a course without intellectual content, except as provided by other disciplines, as opposed to a true writing-across-the-curriculum approach—which could have been a more progressive suggestion—in which each subject is taught as writing-intensive, or with a "write to learn" philosophy in place. Given Morrison's directorship of English A; his past experience chairing the Committee on the Use of English by Students—which controlled the remedial writing courses at Harvard labeled, in various years, English C, D, and F; and his allied interests in teaching creative writing (at both Harvard and at the Bread Loaf Writers' Conference), and writing novels, it is not surprising that he rejected this quasi-handmaid approach to writing instruction.

Morrison's objections are made clear in his written statement to the committee entitled "English Composition in the High School" dated February 1944, which actually discusses both secondary and postsecondary issues in English and writing. Morrison begins his argument by rejecting the label *communication* that has become a standard term in the committee's discussions, noting that it is "not a designation, but a slogan. It is a current catchword, and as a catchword it bristles with false assumptions and betrays a belief that questions have been answered when they have only been concealed" (1). Morrison is speaking of the committee's use of the term, but his objections also may be broadened to the historical moment in which these discussions were taking place—when the idea of *communications* was beginning to take shape in postsecondary institutions and the valuation of generalized writing and speaking was heightened. Morrison traces this valuation to the armed forces, pointing out that, "The word is now in use by the Army and Navy . . . they mean (in part) that they want students trained in writing and speaking to such effect that they can later, in the field, 'communicate' efficiently in a military sense" (1). Morrison goes on to argue, "The fact that the term has now acquired military connotation and military prestige does not increase its usefulness in an educational discussion that aims to be clear and definite" (1).

Morrison's objections clearly undermine the patriotic/civic duty of the Redbook as a whole, implying that acceptance of terminology such as this allies their efforts with military goals and thus nonacademic principles. Morrison positions himself squarely as a humanist—but also as a teacher of writing dedicated to keeping the sanctity of his profession intact.[17] He articulates his beliefs by answering further asserting:

> [Writing] must be frequent enough to constitute a real training and to give the students a chance to acquire proficiency through familiarity with the task. It should, in general education, aim (as a common training for *all* students, in distinction from those of literary taste and promise) at *command of exposition* as a final result . . . the secondary school students should of course write précis, arguments, comments on books, etc.; and "narration" and "description" should never be thought of by the teacher as separate and distinct "forms" of composition. . . . Intellectual responsibility in all expression should be the constant ideal, not mere conformity to genteel usage. (2)

Here, Morrison's recommendations evidence two lines of thinking in his formation of what English composition should be (or do). First, he separates the task of composition, and its students—implying that, perhaps, students with superior writing skills need not take the course (in fact, this was the case, since approximately 25 percent of Harvard students were being exempted from English A during this time)—from those of "literary taste and promise"—that is, students who can both read and write literature due to their innate skills. Second, he emphasizes that the "modes" of composition (though he does not call them that) are false dichotomies— that such divisions are not profitable distinctions, going against the prevailing pedagogy of this era that often emphasized such modes in first-year composition. Finally, though, despite his belief that there are those students of "promise" and then there are students of composition, Morrison asserts that "intellectual responsibility" be the goal—rather than simply surface correctness, which exposes perhaps a more enlightened stance than does his assertion about "promise" among some.

More to the point of the English A proposal, that a General Education A course be implemented that would use as its main texts the material from other courses, thereby encouraging writing as the "responsibility of all," Morrison argues. "In stating the ideal principle that satisfactory powers of written expression are everyone's responsibility, the Committee should not forget the notorious, the inescapable practical principle that everyone's responsibility is no one's responsibility . . . the Committee should not defeat its own ends and aims by putting misplaced emphasis on the joint responsibility of all teachers for competence in writing and thereby impairing or destroying the authority of that class of teachers to whom direct responsibility for training in written expression traditionally belongs" (3). Given that, even as director of the English A course, Morrison held a lectureship—not a tenure-track faculty position—from 1931 until 1962, when he was finally promoted to a tenure-track faculty line,[18] his statement about authority and responsibility certainly may be read through both pedagogical and political lenses.

Harvard had a history of providing extensive writing instruction for its students, even in remedial coursework, as previously noted. But in keeping with the labor practices regarding first-year writing instruction at other Ivy League institutions both midcentury and today, it did not have a history of making these positions tenure-track, despite its perceived institutional position as a leader in writing and rhetoric in the United States. Morrison surely understood the further diminishment of English composition were it to be subsumed by "subject" courses in the general education program. But he also understood, as stated here, that the wide diffusion of writing instruction across other subjects—in the absence of training those faculty, or securing faculty with prior training in the teaching of writing—would be akin to an evaporation of the core instruction necessary, and found previously in the English A course. Morrison ultimately opines, "The Committee should not begin the reform of English teaching by diminishing or impairing the authority and responsibility of English teachers, but by defining for them what contribution they should attempt to make to the general education of their students and what capacities their students should have" (4).

With this stance made clear, Morrison attended a meeting of the committee on April 25, 1944, held at about the halfway mark of the committee's overall deliberations and drafting of the Redbook. Presiding committee member Dean Buck believed, in regard to communication and literature, that the committee "must come out with a program that will make sense for the high schools and the millions of people who do not go beyond them, as well as for Harvard College" (Apr. 25, 1944, minutes). This auspicious and daunting charge certainly must have made a course such as English A—born of a perceived lack among Harvard men, and supported by remedial courses when found itself to be lacking in effectiveness—a complicated charge for revision. Seeing the aim of the committee as stretching from the start of high school through the first two years of college, and seeing the high school itself as the origin of the student's—and citizen's—appreciation for a broad education of "great" works and ideas makes the position of writing instruction primary, in all logical situations. Yet the committee sought a more generic view of writing instruction—one that resisted disciplinary boundaries and, ultimately, greatly diminished or eliminated the position of the English department in such matters, particularly the division of English composition.

The committee discussion focused, in contrast, on the position of literature and the humanities in general in the general education program, and largely ignored the points raised about English A specifically and writing instruction generally. Several committee members were concerned that secondary school teachers would not receive the proper training in "humanistic values" and/or that they would not receive deep enough intellectual training in the teaching of English literature. Others worried that the great texts would not be consistently represented if a particular instructor focused on "some writer or another" rather than the prescribed spread of canonical names that would be put forth by the committee. Morrison's concerns, however, were still about what general education can or should do, and how the "good" of general education would result in the elimination of the very skill training that the committee saw as lacking in the current student body, both at Harvard and nationwide: "It seems a very curious thing for the committee to contemplate the abolition of this long-standing year's training in composition, when I had supposed that more rather than less was needed. I think when the question of English A comes up it ought to be considered at length, and though I do not propose to consider it now, I would like to say that you won't get the equivalent of it by diffusing it through several other courses" (Harvard Committee on General Education, meeting minutes, Apr. 25, 1944). Morrison's comment did not receive a response in the meeting minutes. There are no other minutes reflecting input by Morrison within this pivotal meeting, nor is there evidence of explicit consideration of his views—as the director of English A, and as the only committee consultant trained in or dedicated to the teaching of first-year composition, or English in general.

What does appear in the Redbook regarding composition manifests itself in two recommendations, first in the "Secondary Schools" section and later in "General Education in Harvard College." For the secondary schools, the committee argues that, "Most of the English teacher's time and effort, whether he is aiding readers or not, should be concerned with language" but the "satisfactory exploration of literary terminology is so difficult that it should properly be postponed to the college" (116). Ultimately, in English instruction, "There is a need for versions of the great works cleared of unnecessary and unrewarding obstacles and made by abridgment and reflective editing more accessible to general readers" (114). Such abridgment, focus on language, and deferment of "difficult" literary work results in a philosophy of instruction visualized as such:

> Composition, by pen or tongue, is largely a matter of imitation. But the word, imitate, straddles all levels. In spelling, in pronunciation, and in grammatical conformities we follow the letter, the surface routine. In everything which has to do with the shaping and expression of thought and feeling, "the letter killeth, the spirit giveth life." And if the models we put before them have no spirit our students' progress must be slight. If the reading matter we force them to attend to is not clear, forceful, well organized, and interesting *as language,* in addition to the interest of its content, we are depriving them of the first instrument of their instruction. We are doing worse than this if we make them suppose we want them to imitate modes of speech or writing whose aim and virtue they have not felt. Composition, then, is a matter of good models, in speech and writing, and intelligently graded discussion of what makes them good. (119)

Clearly these secondary school recommendations reinforce the value of "great" literature and the ancillary value of using these great works as "models." This paradigm—whereby students will be asked to model their compositions on the language of "Homer, Plato, the Old Testament, Bacon, Dante, Shakespeare, or Tolstoy" (114) stands in sharp contrast to one of Morrison's recommendations, that the student of composition is a "student of his time" ("English Composition in the High School," 1) who must learn to accept and employ the language of his current culture. In addition, this paradigm asks that students not engage in the actual nitty-gritty interpretation of literature, but instead forestall that training to the college level. The problem with this recommendation is the resulting lack of knowledge of literary texts *in depth*—which was traditionally the litmus test for placement into courses such as English A at Harvard and the first-semester literature course at Yale; students who did not have sufficient knowledge of key literary works were deemed to be "not ready" for introductory literature courses—as contrary as that may sound—and were additionally labeled poor writers, as I have noted elsewhere. So, delaying this instruction, noble though its aims may be, would seem to exacerbate the problem of first-year placement at the college, Harvard included.

Obviously, this secondary school plan also reduces composition to a simple act of modeling, and "intelligent grading" on the teacher's part.

Students are not explicitly encouraged to develop their own writing *voices* (admittedly a very new term in 1945), or even necessarily flesh out their own intellectual positions. Instead, the emphasis is on *imitation*—an exercise certainly prevalent in ancient rhetoric and in creative writing, but less productive, perhaps, in terms of modern first-year composition. Despite his own position as a novelist and creative writing teacher, Morrison's recommendations for the secondary school and college level composition course would seem to contradict this idea that imitation is key to learning, and that said imitation should be done in regards to great works of historical/canonical literature.

The Redbook's second section attending to composition falls under the "General Education in Harvard College" section where, in contrast to the rather fuzzy recommendations for secondary school curricula (other than suggesting this intense modeling, and that students write frequently throughout their English courses), the committee sets forth a very specific plan for the revision of English A, mentioned previously in this chapter. The committee observes that because English A does not count for any distribution requirements, it must be the case that "faculty [believe] that English A has to do largely with the technique of writing and is not primarily a course in subject matter, that it is calculated to develop a skill rather than to explore a field of learning" (199). Given this issue, the committee provides a subsequent justification for its amendment to English A—one that seems to reinforce the very belief feared to be held by faculty:

The present requirement in English composition has the merit of placing responsibility for improvement in the writing of English in a single agency. It has the corresponding weakness of segregating training in writing from the fields of learning. Since the responsibility for training in written communication is vested in the staff of English A, the other members of the faculty too often feel that they have little if any responsibility for the development of skill and facility in writing. This seems to us a serious weakness. What is desired is not primarily skill in writing literary English or about English literature. Training in composition should not be associated with the English Department only. It should be functional to the curriculum, a significant part of the student's college experience. It should, so far as is feasible, be associated with training in general education rather than with a single course or department. We realize that if training in composition is everyone's responsibility, it may become no one's, but we believe that the ends sought by the present English A requirement can be better achieved by the modification of the existing system. (199)

This passage is fascinating in several respects. First, to read this section supportively, one might argue that the committee's vision of writing as belonging to the curriculum as a whole is somewhat forward-thinking. It resembles an early version of writing across the curriculum, but without any notion of how that would be supported or enacted in disciplinary areas heretofore reliant heavily upon English A as both a required course and a sorting mechanism for first-year students. Second, no mention is made of the existing (but absent from this report) English C–F courses that *support* the work of English A, and function as bounce-back required courses for students who either failed to complete English A with a sufficiently high grade, or who need more support in writing later in their coursework. Third, the vision of composition as "not primarily skill in writing literature or about English literature" seems completely in conflict with the committee's own recommendations for secondary school curricula—focused on the great works of literature (and some philosophy) and on modeling one's prose after those works.

Finally, the committee's statement about how "everyone's responsibility . . . may become no one's" is clearly a direct reference to Morrison's remarks in his February 1944 memo to the committee—which appear here without any fuller consideration of, or context for, Morrison's own contrasting view. Despite the clear implication in the Redbook that English has "no subject" and thus carries no credit, the committee's recommendation is not to *grant* the course graduation distribution credit—which would, in theory, go toward solving the problem at hand—but instead to phase out the course by spreading it over other courses' teaching loads, resulting in "no additional course credit for this work in English composition" absorbed by other general education courses (200).

It is easy for us to look back and conceive of this rhetoric as limited thinking put forward by the Harvard committee in relation to first-year composition. We now know the requirements that must be in place—the faculty "buy-in" in terms of support, and compensation, in some cases—in order for Writing across the Curriculum (WAC) and Writing in the Disciplines (WID) programs to flourish. We also know that granting credit for English composition is the first step to making it a "real" course, and we further know that English composition is, in fact, a "subject" with intellectual content that is equivalent in scope to other courses across the disciplines. But as a product of its time, the Redbook presented what may have been viewed as a revolutionary pass-off for beleaguered universities seeking a way out of the dominance that English composition had within, and over, their curricula. Perhaps because the Woman's College felt no such strain under the weight of writing instruction, both inside and outside the English department, it felt little need to emulate the Harvard plan in this or other aspects. A closer comparative look at general education reform at the Woman's College in light of this baseline examination of the Harvard model demonstrates what the faculty at this institution held dear—and held at bay—regarding their own campus and departmental reforms.

From the "Gifted" to the "Forgotten of God": General Education Reform at the Woman's College

To say that the Redbook report failed at the Woman's College simply due to its butting heads—textually speaking—with an enlightened administration harboring deep concerns for women's literacy is only one historical reading to consider. The Harvard report not only elided questions of where and how women should be educated—and where writing fit into that education—but also what "general" education meant to a diverse group of women in a public college setting. One may also see the failure of the Redbook's principles at the Woman's College in the early 1950s as a failure of its chancellor to recognize the abilities of his own faculty to construct a homegrown curriculum fit for its students, and as a failure to meet his own ideals for that student body, who clearly did not represent, in Graham's view, his vision of a cohesive and superior sampling of women scholars.[19] Yet still another interpretation of the problem rests on the struggle between the national and the local, and the Woman's College's prescient moves to create its own postwar plan through two separate committees, as work on the Redbook was only just beginning. In other words, the influence of Harvard—as a potentially negative, or at least a limited, national example—was clear. The resulting measures taken at the Woman's College were both a reactive response to this negative example and a proactive measure to improve the intellectual lives of its students, a measure lost to English studies history and the more famous examples of Harvard and its elite, all-male predecessors.

While the Harvard group was being formed in spring 1943, the Curriculum Revision Committee at the Woman's College—made up of seven faculty (two women and five men) representing the departments of business, history, sociology, biology, education, psychology, and home economics—was already submitting its final written recommendations to its own campus community. On March 15, 1943, the committee produced a report that began with the following rationale:

> This curriculum presented herewith is in keeping with the tradition of this college. The changes recommended are of an evolutionary nature and provision is made for a period of transition. The committee is convinced that our present curriculum is too rigid and illiberal to meet the needs of our students and the demands of modern life. Women are entering many fields today and will enter still more after the war. To meet these new demands our curriculum must be made more flexible. The plan outlined in this report broadens and liberates the elective program, keeps specialization within reasonable bounds, and provides opportunity for new specializations and new types of general education appropriate in a changing world. Above all, it enables us to perform more effectively our function—service to North Carolina and its citizens. (Edwards et al. 1)

This preamble is notable in many respects. First, it invokes some of the same terminology upon which the Harvard report—at this stage, not yet written—would also rely. Second, it specifically names the revisions as being *local* in nature, rather than broadly applicable to institutions outside the Woman's College. While there are many caveats in the Harvard report about widespread use of its recommendations, the implication put forth by virtue of publishing the report *as a book* are clear: this Harvard plan is a model, one that other institutions can, might, or should follow. Finally, the Woman's College committee preamble nods to a revision of general education, but also a possible redefinition of "specialization"—a term that is fairly well shunned by the Harvard committee in its desire to group general education into large categories (humanities, social sciences) and resist overspecialization as a scholarly and pedagogical trend. Most obviously, the Woman's College plan calls for a consideration of women— its student body—rather than a consideration of the world at large, in its postwar condition.

While the general divisions making up the sixty-two-credit-hour core proposed by the Curriculum Revision Committee came to partly resemble those of the Redbook—in that categories such as humanities, natural sciences, and social sciences were posed—its curricular requirements were far more attached to the department level, specifying courses such as Literature in English and Modern European History as well as eighteen hours of electives drawn from some very specific curricular areas such as Dance and Hygiene, as well as Business Education. Given the inclusion of dance and music in particular, it is evident that the Woman's College was accounting for its students' wide interests in the arts—something lamented in the Radcliffe study on general education but not fully accounted for in the Redbook itself. Following this corelike curriculum, students would take twenty-four to thirty-six hours in their majors, and sixty-two more hours in "free electives."

In sum, the plan of this committee looks very much like the plan many large universities follow today, including a twelve-semester-hour requirement for English coursework (composition and introductory literature) and, despite its otherwise forward-thinking and liberal stance regarding the arts and literary education, a provision for remediation, as follows: "Any upperclass student whose work in any course gives evidence of lack of proficiency in written English shall be brought to the attention of a committee from the English department. The committee, after investigating the student's work, will arrange for the removal of the deficiency" (Edwards et al. 5). Such a provision mimics the exact provisions in place at Harvard at this same time, supervised by the Committee on the Use of English by Students.[20] It also evidences that the Woman's College, despite its very different populace, was dealing with similar issues of ability grouping in writing instruction, just as Harvard was during this early postwar era.

Even with this highly specific and detailed curricular plan, the Woman's College was still concerned about the new types of students it would face postwar, and how to best help these students at the micro as well as the macro level. As such, a second committee, the Committee on Postwar Planning, made up of five female and one male faculty from the Woman's College, was formed and drafted its own report on May 10, 1945—just three months prior to the publication of the Redbook. The postwar committee's report references the flurry of general education reform beginning to take place nationwide (and about to explode as a discussion topic following the Redbook's publication), noting that, according to R. H. Thornton's article "What the Colleges Are Doing," "the conclusions reached by most of these special committees are strikingly similar, and the objectives of a liberal education as set forth in these reports show few differences in ultimate aim" (Lockhart, "Report," 2). Yet this committee's report—while acknowledging that in most reports, "a 'core' curriculum in the liberal arts is recommended" and that this core "usually includes English composition, some modern foreign language, and some courses in history" (2–3), also commented that such a vision "of what college education may become is magnificent. The difficulty will be putting such a conception into practice" (3).

Rooted in this national context, the postwar committee's report goes

on to recommend that the Woman's College take care to consider returning servicewomen and their needs in the college. Unlike the general disregard for women's academic and personal counseling postwar as articulated
in the Radcliffe report, the Woman's College, as part of their "Information
for Servicewomen" pamphlet, set up a special (and separate) counseling
program specifically for women veterans enrolled at the Woman's College, per the general guidelines of the Serviceman's Readjustment Act of
1944, Public Law 346. The pamphlet notes, "The Woman's College in its
long experience in working with women is well organized to advise and
counsel on the educational programs of women and to give careful consideration to their vocational plans and placement upon graduation. Special faculty advisers are appointed to all students and for servicewomen a
separate committee has been set up to consider their particular problems.
In the residence halls trained counselors are employed to give attention
to social and personal development" ("Information for Servicewomen,"
1). In addition to these counseling programs, the postwar committee also
advanced specific recommendations regarding these students' curricular
needs, such as offering language courses on six-day schedules to accelerate completion; the construction of new courses in physiotherapy, home
economics, and recreation; and the allowance of a two-year plan for army
and navy nurses who desired completion of their nursing degrees at Woman's College (3). These recommendations are far more specific regarding
armed forces personnel than those covered by the general aims of the Redbook. In addition to these curricular recommendations, the committee
also asked the faculty and administration to consider more general provisions for the postwar Woman's College student, including the returning
servicewoman, within each department of study:

> In order that we may more adequately prepare our students for the com-
> plexity of Life in "one world," the committee would recommend that as a
> beginning each department take stock of itself . . . [by considering] (a) Is my
> department doing the utmost to prepare young women for living in the post
> war world? (b) Are the courses as coordinated as to give the student a broad
> as well as a deep grasp of the subject? (c) Are the courses so coordinated
> with courses in related departments that the student cannot fail to grasp the
> relationship? (d) Am I, as an instructor, doing my utmost toward achieving
> these aims? (e) Would a returning service woman, with her broadened expe-
> rience, feel that it was worthwhile to take my course? (f) Is my course, or can
> it be made, one that will add to the achievement of a satisfactory preparation
> for living and working in the post war world? (4)

This committee's recommendations, like the Curriculum Revision Committee before it, are also notable when set against the broader aims of the Redbook. The Committee on Postwar Planning quite specifically put responsibility on the *departments*—rather than the college in whole—to align their courses both internally and externally, against those of other departments, in order to build logical and visible relationships between perhaps disparate courses. Such a charge seems somewhat anathema to the Redbook, which envisioned a larger organizing principle of general education that, to a degree, elided departmental authority over curriculum. This charge to the departments would be one that the English department would take up between 1954 and 1956, when attempting to revise its first- and second-year offerings in composition and literature. What the postwar committee also focuses on that is perhaps ignored, or certainly glossed, in the Redbook is the sanctity of the department. Whereas the Redbook posits general education as a collegewide task and responsibility, and frequently resists talk of either specialization or fragmentation— dividing and conquering at the department level—the postwar committee's report, like the Curriculum Revision Committee's report, promotes a deep understanding of the Woman's College student at the departmental level and asks that faculty think from within their disciplinary ranks about how to best meet these special students' needs.

Given these earlier (and apparently agreed-upon) curricular and student-centered recommendations for postwar education at the Woman's College, it comes as some surprise that the college would again take up a wide-reaching study of the general education curriculum some six years later. But this charge was attached to the college's new chancellor, Edward K. Graham Jr., who from his earliest days in office sought to align the Woman's College with the most elite and prestigious institutions around the country. Graham, whose father had been the much-revered chancellor of the University of North Carolina—Chapel Hill, and who was known on the Woman's College campus as a polarizing figure for the six brief years he held office, took the reins of general education reform, and failed in his attempts to position the Woman's College as a local enactment of the Redbook report.[21]

Early correspondence evidences that Graham was feeling very positive about the prospect of the Woman's College reforms, and equally confident about his ultimate success in implementing them. He wrote to Ralph McDonald, executive secretary of the Department of Higher Education in Washington, DC, about his plans, using the extended metaphor of a football game (perhaps ironic—or clueless—given that he was talking about *women's* education):

The first play from scrimmage was the first faculty meeting. The entire faculty of 204 was appointed a committee of the whole to undertake a study of what an educated woman should have in terms of understandings, knowledge, and skills. . . . Throughout the fall and winter, the steering committee has been moving ahead with the formulation of the study—both in planning sessions and in open meetings. Interim reports have been presented and discussed with the full faculty. . . . At the present time, about five minutes of the second quarter have elapsed. No score, but we have the ball and are moving it. All goes according to pre-game strategy so far. . . . It would take a genius to fumble this. I'm no genius. (Mar. 10, 1951, letter)

Just one month later, on April 24, 1951, Graham submitted a budget to the Consolidated University of North Carolina system office for "a grant of three thousand dollars in support of a faculty study looking toward development of a program of general education at the Woman's College" (Grey, letter to Carmichael). This included a provision for two faculty to attend the Natural Sciences at Harvard workshops in summer 1951; summer salary for three faculty members (natural science, social science, humanities) to develop courses in their areas; travel for three faculty in these same areas to visit institutions "whose programs we wish to observe at first hand"; and honoraria for three consultants in general education to visit campus during the 1951–52 year, plus "stenographic assistance." He also invited several figures from other universities and from government educational foundations to visit campus, writing personal letters to each that outlined his ideas in brief and promising hospitable accommodations.

Indeed, Graham's plan for the Woman's College was built explicitly on the Redbook study from Harvard, and his desired consultants were those who either taught at elite universities or who had extensive knowledge of the work done at Harvard. As he writes in a letter to O. C. Carmichael at the Carnegie Foundation on April 24, 1951, seeking external funding for the project as he had also sought internal funding, Graham invokes the language of the Redbook when he explains, "During the present school year, our faculty, under the direction of a steering committee on General Education appointed by the Chancellor, has undertaken a careful examination of that part of our students' education which we believe should be the possession of every graduate of this college as *an educated person in a free society*" (emphasis added). In addition, in a statement in his letter to Carmichael titled "Summary Descriptions of the General Education Program at the Cooperating Institutions," the curricular revisions at Yale, University of Chicago, Harvard, and Columbia are noted as models. Graham's division of the committee's work into the areas of humanities, social sciences, and natural sciences exactly mimics the divisions that house the "elementary courses" at Harvard. This despite the strong presence of fine arts at the Woman's College—including theater and music—which would have, consequently, been a fourth logical subdivision to offer in the revision plan. But it did not exist in the Redbook, so it does not exist in Graham's template.

In addition, the divisions of teacher education, as well as home economics, also obviously strong presences at the Woman's College, are also ignored in this general education charge of Graham's. One might argue that an education program or home economics program is too "specialized" to be considered within general education. But given the original charter of the college and its significant number of majors in education and home economics, it seems equally odd to completely ignore these units in a study of the "educated woman" as she was produced by the Woman's College. These are baseline curricular areas for which it becomes difficult to apply a large, private, all-male university's plan to that of a small, public, all-women's college steeped in normal school traditions.

But Graham's goal was clearly, in many ways, to erase some of the college traditions that spoke to those normal school origins and instead position the college among the elite institutions of the eastern seaboard (and their peers, like the University of Chicago). In a one-page draft document in Graham's personal papers entitled "Tentative Statement of Objectives in General Education," marked by edits and handwritten changes, these parallels are made even more clear, and their indebtedness to the Redbook study is explicitly noted:

> General education is part of a student's education directed toward understanding the knowledge and the skills that should be the common possession of every man and woman in our society. This education should give some understanding of man in relation to himself, to society, and to the physical world. The student must accordingly master something of the factual content of the three main areas of study: the humanities, the social sciences, and the natural and physical sciences. With this must go some grasp of the methods appropriate to each area, i.e., aesthetic, historical, and scientific. The concern of general education is the enrichment of the inner experience of the individual. Of equal importance, general education must contribute toward the development of the citizen in a democracy, a person aware of his cultural heritage, and committed to the values that make a democratic system possible. Knowledge should be presented to the student

in as integrated a manner as possible. Every effort should be made to clarify the relations among the disciplines of each area, and among the areas themselves.

Through general education the student should develop certain basic abilities. Perhaps the most important are those singled out in the Harvard report: ". . . to think effectively, to communicate thought, to make relevant judgments, to discriminate among values."—*General Education in a Free Society*, 65

Yet these lofty assertions—common to many an institutional "vision" or "strategic plan," as is the parlance of the twenty-first century—are very nonspecific to the goals and history of the Woman's College. Its roots as a very special kind of institution seem to be ignored in this overview—right down to the idea of "man in relation to himself" and "his" cultural heritage (though of course such sexist language was common midcentury, even in syllabi and materials from Woman's College courses). Indeed, Graham's statement seems so broad as to be applicable to any institution serving any population—which, apparently, was his goal, following Harvard's published lead. This despite a report from the executive committee of the Cooperative Study in General Education, American Council on Education, in 1947—also filed in Graham's personal papers on general education—which makes a series of conclusions and recommendations regarding general education reform using twenty-two colleges as sites of study between 1938 and 1944, prior to Harvard's own work, and including an unnamed "state teachers college" and a "four-year college for women." There were no elite private universities included in this study; rather, it appears to have been—perhaps unintentionally so—a study of general education *outside* the confines of Harvard and other elite institutions authoring such plans. This study notes,

> The primary obligation of general education is to develop an intelligent, socially sensitive layman able and willing to discharge his responsibilities as a citizen, a community member, a friend, and a member of a family, and equipped with interest and powers to give meaning and satisfaction to life. The ends of general education should emphasize understanding, intelligent problem solving, and clarification of values rather than memorization and habits and skills for which the rationale is not understood. . . . Definite objectives for a program of general education in a particular college can be most helpfully made by *studying the needs of the students in that college*

[including] data about students, and learning processes, and the educational philosophy of the institution. ("Some Characteristics of the General Education Movement," 1–2)

It is unclear from the archived general education documents how Graham responded to this report, which notably valued the local over the national in curricular construction, and the history of the particular institution at hand. Certainly archival documents show that individual steering committee members visited and profiled the curriculum at similar institutions of the time, such as the Pennsylvania College for Women, and discussed women's colleges in general as being a segment of their institutional comparatives.

But even as Graham's view of the local is not explicitly stated in his general education draft documents, his concerns regarding the *abilities* of the local student population of the Woman's College are clear in two of his personal letters. In the first, sent to Clarence Faust—and excerpted at the start of this chapter—Graham expresses his frustration and provides a preview of discontent to come among the faculty regarding reform:

> The situation at our school is this. We have here some 2450 girls. They come to us with all sorts of academic and family backgrounds, and with the widest conceivable range of interests and aptitudes. When I came here last summer, I was immediately impressed with the remarkable potential of the place, and appalled by the prospect of rapidly mounting enrollments and the prospect of failure in carrying out our mission unless we gave aggressive and far-sighted attention to our academic dimensions. . . . At our opening faculty meeting last fall, I proposed a re-study of our program, by the entire college community, in terms of general education. This has been assumed by the faculty with the usual mixed reactions of enthusiasm and anxiety . . . every member of our faculty of 204 appears to have developed very strong feelings favorable or unfavorable. (Apr. 7, 1951, letter)

In another letter to Frank H. Bowles of Columbia University, whom Graham asks to speak to the Woman's College faculty during his visit to campus in May 1951, Graham again describes his current students' range of abilities, and Bowles's role, as such:

> You will remember that in an earlier letter I mentioned my concern over our problem of handling more than 2400 girls who ran all the way from the gifted to the forgotten of God. While you are here, we shall use that problem

as one of the major bases for your conferences with members of the faculty. I should like to have you appear at one open faculty meeting . . . [to speak on] Columbia's approach to general education, or on anything else that you think would be of interest to a faculty group which is currently engaged in taking a look at what it is doing and trying to decide whether it is good or not. (Apr. 20, 1951, letter)

In fact, in his correspondence, Graham repeatedly took some issue with the less-prepared students of the Woman's College, and used their perceived plight as his chief justification for designing a revised general education plan. He sought—by elite national examples—to improve their lot through a rigorous and fairly standardized plan of general education. Perhaps Graham felt these lower-ability students were akin to the vast number of returning soldiers appearing on college campuses—those who did not "belong," in some educators' view. Or perhaps Graham wanted to raise the profile of the Woman's College outside the South and beyond the circle of women's educators who were aware of the past prestige and rigor of the Woman's College curriculum, and the quality of its graduates. Either way, his private correspondence evidences a sharp disapproval for the status quo, and an almost zealous desire to improve upon it—given the flurry of year-end correspondence alone on this subject for a chancellor barely nine months in office.

Graham's wishes, ultimately, went unrealized. The general education reform that he so longed for did not materialize in a specific plan for or by the Woman's College faculty. Though the individual statements drafted by the humanities, natural sciences, and social studies groups passed by a fairly wide majority (77–22, 83–16, and 79–20, respectively), no further curricular plan was developed using these statements, and neither the Harvard study nor its counterpart curricula at Yale or Chicago were implemented. Beyond the general inapplicability of the broad Harvard goals to the specific Woman's College student body that precluded, perhaps, any measurable changes to the curriculum stemming from Graham's study, what were the specific objections to such implementation, and from whom did they originate?

One may view the archives of the steering committee and its subcommittees as detailing a struggle with departmental autonomy and faculty's values as in conflict with those being imposed upon them by the Harvard plan and Graham. It is raised on several occasions that new core courses would take a tremendous amount of time and work for departmental faculty, and that such work would be better spent designing courses that were already rooted in local values and principles, as noted by M. Isenberg of the classics department, who confided to Marc Friedlander (English department) that "to defend adequately [my above proposal for a humanities course] would entail living together with a staff for the next year and probably the next two . . . [but] you will come up with something homegrown and native to W.C. which would be better for W.C. than something you have not reasoned out for yourselves" (May 11, 1953, letter).

Additionally, these new general education courses would have to be positioned clearly against or allied with existing requirements in order to be sensible to the students of the college. For example, the September 24, 1951, steering committee minutes include the expression of a member that "some misunderstanding on the campus is evident about the place of General Education Courses as opposed to Basic College Required Courses and that such questions as 'Are General Education Courses equivalent to the first two years of Basic Required Courses?' are being asked" (minutes, Sept. 24, 1951). These "basic required courses" seem to be health, English composition, and foreign languages, which at the October 25, 1951, meeting became a topic relevant to the general education proposal. Namely,

> It was recognized that there will come a time when we shall have to consider how to fit the newly developed courses into the time available in a student's program. It was felt, however, that this could hardly be done until such course planning makes clear how much time the work in the area courses will require. The impact of development of general education courses upon such existing courses as English composition, foreign languages, and Health 101 can best be examined after we have a clearer view of the content of the new courses that may be developed . . . several departments which teach elementary courses might be encouraged to re-study their courses before our study reaches that stage. (minutes, Oct. 25, 1951)

Here the steering committee begins to recognize two truths: (1) there are core courses that already exist that sit at the heart of the curriculum, required for all students, and are undoubtedly affected by any widespread reforms—such as English composition; and (2) it is difficult to create a new curriculum at the first and second year without recognizing what already exists in these core courses, and whether that will—or should—change. Of course, in Harvard's plan, English composition was sweepingly revised to play second fiddle to the general education curriculum. That idea is noted in these minutes, reporting, "Harvard has come to a major modification in its English A course only this year." The Woman's College, however, resisted explicitly any emulation of this English A paradigm.

Instead, the committee saw a reverse relationship to that articulated at Harvard; since composition was at the center of the first-year student's curriculum in particular, it was the course that should stay constant—pending full-scale success of the general education courses—rather than the other way around: "English and foreign languages possess unique characteristics: Any general education course of study in English for communication would probably be largely dependent upon the courses developed in other areas. Since the natural sciences, the social sciences, and the humanities are our major consideration at present we do not feel that any proposal should be made now in regard to English, though it should be clear that consideration of this important aspect of communications may normally come at a later date" (minutes, Oct. 25, 1951). Complicating this stance even further was the humanities group's proposal regarding its own path of courses, which Warren Ashby, professor of philosophy,[22] communicated to the chancellor on November 20, 1951:

> First, there was unanimous agreement on the committee that an adequate evaluation of our present program in terms of any objectives which the faculty may find acceptable should be made before new courses are added to the curriculum. Second, there was the consensus of opinion that if the faculty should decide to adopt a program of general education work in the Humanities it should be considered in terms of a four-year program rather than one course offered to freshmen and sophomores. There was agreement with this view both because of the obvious fact that the objectives which we have stated could not possibly be realized with one course and because of the importance of relating the general education to the special education of the student, especially to her major study. (minutes, Nov. 20, 1951)

So we now have two snags in developing at least the humanities arm of the general education plan: first, the recognition that there may be existing *successes* that need not be overturned, or should be examined before large-scale course revisions take place; and second, that the proposed single course would be insufficient to the learning needs of the women of the college, and (as a final complication) not always valid depending upon her major—an intrusion of the lesser "specialized" curriculum onto the outlines of the Redbook.

These problems come to a head in 1953, when the steering committee filed a report to the general faculty that is, in sum, a nonreport. The memo, dated May 19 and authored by Marc Friedlander of the English department—who was, incidentally, a staunch supporter of Graham's aims (Trelease 220)—begins by stating that "The Steering Committee has no recommendations and no formal report to make to the Faculty at this time." It then outlines the timeline for the two years' worth of work of the committee and the faculty, starting with the approval of the group/division statements in December 1951; the creation of the three course planning committees in March 1952, and the chancellor's directive to those committees that "We are committed to no particular type of program or course. We *are* committed to the encouragement of experimentation where there is reasonable hope of an educational benefit" (General Education Steering Committee, meeting minutes, May 19, 1953). The memo then notes the institutional internal studies done in service of the report—including student opinion surveys directed by Chapel Hill testing officials—and the committee's hope to do further evaluations of this kind.

But then the report notes that first, the social studies committee could not come to terms with the History 101–102 course that was proposed as the core in this area, instead believing that "the offering of these sections is purely a departmental matter, and since one of the most important decisions regarding any offering is whether it shall be given, the committee . . . wishes to withdraw its recommendation." Second, the humanities group "received and considered several proposals for experimental courses [but none] received the committee's endorsement. [Therefore] it made no recommendation to the Steering Committee concerning an experimental course or courses." It did, however, suggest a six-hour sequence across two years, including "three semester hours of art, and three semester hours of music," notable in its contrast to the Harvard report, which indicated a lack in these very areas for Radcliffe women. Yet even this recommendation "was defeated in the Steering Committee, [as it was] unwilling at this time to bring to the Faculty any proposal that would have the effect of increasing the number of required hours in the curriculum," a concern that would have been common at a public, specialized institution such as the Woman's College—where students are likely to be more mindful of their tuition costs and eager to enter the workforce to support themselves or families, versus Harvard students, whose elite status alone, perhaps, precludes these kind of considerations in the Redbook or its archival committee records.

Friedlander closes this memo by stating, "In my opinion, Mr. Chancellor, for whatever it may be worth, that the difficulties which have been encountered in the course-planning committees in evolving courses, center about the problem of control." Indeed, the failure of the committee to enact any specific curriculum does seem to be largely about the position of the department versus the position of the university as a whole in terms of controlling coursework and, beyond that, the values and ideals that stand behind those courses. By September 1953 the steering committee had been dissolved, and the study therefore abandoned on any large scale. In December 1953, Graham again writes to Frank Bowles of Columbia about a statement he is drafting to the general faculty. Clearly defeated and discouraged, and absent of the jovial tone found in his previous correspondence, Graham calls this statement in progress an "effort toward solving the familiar problem of departmental autonomy hiding behind the skirts of faculty responsibility." He further notes, "It is a sort of rough case study in academic political theory, and the title is misleading. It actually has nothing to do with general education as such." This contrasts sharply with his early optimism of April 1951, at the start of the study, when he had written: "If we never got another dividend, the faculty ferment would have made this thing [general education reform] more than worth while. I understand from some of our people that the results have been amazing, although I am not able to judge because I never knew this campus until this year. My impressions, however, are that something important is in the process of happening, and that some old fires that have sputtered out years ago are beginning to burn again" (letter to Thomas S. Hall, Apr. 27, 1951). This letter reflects Graham's position that the self-study *process* was more important than the *subject* of that study, general education reform (Trelease 221). The letter also, however, is evidence of defeat by a strong and fairly united faculty against outside mandates for curricular change.

As I transition now into a brief look at the 1954–56 study of English 101–102 and English 211–212 (composition and literature, respectively) I aim to address this phenomenon of "faculty responsibility" in the English department specifically, as a postscript to the earlier collegewide reforms (and failures), and as a reflection of the nationwide question that haunted English departments postwar, and continues to do so today: What is the *best* way to teach writing, and who decides what *best* means in any given historical and local context?

What Is an Educated Woman (Writer)? Attempting Reform in the Woman's College English Department

On December 29, 1953, not long after the schoolwide curricular revisions requested by Graham failed to materialize, English professor J. Benjamin Townsend wrote to the chairman of English, Leonard B. Hurley, requesting that the department review its offerings in first- and second-year English. Townsend proposed that instead of seeing composition and literature as separate entities able to be altered in isolation—as might be closer to the Harvard Redbook plan, which separated English composition from other humanities courses—the department alternatively see these as linked offerings: "In debating in my own mind proposals which I should like to offer for the improvement of Sophomore English, I find myself confronted with the impressive fact that English 101 and English 211 are inseparable parts of a single, unified program in English for *all* underclassmen at the Woman's College. Any changes adopted in the Sophomore English course would by this premise affect the Freshman course, and in all probability require concomitant changes in Freshman English. The same situation prevails for any changes adopted in that course" (memo, Dec. 29, 1953). In requesting a "*concerted* revision of both courses," Townsend set in motion a two-year review of the English 101–102 and English 211–212 curriculum in the English department of the Woman's College, a review that would engage a variety of faculty, including those in creative writing, and would raise questions about how best to produce an "educated woman" writer, and reader of literature, in a public women's institution postwar. The review would also contradict assertions made in both the Redbook and the Woman's College general education committees regarding humanities education and the relationship between writing and literature, particularly for these women students.

The Committee to Examine Freshman and Sophomore English Courses met weekly (and sometimes more frequently) between February 1954 and May 1954, and then every few weeks in spring 1956.[23] The committee was chaired by Friedlander, and members for spring 1954 included Professors Bridgers, Hall, Tillett, Painter, Watson, Bush, Townsend, Summerall, and Hurley. May Bush was the director of composition, and Professor James Painter's wife, notably, was the primary instructor for so-called remedial composition, or English A (its title an interesting mimicry of the Harvard *standard* composition course of the time). Professor Watson was a new, and increasingly prominent, member of the creative writing faculty. In 1955–56 the committee membership changed and included the poet Randall Jarrell, whose importance to the English department, and to the shape and political import of writing in general at the Woman's College, will be a focus of chapter 4.

The English department committee set a number of broad goals for its internal review of the first two years of study. Some of these goals, authored by Bridgers, would not be realized by the end of the two committees' aggregate eighteen-month endeavor:

1. Determine a good sound course for each of the two years with due regard for high standards;

2. Offer other objectives in addition to those stated.

3. Interpret the first objective to mean skill in reading English.

4. Determine whether the statement of objectives presupposes a consideration of how these objectives might be attained;

5. Use whatever material in the sheets bears on these objectives;

6. Interpret skill in reading to mean growth in vocabulary and capacity to extract meaning;

7. Consider whether the department should state what the minimum levels in reading should be;

8. Keep a critical attitude toward the value of standardized tests. (Dept. of English, minutes, Feb. 15, 1954)

These initial goals emphasize curricular rigor; a strong (if not dominant) emphasis on reading in addition to writing; and skepticism toward the validity of external measures, such as standardized testing, in assessing the students of the English department. Perhaps because these goals were so very broad—and not fully articulated (for example, points 2 and 5)— an alternate proposal is included in subsequent minutes, which is likely authored by Friedlander, but is left unsigned. This "corollary" to the initial proposal asks in turn for the committee to consider these overarching questions, among several others, in its work:

What is an educated woman? What contribution to the education of such a woman should a two-year college course in English make?

What becomes of the student after she has received a two-year basic training course in English? Should the English department be regarded as a service station for other departments?

If composition is the teaching of students to read with understanding and to write well, what is the best method of teaching composition? Does it vary with the student? If so, what can be done about it?

Should students at the Freshman and Sophomore levels be taught complex, difficult masterpieces of literature? Should they study only such masterpieces?

To what extent should Freshman English be a preparation for Sophomore

English? And Sophomore an extension of Freshman English? To what extent
or should they be integrated?

Can the inevitable and ubiquitous course in remedial English be enlarged
and elevated to where it can be offered for credit as a co-equivalent course?
(Friedlander, "Some Points," 2)

These questions illustrate a deeper desire to create (or re-create) a two-
year general education curriculum in English that would not only address
best practices, but also consider these students *as* women who not only
needed a college education, but who also would hold positions in general
society after graduation—positions that were, in part, dependent upon
the success of their training in writing and reading. These questions also
point to the question of sequence and curricular connections—between
first-year writing and second-year literature, between remedial composition and first-year writing, and among the various aspects of the courses
themselves (for example, masterpieces of literature as either one, or the
only, type of reading required).

In addition, Friedlander's memo asked that the committee consider
allied issues, such as whether 101–102 instructors should "meet from time
to time to read students' themes and to exchange ideas relative to the
teaching of composition" and whether 101–102 should "remain primarily
a course in composition." The memo specifically noted that the committee
should *not* consider what "comparable institutions" were doing in these
first- and second-year courses, the "quality" of the students in the Woman's College, or the "strengths and weaknesses" of the current courses (1).
Still, these issues were raised in various contexts during the deliberations,
namely regarding remedial instruction and the position of grammar in
composition courses.

These aggregate proposed guidelines for the committee illustrate very
different operating principles than those of the Redbook group, or even
those of the General Education Committee commissioned by Graham. To
aim to *not* consider either the quality of the student body or the practices
at other peer institutions means that the department would focus only
on the sanctity of the courses, essentially, in the abstract—not how they
related to other courses at other colleges, or how they spoke to Woman's
College student "quality"—a clear concern of Graham's. The issues before
the committee, as proposed by Friedlander, also emphasized some progressive views of composition that were, the committee would find, not
present in other state universities at this time. These include the sugges-

tion that instructors might meet to exchange ideas about writing, and that remedial writing might be an "allied" course in credit and design rather than a precursor to standard sections of English 101. Certainly this was not the case at Harvard, or at many other universities across the country that struggled with underprepared students. Finally, the committee suggestions proposed here explicitly ask the faculty to question whether the department is a "service station" for other departments—implying that to be such a station might be less than ideal. This position is borne out in the discussions of the position of literature—the core of this English department's interests and practices postwar—in the composition classroom.

From the start of their deliberations, the committee argued over whether, and how much, literature would be included in English 101 and 102, Composition I and II. A chief concern behind these discussions was not only the breadth of coverage of literary texts, but also the students' ability to read the texts in a meaningful way. At the March 1, 1954, meeting, the two contrasting views were clear in the form of Professor Townsend, who urged, "We should remember we have a golden opportunity in two years of required College English. We should ask ourselves if we introduce students to as much literature as we should," and in Professor Bridgers, who argued that, "Our girls have read very little, but it seems that in high school perhaps they have neglected writing for the sake of reading. . . . Should hate us to take time now devoted to writing and use it for literature." Secondary to this question of literary texts was the concern over level of preparation; Professor Watson asked the committee to "think of the good student" while Professor Friedlander asked, "Isn't our present freshman course conceived to meet the needs of the students who come badly prepared?" and Professor Painter responded, "No, it hits the middle" (minutes, Mar. 1, 1954). These two concerns—that literature was important, but perhaps not as important as increased writing instruction, and that, implicitly, literature benefited the "good" student whereas writing benefited the "middle" or below—would become the elements of a significant paradox throughout the committee's deliberations.

In some contrast to the concerns of the English faculty, the students in the English department of the Woman's College were themselves desirous of more instruction in the fundamentals of writing—specifically grammar and usage—and less certain about the esteemed position of literature, especially canonical or historical works. They were also uncertain about their professors' attention to their ability levels in the courses in general. In a May 1953 "Survey of Student Opinion on General Education at Woman's College," which was based on oral interviews and group conversations with different sets of undergraduate majors, the group of

English majors surveyed by the college testing office indicated that first, more students indicated that "remedial classes are valuable" and that "not enough grammar [is] provided" than in any other response category. At the same time, students noted that they desired "interesting and meaningful material, especially for freshmen" and that "not enough attention [is] given to modern writers" in the required courses. Further, the survey administrators noted that some students contended "their richest experience in Freshman English was from theme writing. Many of these would sacrifice literature study for more writing," and that "it was felt that grammar could be stressed in other courses, and that writing of various papers in other courses could be used in the English courses through some means of coordination" (University Testing Service 21–22). Survey administrators also noted a criticism of the teaching staff, which was that "they made little effort to find out the backgrounds of the class—all students were assumed to be on the same level" (18–19). One conclusion of the survey was that the "sequence of courses is poor in many departments," especially in history and English (73).

This last conclusion about course sequencing was likely an impetus for the first- and second-year study of English 101–102 and 211–212 in the months immediately following this survey. But the survey's other findings about the place of writing versus literature, the modern versus the historical, and the abilities of the individual versus the group, seem to contrast with the desires of the department faculty to keep a literature-centered, uniform approach to these courses. Previous department meeting minutes include concerns over the ability of Woman's College students to "cope with the complex literature—except on a very elementary level—in Sophomore English" with the hopes that the freshman-sophomore committee would "perhaps alter [the courses] so that the students would have more time to learn literary analysis" (Dept. of English, Jan. 11, 1954, meeting). Other faculty raised this issue of time versus content even earlier— for example, Nettie Tillett noted in May 1951 that "Freshman English has become such a hopeless jumble" and thus questioned adding more texts of any sort to the mix. As was the case at many institutions—and still remains the case today—the committee and department struggled with how much the first two years of English can "do" for students, and how to balance skill levels and desired coverage of various texts and concepts.

Nonetheless, several members of the committee noted that improvements were being made in writing instruction; Professor Hurley commented in the March 8, 1954, meeting that "more writing is being done now [1954]" than in 1927, referencing a copy of that year's manual of instruction. This seems like a significant claim, given the rhetoric-centered rigor of the 1920s-era writing curricula discussed in chapter 1 of this book. Bush seconded this observation, noting that "not only more writing is being done, but more attention is being given to writing, i.e. to reading of papers in class, and to preparation for papers" (Dept. of English, Committee on Freshman and Sophomore English, minutes, Mar. 8, 1954). Yet at the next week's meeting, Friedlander persisted in his desire to improve "the literary quality of the freshman course" and that students "might read poetry when [they] study exposition" (minutes, Mar. 15, 1954). Tillett also "reminded the committee that one of its purposes is to get rid of all the journalese stuff that we read in Freshman English." Bridgers and Bush protested, noting, respectively, that one could "not teach formal exposition writing on Lamb's essays or by short poems," and that "the staff had recently felt that what our students needed was more exposition." Ultimately, Bush argued that "a freshman course which was all literature might endanger our present two-year English requirement," a requirement unique to the Woman's College among other like institutions, and one that was at the center of the writing culture upon which the department was based (minutes, Mar. 15, 1954).

These snippets of the argument among committee members show a department divided by the differential valuation of literature among its members—or, more accurately, a differential valuation of the *position of literature* in the composition classroom. While some members saw the value of literature as a model, a text to be emulated by students in their exposition (much as the Redbook group did), others argued that exposition could not be modeled on artistic texts or literature, and that to re-label composition *as* literature endangered the sanctity of the sequence, as well as compromised the larger purpose of the two-year requirement—a curricular stronghold for the English department and a large factor in its well-being in the larger university curricular structure.

By March 24, 1954, the committee had created a provisional recommendation to the department, presenting a plan that indicated that English 101–102 and English 211–212 were an "integrated, two-year program" that had as its objectives "skill and facility in writing; skill in reading; knowledge of literature; the appreciation of literature." It noted that in English 101–102, there would be a "greater emphasis on skill and facility in writing and skill in the reading of prose," and that the "practice in writing in the combined program should primarily serve the useful purpose of training the student in the kind of writing she will do in her other courses in college and in her personal and professional life after college. Most of the writing will therefore be expository" (Dept. of English, "Tentative Language").

This statement about the general nature of writing in the first-year course sequence is notable in its attention to expository instruction—noting specifically that this would be "most" of the course, perhaps in response to earlier versions of English 101–102, from the late 1940s through early 1950s, evidencing some significant attention to other creative forms, such as the short story, memoir, and poem—as is clear from the aggregate issues of the *Yearling*, discussed in chapter 2. The statement is also notable in its rationale for making said choices about the course in order to serve the student's "personal and professional life after college." This contrasts somewhat with the Redbook general education goals for humanities courses—which imply, as part of the larger general education sequence, a preparation for civic participation and postcollege life, but in fact are broad surveys of canonical works that every student "must" know. Their latter usefulness depends upon, ultimately, whether the student achieves such a station in life as to draw upon those texts for his or her own further advancement. The Woman's College plan is far more vocational in its implications, as is also clear in the statement about reading, which "should be chosen primarily for its usefulness as a means of teaching writing: that is, for its organization, its paragraphing, its sentence structure, and its diction. It should also serve as a means of teaching close reading" (Dept. of English, "Tentative Language").

Yet as a conciliatory gesture to the other members of the department who argued vociferously for literary study in the first year, the proposal also calls for "literary distinction" as the test for the chosen texts, rather than "the timeliness of the matter or its relevance to the student's immediate problem." This directly contradicts the English major survey results, which show a desire for more "modern and contemporary" works. But it is more importantly a reflection of the canonical values in the department, and the department's adherence to a traditional literary focus in its curriculum—evidenced by the perpetual inclusion of the Bible in its course texts for 211–212, as well as the *Odyssey* and "extensive reading in myth . . . epic, novel, and drama" (Dept. of English, minutes, May 28, 1954). Indeed, once the committee's proposal reached the department for a full vote in May 1954, the recommendations for texts in 101–102 had been revised to include "reading and analysis of short literary pieces, short stories, and poems," which would be "intensive" in both parts of the course sequence. As was the case with many departments of the era (and some to this day), the readings were prescribed by the department to be in use for the department as a whole—in other words, individual instructors were not left to choose their own specific texts from a broad type required. In English 101, selections from Shakespeare, Frost, Hardy, Dickinson, and Herbert were required, and in English 102 the focus was on larger texts, that is, the *Odyssey* and the Bible.

Still, the proposal noted that "the same amount of writing to be required in the course should be no less than that now stated and required in the Manual." In other words, the reading load would potentially increase—and focus more sharply on difficult, canonical texts of literature—but the writing load would stay as it was. In the meantime, instructors were to concentrate on "grammar—the sentence, punctuation, mechanics; the paragraph; letter-writing; summary and précis; organization and outlining; word study; and formal study of exposition" (Dept. of English, minutes, May 28, 1954). The course was bursting at the seams with the various skill sets that the department found vital, with little indication of how all of these goals would be accomplished, even across two semesters of coursework.

In fact, in the May 3, 1954, meeting of the committee, Professor Watson declared, "there does not seem to be much agreement about the best way of teaching students composition. We have agreed that writing is fundamental, but that agreement does not solve the problem of how the literature is to be used to teach writing" (Dept. of English, "Minutes of the Committee on Freshman and Sophomore English," May 3, 1954). Townsend noted at the May 10, 1954, meeting that "there is not agreement on the best method of teaching expository writing or on the models that should be used." This comment came after six different committee members each proposed a different possible core reader for the 101–102 course, with titles (and implied foci) ranging from *The Creative Reader* to *Introduction to Literature*, to *College Omnibus* and *A Century of the Essay*. Ultimately, two compromise texts not proposed by members—*The MacMillan Reader* and *Better Reading, Volume 2—Literature* were proposed as the core readings for 101 and 102, respectively. Perhaps ironically—and now as a footnote to history—one of the five required essays proposed for English 101 was also "The Scientific Education of the Layman," by Harvard president James B. Conant. Despite these behind-the-scenes disagreements, and a general consensus that there *was* no consensus, the proposal passed the department with a slight majority. At the final meeting of the semester, Nettie Tillett—who had proven to be a polarizing figure in the department—asked the following statement to be entered into the meeting minutes of the committee: "The minutes of the meeting of the committee do not reflect the tone of the meetings. Deplorable as the acrimonious tone of most of them (at times, really vicious) is, it should be reflected in the minutes" (Dept. of English, "Minutes of the Committee on Freshman and Sophomore English," May 3, 1954).

For reasons that are not completely clear from archival records, the committee was reconstituted in early 1955 in order to revisit the course sequence. These discussions focused much more heavily on ability levels in composition and the problem of students moving from 101 to 102 and experiencing repeat content or instruction. The February 21, 1955, minutes—the first archived for this constitution of the committee—note that only fifty-six of approximately four hundred students across the nineteen sections of English 102 were being taught by a *new* professor (someone whom they did not take for English 101). This led to concerns that there was too much overlap in instructional methods and approaches; in contrast, Bush noted that she "could do much more for a student if she has her for a year rather than a semester." A secondary concern was how the course sequence compared to those at area institutions—despite Friedlander's original charge that the committee not consider the work of peer colleges in its curricular revisions. Hurley noted that since "Woman's College is a part of the Greater University of North Carolina," such comparisons were timely and necessary.

Hurley reported on March 7, 1955, that based on his discussions with the chairmen of English at the University of North Carolina–Chapel Hill and North Carolina State College (now University), the Chapel Hill course focused on grammar and usage "one hundred percent" of the time, and used a dictionary and English handbook as its main texts. The State College course required use of a dictionary, a handbook, and the text *Toward Liberal Education* by Locke, Gibson, and Arms, with the "practical application of matters of grammar, punctuation, syntax, and rhetoric" as the basic objective. Neither course included literature in the first-year sequence, except at State for "special sections of superior students." These observations caused Hurley to note that these institutions "have no more integration in their freshman and sophomore courses than we have" and made another committee member remark that the Woman's College course was "certainly richer" in its use of literature than the courses at these nearby campuses. Hurley finally noted that "both Woman's College students and those at Chapel Hill were far superior in performance to those at State, and those at Woman's College slightly above those at Chapel Hill." As a side note, Bush commented, "from all the material she has studied on the organization of freshman courses in other institutions throughout the country, she has concluded that we are not out of line with the practice elsewhere in putting emphasis on composition and expository work" (Dept. of English, "Minutes of the Freshman-Sophomore Study Committee," Mar. 7, 1955).

Setting themselves against these all-male institutions, and positioning themselves as the more liberal arm of the larger system, the Woman's College showed significant concern for the viability of the college as the 1950s progressed and talks of unification of the campuses began to emerge. Reinforcing among themselves that their first-year course was "in line" with other campuses nationwide helped to secure the notion that the Woman's College was competitive on a national scale in its English program, and that its curricular aims were not, in fact, particular to its status as a women's institution or a former teacher's college. The department struggled to create its own "homegrown" curriculum for its students rather than adopt an external model or even adopt the school-specific model of general education that Graham had proposed. But the overriding pedagogical concerns of reading versus writing, literature versus exposition, and, more generally, the endeavor of a composition course versus that of a literature course, resulted in a proposal that was not radically different than the existing curriculum, if now simply more open in its aims to cover a wide variety of subjects and skills in a relatively short amount of time. Still, the overarching concern that this be *unique* to the Woman's College within the UNC system, yet reasonable and customary when set against the nationwide swath of writing courses, reveals a deep need for the English department to sustain itself and stake out its own intellectual existence in this era of competing, charged, and sometimes overzealous curricular reform. When all was said and done, the general education movement rolled through the Woman's College like a passing freight train, but the department held firm and resisted becoming a Southern version of Harvard, or any other institution. It ultimately held tight to its local values and used those to make critical curricular decisions.

It would be wrong, however, to imply that there were no lingering doubts among committee members about the general ability of the English department student writers. There was undeniable talk about the need for remedial work in English, such as the aforementioned "English A," and how to best offer this work without compromising the department's now-benchmarked standards for writing instruction. Having put in place a committee to create the English A course in October 1945, and having offered the course for a number of years since that time, the department continued to struggle with whether its plan was really working for its women writers. In the 1956 "Recommendations of the Freshman-Sophomore Committee," the members collectively note that:

> The courses are not, at present, well enough coordinated. . . . There is a very great distance between the best and worst students in the regular freshman classes; because of this, the level of teaching and class discussion sometimes has to be lowered more than we should like to lower it. . . . At present, the

weakest of our freshmen get special training in English A. We would like to
set up, in addition, four English fundamentals sections, each of about eighteen or twenty students, for the worst-prepared members of English 101 and
102. By doing this, we can give these weak students the detailed, intensive
training that they need; at the same time we can elevate considerably the
level of the teaching and discussion in the other sections of English 101 and
102. These sections will . . . leave more time in teaching the [advanced] student to write a vigorous, cultivated, and idiomatic English. (Bridgers et al. 2)

These discussions of ability grouping and the kind of writing needed—
versus the kind of writing that would put the English department on the
map—became a significant issue during this postwar era of the Woman's
College.

The Woman's College would enter the last fifteen years of its independent existence firmly hitched to the wagon of creative writing, and the
promise of making its mark in a manner no other institution of its kind
would be able to even imagine in the postwar era.

4

The Double-Helix of Creative/Composition

Randall Jarrell, May Bush, and the Politics
of Writing Programs, 1947–63

ACHIEVING A BALANCE between local needs and national trends in writing instruction was a compelling quandary facing the Woman's College
postwar. The politics of this balance were powerfully affected by national
movements such as general education, and by the social history of the
college as a site of not only diverse writing curricula, but also properly
rigorous whole-person training. Yet as much as general education, normal school traditions, and southern social culture shaped the relationship
between composition and literary studies during the postwar era of the
Woman's College, the third player in the department—creative writing—
emerged as a final, critical factor in how literacy was defined for students
in the years immediately preceding its rebranding as a coeducational university.

Examining the forceful addition of creative writing to the literacy
concerns of the Woman's College English department will allow me to
reveal yet another dimension of local programmatic research, that which
makes lesser-studied historical connections between the aims of rheto-

ric and composition and the aims of creative writing in the shaping of women's public college student literacies. This examination also reinforces my initial contention that individual accounts of women's college writing instruction provide us with more nuanced definitions of our field history, including our histories of writing program *administration,* than whole-scale overviews of the field (often privileging more well-known settings and larger institutions) might provide. Further, by focusing on two important figures in this case study—the well-known poet Randall Jarrell and the unknown writing program administrator May Bush—I aim to recognize the importance of untold stories, buried narratives, and previously unconsidered cross-relations among the people most in charge of defining and shaping writing instruction on a given campus: department faculty.

The Woman's College in the 1950s and early 1960s was arguably a primary instantiation of the creative arts movement flowing through college campuses, led by a surge in creative writing courses in English departments that may be seen as both an embrace of the more lofty, if unrealized, aims of the Redbook and a push-back against the move toward communicative "efficiency" in writing instruction. Such calls for efficiency were motivated by the influx of returning soldiers and other new college student populations desiring quasi-vocational training for the workforce and enrolling in institutions wherein literacy had previously been defined chiefly by markers of taste, refinement, and appreciation of canonical (literary) texts—as opposed to basic fluency in ideas and execution of those ideas, in catch-all courses teaching writing, reading, and speech in rapid-fire classroom sessions

Due to the already tangible investment in writing and the arts earlier in the twentieth century at the Woman's College, its embrace of creative writing as a full-fledged area of study in the postwar era is not surprising. This allowed the college to expand its advocacy for women as writers while also making significant social and political strides within the North Carolina university system, all the better to solidify the college's unique status and singular mission. It followed other large state and private universities in reshaping the ways in which writing would be regarded and taught in English departments; for example, at Yale, "Daily Themes" courses were assigned to poets and novelists such as Robert Penn Warren during this postwar era, and were characterized by concomitant shifts from expository writing to belles-lettres or personal essay writing classes. This movement to accept and welcome with open arms the popular and somewhat mysterious genre of creative writing into the English department aimed to supplant the less desirable, and required, composition course (perceived as difficult and often unrewarding to teach) offered at most other public and private colleges, with the more attractive, and popular, creative writing course, subsequently redefining writing literacy in terms of art/poetics rather than argument/rhetoric.

Led by the curricular and social growth of masters of fine arts (MFA) programs in creative writing, American universities of both coeducational and single-sex design midcentury—including the Woman's College—became hotbeds of academically sponsored creative instruction, while composition and rhetoric, comparatively, took a significant backseat in both the institutional and public eye—an ironic curricular condition, given the advent of the Conference on College Composition and Communication (CCCC) in 1949. As the training of returning servicemen and women became the basis for expanded campuses, increased introductory course offerings (in English and other areas), and an attention to the tension between eloquence and efficiency in writing instruction, campuses searched for a way to reclaim their standing as intellectual and artistic sanctuaries rather than purely functional sites of rote instruction. This reclamation mission arguably has continued throughout the twentieth, and now twenty-first, centuries, as the figure of the creative-writer-as-artist remains set apart from other types of faculty, even those faculty within English departments themselves.

At the Woman's College, the movement in the creative arts provided a keen opportunity postwar for a highlighting of the progressive stance that the English department, and institution as a whole, had long since taken toward writing and the arts, since nearly its institutional inception. This new cultural recognition of creative writing as a legitimate academic field of study allowed the college to step forward as a seasoned, if surprising, leader in literacy instruction within the southern United States, as manifested in two key ways. First, creative writing and the arts had held a core curricular position in the college since the 1930s, when the English department first began to offer courses in poetry and fiction writing. Thus, the heightened focus on creative writing in the postwar era was indeed an extension of an existing impulse to imbue women students with an artistic aesthetic; as such, the presence of creative writing postwar simply became more formalized, in regular upper-division offerings and, importantly, the department's proposal for, and receipt of, an MFA program in creative writing.[1] Though the first MFA degree was conferred upon a Woman's College student in 1953 (Hurley, "Annual Report," 1952–53), the formal program of study was not officially recognized until 1963, just before the college became a coeducational branch of the University of North Carolina.

Second, the role of creative writing in the department's educational and public mission—and unique institutional identity—became of primary importance postwar. If one recalls Harriet Eliot's 1944 admonition in chapter 2, that the Woman's College must solidify its status and identity or else be claimed (or overrun) by the campus at Chapel Hill, it is clear that creative writing provided a unique entrée into the high-status position that the Woman's College ultimately desired for its students and faculty. This high status would be ushered in by the faculty hired to teach creative writing in the department, chief among them the renowned poet Randall Jarrell. As noted previously, Jarrell held leadership roles in the proposed restructuring of English 101–102 per the department's contributions to the Woman's College General Education plan. Jarrell was also somewhat of a progressive in terms of his views on composition, notably arguing in department meeting minutes that separating basic writers from "standard" or mainstream composition students was not a beneficial pedagogical act for teacher or student.[2] But Jarrell can also be read as a controversial figure in terms of his economic value to the department—painstakingly illustrated through archival records detailing pay raises designed to keep him on the faculty at the college despite regular external offers of employment from other colleges throughout this decade. Jarrell's standing as a well-known and respected literary figure brought an undeniable cachet to the English department of the Woman's College, one that would potentially grow and expand the strength of the department, and the reputation of the college, in and outside of North Carolina.[3]

What makes this steadfast devotion to creative writing on the Woman's College campus significant for study, in the context of the rise of the MFA as a degree and the general embrace of the creative arts on campuses nationwide postwar, is not simply its lasting power, however, nor its ability to put the campus on the national map where writing was concerned. This devotion is important, and worthy of analysis, due to its undeniable influence on how the very idea of literacy was locally redefined for both students and faculty—as purveyors of the curriculum, and curricular values—with a clear detrimental effect on the allied field of composition and rhetoric. Examining creative writing politics at the Woman's College, specifically the machinery required to keep the MFA alive and the creative writing program generally healthy and happy, requires acknowledgment of key players in this era. Randall Jarrell becomes the historical embodiment of the program and its ambitions and also stands as the economic lynchpin for writing as a discipline. Readers familiar with Jarrell's reputation in the literary world would not be surprised to learn that he was sought after; what has gone unsaid about Jarrell's situation, and what thus is the more significant factor in this study, is how his status affected other faculty and programs in the department. In order to keep Jarrell, other departmental faculty had to receive less—again, not surprising to readers familiar with typical past or current university politics. But in the case of the Woman's College, it becomes clear that one figure in the department deeply—and ironically—affected by Jarrell's raises and salary packages was May Bush, director of first-year composition, who was denied promotions and raises year after year, despite pleas from her department chair, while Jarrell was, simultaneously, generously compensated.

Investigating creative writing and composition as represented by Jarrell and Bush offers us insight into how literacy instruction (and, on a more personal level, professional standing) for women—particularly those invested in rhetoric and composition, and general education—was deeply complicated at one institution by the intersections of these fields of writing during the postwar era, intersections that sometimes boiled down to economic contests with clear winners and losers. It also recalls my assertion in the introduction to this book that the history of composition—and by extension, college writing instruction within various genres—is a history of its people, both those who can speak for themselves, through archival documents, and those who need to be spoken for, through multiple layerings of these documents against other institutional remembrances.

What I ultimately illustrate in this chapter, using this human scale, is how the Woman's College, as an institution already heavily committed to writing and the arts prior to the postwar era and at the forefront of the surge in MFA offerings nationwide, responded to this visibly dynamic decade in writing—specifically, how it came to redefine its priorities where writing instruction was concerned, and how it came to define itself as a primary department of *creative* writing both internally and externally. This redefinition would be one last way in which the college distinguished itself from stereotypical traditions expected of normal schools, and became a case study in cross-pollination of writing pedagogies, as well as administrative priorities, in the postwar era.

Creative Writing and the Academy

Without the surge of MFA degree programs that occurred in the postwar era, the story of creative writing in the academy would have a far lesser position within our institutional narratives. Certainly the figure of the writer throughout the history of print culture has been a revered one; the notion of the author as an entity somehow above the common person, however, separated from mass society by his or her innate, mysterious talents, is a decidedly modern construction that has been supported mightily by the enterprise of (for pay, or by patronage) writers' colonies, writers' workshops, and, ultimately, MFA programs—as a codified system of training writers, led by successful writers-in-kind, who employ an apprentice model that relies on both intimacy and loyalty in its design.

The move on the part of English departments in the twentieth century to not only embrace, but potentially exploit, the popularized notion of romantic creativity in the humanities permanently changed English studies from a collective body rooted in the study of the past and its "correct" articulations (wherein composition serves as the translation and recitation of literary principles and specific textual ideologies) to a body of scholars and writers of past *and* current literary practices set against a growing and evolving literary canon, and participating in this canon's evolution. In this paradigm, however, composition as *the* representation of writing in English studies (and rhetoric as the embodiment of aesthetic and social truths) is overridden, both in spirit and in practice. Creative writing faculty become the alternate representation of writing—one in which the writer as an institutional and public figure is as important, if not more so, than his or her own writing, or even his or her relation to other members of the English department (such as PhD faculty in literature). The writer becomes the tangible investment on the part of the institution, a living success story that can be displayed for, and shared with, the university and the community at large. This investment paradigm was clearly the case with the figure of Randall Jarrell at the Woman's College, and with other writers at parallel MFA programs around the country.

The MFA, as the professional "terminal" degree in creative writing,[4] solidified this attractive theory of the practicing writer versus the literary scholar, the latter being the previous lone tenant in English departments. In *Keywords in Creative Writing*, Wendy Bishop and David Starkey note this division, as they define the MFA as "a studio degree that invites comparison with terminal arts degrees in dance, theater and the visual arts. Consequently, the MFA privileges writers as artists while minimizing their stand as academics" (115). Bishop and Starkey's definition is an important anchor for any look backward toward the history of creative writing within the university, since, for many students, the MFA as a degree represents a chance at public recognition of one's own poetry, fiction, or drama, as well as a means by which universities seeking to legitimize and expand their writing programs as a critical component of English departments may most easily do so. As D. G. Myers notes, the rapid growth of creative writing programs in the United States postwar was directly tied to "expanding the university's role in society" as the university aimed to be the "permanent center of artistic activity" in this country (148). Myers argues, "Creative writing reached its full growth as a university discipline when the purpose of its graduate programs (to produce serious writers) was uncoupled from the purpose of its undergraduate courses (to examine writing seriously from within)" (149). Seeing the MFA as, historically, an *arts* degree, designed to professionalize writers as artists and training future artists, rather than a *humanities* degree—and without the critical research component or scholarly impulse endemic to other graduate degrees in English—is critical in understanding both the MFA's appeal and its divergence from more staid academic views of writing, and writing instruction, including first-year composition.

For the Woman's College, the MFA symbolized the ultimate achievement for its creative writing program and its foray into the big-business writing instruction usually available only at larger, coeducational colleges and universities. As noted elsewhere in this book, the Woman's College—as a former normal school and as the only public single-sex institution in the state—sought and maintained a separate and specialized identity within the University of North Carolina system of colleges for over thirty years; it fiercely held to its mission of educating women, per Charles McIver's original decree, and deeply valued its ability to produce women graduates of intelligence and taste. The college resisted threats for many years from the "men's" campus (University of North Carolina–Chapel Hill) and had long prided itself on the niche it filled within the state, and within the South, in public women's education, as articulated by Dean W. C. Jackson himself back in 1934. With the rise of creative writing as a discipline and the college's existing history of employing working writers to guide and shape students—faculty that included Jarrell as well as Peter Taylor and Robert Watson, and others before them, such as Jane Summerall and Robie Macauley—the Woman's College would now be able to argue, with the addition of an MFA program, that its English department was, without any doubt, a unique regional foothold for the fine arts.

These local conditions affecting the Woman's College as an institution, and as a site for women's literacy instruction, would indeed seem to create a logical breeding ground for an MFA program, since, as D. G. Myers argues, creative writing was perhaps the most successful discipline in allowing women students and faculty to gain a greater agency within the academy. This was clearly contrary to the growing notion that the field of composition was, to paraphrase Sue Ellen Holbrook, "women's work," and that theme correction was an arduous task that did not, in fact, promote a joyful connection with or relationship between writer and text, or text and teacher, and thus was the province of women—as a kind of motherly, housekeeping act. In sharp contrast to the negatively feminized work in rote theme correction for composition, creative writing opened the door for women to be not only *teachers* of writing (in the classroom, or in the home), but also *producers* of literary work—ergo *art*—themselves, and to be recognized both inside and outside the academy for their pursuits. This artistic production, when set within the culture's predilection for valuing the author as a kind of mystical star among the masses, was far less negatively gendered than any work, whether teaching or administration, in composition (which, during the postwar era, had, importantly, no corollary scholarly or artistic *production,* other than the production of grammar handbooks and teaching primers, themselves texts of classroom-based value only).

Beyond these material conditions that positioned the creative writing teacher above the composition teacher and elevated her work above the mundane practice of "correction" in a larger sense, Myers also notes that creative writing shifted literary study from the "past to the present," providing women with a chance to become a part of a growing body of evolving, dynamic work-for-study, and further presented women with the opportunity of engaging in practical criticism, which "desexed literature by inverting the categories and values of the older literary and educational establishments," transforming literature into an "impersonal constructive technique" that did not discriminate on the basis of gender (140). Indeed, Katherine Adams contends that between 1880 and 1940, "American women came to college to learn to be writers. They took advantage of every opportunity to form groups of colleagues, and they continued to rely on this model after they left college, creating new types of personal/professional groups. And from this home base, they crafted very influential texts that helped shape their era" (xviii–xxiv). We can see this desire to build writers' groups in the artifacts of the *Yearling* and the allied collectives formed to create and sustain *Coraddi;* clearly, the grassroots production of these publications built upon women students as literacy collectives, and the influence of working on these publications extended into women's postgraduate lives, as illustrated in the cases of Elizabeth, Jacqueline, and Lucy in chapter 2. Certainly at the Woman's College, the MFA would have been a logical progression of not only the department ethos regarding writing and the arts, but also the department philosophy that women *were all* potential writers—whether in rhetoric and composition or in the creative arts.

Indeed, Adams notes that even though women's colleges, starting in the 1920s, were inclined to reduce their overall offerings in the fine arts, such as dance and theater (clearly a controversy represented in the Radcliffe Committee on General Education for Women, as discussed in chapter 3), *creative writing* offerings were generally not cut, as they were seen as a combination of "academic study and arts practice" (42). Adams comments that as early as 1915, private women's colleges (and coeducational colleges of both public and private origins) such as Smith and Barnard were offering a much wider range of creative writing courses than their elite men's college counterparts, who lagged behind this movement for some twenty years (51). Yet Adams does not include *public* women's colleges such as the Woman's College in her study, where such creative work was also thriving throughout the first half of the twentieth century. Here is where a deeper look at the Woman's College becomes particularly salient in both adding to this history of women's education in creative writing and in recognizing the truly nationwide influence that creative writing as a field, and social movement, had on college writing instruction postwar.

The Woman's College MFA program in creative writing was ideally positioned, both in terms of its population and its geography, to be the first of its kind for women *only* in the South; such was the original plan in the curricular proposal, drafted well before the college underwent its inevitable transformation into a coeducational university. In 1945, just two years before the Woman's College hired Randall Jarrell to join its faculty, there were only eight MFA or MA programs in creative writing in existence nationwide. By 1965, not long after the MFA at the Woman's College was formalized, just ten more institutions had joined these ranks (McGurl 25). Yet of these total eighteen programs, only one, the MFA at the University of Virginia, was in the southern United States; the remainder were clustered in the upper Midwest, the Northeast, and on the West Coast. Additionally, none of these MFA programs were housed at single-sex colleges or universities (ignoring for the moment that Brown and Columbia did not admit women, and were thus single-sex *male* institutions, in their earlier years), nor did any have the history of educating women, or for that matter, *teachers,* that the Woman's College possessed. These institutions with MFA programs were all either flagship state universities or prominent private colleges and universities. So for the Woman's College to embark on, first, an expanded creative writing focus in its English department and, second, an MFA program, in the context of these other national models was, indeed, a revolutionary step that would put the college squarely on the map where graduate study in the arts was concerned.

The formal proposal for the "Petition for an Allocation of Graduate Function in the Creative Arts and for the Establishment of a Creative Arts Program at the Woman's College," first put forward at the Woman's College in 1948, was finally realized in 1963 in the form of a master of fine arts in writing program. A January 1963 publicity flyer for the program states that its core faculty, or "writing faculty in residence," were Randall Jarrell, Carol Johnson, Peter Taylor, and Robert Watson, with an upcoming March 1964 writing forum (the twenty-first annual event) featuring "special lecturers" Fred Chappell, Elizabeth Hardwick, and Robert Lowell, Jarrell's longtime personal friend. The program description notes that it is "offered to a limited number of students with ability in the writing of original works of poetry, fiction, and drama. The program is a flexible one that permits the student to develop his particular talents in small classes and in conferences with the writers in residence and also to increase his general knowledge of literature and the other arts in courses offered by the general faculty" ("Petition for an Allocation"). This description builds upon the earlier creative arts concentration proposal of 1948, which originally included writing as just one of many concentrated interdisciplinary studies in art, music, and drama, and articulated a series of writing courses designed for advanced undergraduates and graduates. The MFA proposal limits and delineates the pedagogical endeavors to core instruction in three primary genres of publication, and emphasizes individual faculty attention and close-knit program relations of the type that would become the hallmark of the typical MFA program postwar ("Petition for an Allocation," 28C–28H), and would popularize these programs among young writers seeking singular guidance from a well-respected mentor and, in many cases, career role model.

But the Woman's College foray into graduate instruction in creative writing postwar was not necessarily a unique request in the context of colleges nationwide, despite the revolutionary move for women's graduate education that its initial program proposal constituted. One may observe that while doctoral studies experiences a comparative stagnation, due to an unsure job market in academia and a general decline in funding for less visible or financially profitable PhD programs (such as religious studies, philosophy, and, more recently, American studies) the MFA is, and historically has been, one of the fastest-growing graduate specializations in the humanities in the United States.[5] The MFA, unlike the PhD, has historically served the dual purpose of drawing writers and artists into the academy when they might otherwise eschew such a restrictive setting, and calling the public's attention to the academy as a patron of the fine arts.

The growth of the MFA may be traced to several more specific impulses related to this dual purpose of politics and aesthetics, as situated within English departments such as the Woman's College postwar. One of these impulses was to reinforce the notion of writers as living, breathing entities rather than historical figures, which was to reify the English department as a colony of working writers passing on their trades, in real time, to students. As posted on the main page for the Associated Writing Programs (AWP), David Fenza, executive director of AWP, notes that in the 1960s, "on most campuses, the best, most respected writers were those long dead and safely entombed in anthologies and libraries" and thus AWP was founded "to support the growing presence of literary writers in higher education. Because, at that time, Departments of English were mainly conservatories of the great literature of the past, scholars fiercely resisted the establishment of creative writing programs. To overcome this resistance and to provide publishing opportunities for young writers, AWP was founded by fifteen writers who represented twelve writing programs."

The apposition here of "writers" and "scholars" is telling, as it signals the root division of creative writers as artists versus literature scholars as academics, researchers, nonartists. Such a stance, however, glosses over the position of composition and rhetoric, or in curricular terms, the enterprise of rhetoric and expository writing, within this paradigm. Indeed, the meteoric rise of creative writing has been documented in relation to literary studies, and as either the root of, or the inspiration for, more expressivist tendencies in composition, particularly the use of the workshop model for peer review of student writing and the multiple-draft, pure-process pedagogy of early 1970s composition scholars such as Kenneth Bruffee, Donald Murray, and Peter Elbow. But the politics of creative writing versus composition is in large part undertheorized, despite the clear declarations from the AWP about the identity of the writer as exclusively the *creative* writer, that is, the poet or novelist, or perhaps playwright— not the writer of expository works or rhetorical criticism. As R. M. Berry notes, "as the academic contact with political and economic power has increased, Creative Writing has been in the thick of things while theory has remained aloof. . . . Despite a generation of critical theories insisting on the historical situatedness of all literary practice, literary criticism still treats the institution for forming American writers as a world apart" (58). Because this philosophical separation exists, creative writing "is less likely to consider itself a sub-specialty of literary scholarship than to *define itself in contrast to* literary scholarship" (Berry 66; emphasis added). A similar separatist philosophy exists when one seeks out a disciplinary history of creative writing in relation to composition studies more generally, even when there is an explicit attempt to marry the pedagogical concerns and pursuits of these two related fields.

Another import of integrating creative writing programs into post-secondary English departments was the (positively) liminal status of the writers working in these programs. A forceful piece on this subject appeared in 1955 in *College Composition and Communication (CCC)*, titled "College and the Writer." This piece is notable for its previous life as the address to the CCCC luncheon in November 1955, given during that year's National Council of Teachers of English (NCTE) annual convention, and for its attempt to characterize the academy as a site ripe for infiltration by those who did not typically share its value systems—chief among these, creative writers. This piece illustrates some of the separatist philosophy that would distinguish poet and creative writing director Randall Jarrell's status and position at the Woman's College from that of writing program administrator May Bush.

The author, Donald Adams, opens his talk by observing, "Increasingly, [the university's] faculty members take part in the work of the world outside, whether in government, in business, or in the arts. And its student body is immeasurably more aware of that world outside. One result of this development has been the welcome extended by the colleges to the professional writer whose concern is not primarily, or perhaps not at all, with scholarship" (5). Adams further observes that this professional writer is "most frequently . . . a poet" but can also be a novelist, either way serving as a "writer-in-residence" (5). Adams argues that this "welcome" figure of the working writer makes "college a more exciting place" for students, who benefit from this other-world presence in their lives (5). Significantly, Adams lays down a foundation for the importance of the *person* of the writer when he states, "If he is a good teacher as well as a good writer, and even if *sometimes he is not,* he performs a useful function" (6; emphasis added). This statement—despite its bold implications, tossed out in the middle of an otherwise pedestrian paragraph—invites the person-writer to take importance over the teacher-writer, a rather shocking statement for someone speaking to a luncheon attended by college teachers of writing. While there is no evidence that writers such as Randall Jarrell at the Woman's College were anything less than stellar teachers who chose to teach, opening the door to the writer as a mere *valuable presence* on campus certainly paves the way for the commodification of the MFA program and the deeply corruptible term "writer-in-residence" to be rationalized on a variety of college campuses, both midcentury and today.

Adams's concluding thoughts on writing about literature, as it was then taught (in 1955), were that it was "too much concerned with the techniques of fiction, and with critical theories regarding the function and nature of poetry" (7). As a result, a student should not be engaged in such teachings until "he has found his own medium of expression" and "an increase in his power over words" (7). Such a notion that literature study is the curricular reward for youth who can prove themselves to compose clean and error-free prose recalls the position of the English departments at Harvard and Yale, and their regard for all first-year composition as, to an extent, remedial. Adams argues, however, for a position of equality in instruction, namely that we must "broaden the sense of the forms which creative writing can assume . . . [and] see the students who are enrolled in what are known as creative writing courses encouraged to express themselves in any form which they would like to try. . . . Let us shake ourselves free from stupid literary snobbery and get down to brass tacks" (7).

In making this declaration, Adams also "shake[s] free" the *teachers* of creative writing from the staid forms of literary criticism and analysis, and simultaneously critiques the teachers of composition, who similarly adhere to rules of rhetoric and genre divisions, even as they are seemingly necessary precursors to the more advanced study of literature and creative writing. In a sense, Adams sounds a call to arms, elevating the status of the writer-in-residence above all other faculty and absolving him or her of any dutiful participation in the lower traditions of the English department.

In broad strokes, the postwar era welcomed the rise of creative writing against the decline of other academic conceptions of writing—chiefly composition—within the larger view of literacy and the role of the English department in educating students as writers and scholars. Such privileging of creative writing over expository writing and rhetorical studies, while institutionally striking and far-reaching in its curricular and cultural implications, is even more apparent within the human elements of this postwar dichotomy, namely, the position of the writing program administrator (WPA), as compared with the figure of the creative writer(s) within the English department. The WPA exists as a separate figure, but one always negatively defined: his or her separation from literary studies, like the course that he or she governs, serves to annex the administrator from any departmental agency, as compared to the creative writer, whose intellectual separation from, but curricular ties to, literature *increases* his or her agency (politically, financially). This relationship allows, on the part of the creative writer, the sports-related status of "free agency" from the shackles of English, whereas the WPA is saddled with being, in sad contrast, the last-round draft pick.

"Surely You Have Enough about Me": The WPA and Historical Views of Writing Program Leadership

While the general published discourse surrounding creative writing as a new and promising course of study in universities makes clear that this field had primary agency within many English departments postwar, the human consequences of this agency are best illustrated through local examples of personal gains and losses in the politics of writing instruction. In order to understand how highly valued creative writing *faculty* were in postwar English departments, or how specific figures such as Randall Jarrell became so central to the Woman's College English department in particular, one must understand how comparatively unprestigious were the status and visibility of leaders of expository and first-year writing programs during the first half of the twentieth century, at both single-sex and coeducational institutions alike. Unlike creative writing, which is appealing and understandable to most as a certain aesthetic, or simply as "art," composition has long been typically associated with the opposite: an uglier, if necessary, cousin of creative writing, whether inside or outside of schooling, short of public patronage and ostensibly driven by grammatical correctness and other drill-based learning. With this contrasting disciplinary standing for composition as a course, and composition studies as a field, comes the lower status and visibility of the writing program administrator.

As scholars of the history of writing programs have noted, the figure of the WPA through the 1960s is a shadowy one at best. English departments did not always give their writing program administrators an official label, and frequently they did not bestow upon these administrators any particular status—including extra compensation or reassigned time for their work beyond their regular teaching and scholarly duties as faculty. The WPA typically existed in these earlier decades as a beleaguered and bitter paper-pusher who has been assigned the intractable task of overseeing freshman courses—courses that students do not want to take (but must), and faculty do not want to teach. This lose-lose impression of first-year writing administration extends into our departments today, despite early attempts on the behalf of professional organizations in composition and rhetoric to resituate the position in a positive way. As noted in an October 1964 report of the CCCC workshop on "Administering the Freshman Course":

> Several representatives deplored the fact that most experienced members of the faculty wish to withdraw from teaching Freshman English as soon as they can. Some reported that their schools make Freshman English more palatable by . . . giving credit toward promotions and salary increases to those who distinguish themselves in teaching Freshman English. Several schools require all staff members to teach at least one section of Freshman English each year. Representatives from these schools said that this practice

helps raise the status of the Freshman Course. Most participants agreed, however, that these and other devices have done little to lessen the belief that Freshman English is a drudgery which the experienced teacher will abandon as soon as he can. (CCCC 197)

This lingering impression of composition teaching and administration as undervalued and lacking in meaningful institutional recognition is in sharp contrast to the perceived task of the creative writing faculty, or creative writing program administrators, who are charged with teaching and overseeing attractive, elective courses that enroll mightily with students seeking "alternatives" to traditional literature-based courses in English. Since rhetoric and composition was not a field of graduate study until the mid-1970s, these early WPAs were almost without exception scholars and teachers of literature, often with no particular training in, or inclination toward, the administration of lower-level writing courses, and with no organized community for professional support. Rare exceptions were the occasional writing faculty member such as Theodore Morrison of Harvard, profiled in chapter 3, whose biography and public reputation within other historical accounts of English at Harvard minimize his role in expository writing management in favor of his (successful) identity as a published novelist.

In fact, the prototypical literature professor serving as WPA in these earlier decades of the twentieth century was relatively unproductive as a *scholar* when compared to other faculty in his or her English department, existing instead at the intellectual margins. Since composition studies was not yet a bona fide field, these WPAs were not expected—nor were they even perhaps inclined—to produce substantial scholarship on writing, rhetoric, and language. There were few outlets for such scholarship, even as *English Journal,* and later, *College English* and *College Composition and Communication,* themselves devoted to the work of this field, published in these early years only short "how-to" pieces on the teaching of writing, or more lengthy, but less scholarly, program reports or studies—hardly the sort of work upon which most literary scholars could achieve tenure. As Maureen Daly Goggin observes, early articles in these journals often "pose no argument, interpretation, evaluation, or critique. Instead, these essays typically explain in narrative form a practice or process in which the author engaged" (46). Goggin notes that the descriptive and testimonial essay genre is prominent in *College Composition and Communication*—as 45 percent of the published work for its first decade and a half (46). Certainly the various *CCC* articles excerpted and discussed in this book evidence the prevalence of this narrative genre, which itself stands in stark contrast to more interpretive, text-based work being published in literary criticism, and being more typically valued by promotion and tenure bodies. Save for those few linguist scholar WPAs who may have been working on scholarship related to philology per se, these faculty administrators were largely literary scholars who were assigned duties in composition administration, sometimes as part of a faculty rotation, sometimes by drawing the short straw, and often prior to receiving tenure, without real hope of connecting their own scholarship to their primary administrative duties.

By comparison, where and when creative writing programs exist, the faculty who administer these programs have historically been frequently prolific writers themselves, securely publishing their own poetry, fiction, or drama to institutional accolades, not selected as administrators for any compelling reason beyond their writing talents, and/or ability to draw students and faculty to the program itself. These administrators also are usually assisted by a variety of staff regarding student writing, student-faculty complaints, or other budgetary or structural aspects of program management, to further contrast the philosophy of their position versus the WPAs. As noted above, they are already typically separated from the daily duties of the English department by curricular design, and are responsible for oversight of either a menu of elective courses (in contrast to the nearly universal requirement of first-year composition) or a degree concentration in creative writing that is positioned beside, but not necessarily beholden to, either literature or composition.

While narratives of creative writing program directors are scarce—with one notable exception being Sharon Crowley's narrative of Norman Foerster,[6] and lore-based stories of program directors through studies of prestigious programs themselves[7]—scholars of the archives in composition have compiled historical evidence of the clear thread connecting WPAs in the early to mid-twentieth century with the existing concerns and work conditions of WPAs in many institutions today. The most comprehensive collection of these narratives is located in L'Eplattenier and Mastrangelo's *Historical Studies of Writing Program Administration*, wherein several contributors present research that reinforces the common instigating image of the undertrained, undervalued, and frequently exhausted WPA pre- and postwar.

D'Ann George, for example, tells in this collection the story of Regina Crandall, Bryn Mawr's "Director of the Essay Department" from 1903 to 1916 who, frankly abused and misunderstood by her college president (ironically also a woman), and frustrated by the work required to teach and oversee first-year composition, was replaced as WPA by Howard Savage, coincidentally trained in Harvard's English A program (George 23, 29). As George narrates, Crandall felt that as a field within English, "Composition, like trades accounted 'dangerous,' ought to command a premium" (28). Yet her low status and lower pay (in comparison to her English department colleagues) belied this assertion and precipitated her dismissal. Similarly, Randall Popken describes the work of Edwin Hopkins, WPA at the University of Kansas from 1889 to 1923, as that of a man dedicated to exposing the "deplorable conditions endured by writing faculty" in his programmatic research, yet "frequently at odds with administration over the legitimacy of his project" (8, 11). Popken notes that Hopkins was even hospitalized for four weeks during the summer of 1919 as a result of teaching as many as six classes per semester in addition to his WPA duties (11, 15). Hopkins is presented as a WPA who, like many who would follow in his footsteps, was regretful that his "research always [came] last" (15).

Of course, as Amy Heckathorn argues in that same volume, these administrative faculty were still decades away from the era of WPA as an identifiable area of research and labor within composition studies; not until the inauguration of the journal *WPA: Writing Program Administration* in 1977 does WPA work become associated with an "identity" that one can possess, and with that access a like-minded group of (equally suffering) individuals (206). Heckathorn asserts that only for the last forty or so years have WPAs had adequate outlets for their professional frustration, and that these outlets have risen in importance as the field has also taken a firmer intellectual stand within English departments, and within colleges and universities in general. In today's twenty-first century academia, WPAs—who are historically, overwhelmingly women—are able to share their stories and receive (professional) validation that they are not alone—that they are valuable teachers and scholars whose work is of significance to composition studies and rhetoric.[8] Indeed, as Shirley Rose argues, "WPAs frequently turn to narrative as a way to impose order, meaning, and value on their experience" (221) even as they are accused, by labor scholars such as Marc Bousquet and Tony Scott, of being little more than middle management in a business-minded university set on self-destruction of the field of English studies vis-à-vis the maintenance of the first-year composition requirement.

The narrative of writing programs from an administrative perspective, however, is fraught; for public women's colleges, it is additionally underresearched and thus largely mysterious as a subset of composition's history. L'Eplattenier and Mastrangelo's work profiles WPAs at the aforementioned Bryn Mawr, as well as Vassar, and also discusses the influential 1919 meeting of WPAs from other Seven Sisters colleges. They argue that the networking done by these Seven Sisters WPAs "refutes the notion that these women, like so many other participants in rhetoric and composition's history, were individual actors, toiling in isolation, with little or no support from those around them" (118). Indeed, representatives from Radcliffe also attended the summit on women's education in 1944 that illustrated this professional women's academic network in the mid-twentieth century. But public women's colleges were not represented in this historical re-visioning of WPA agentic collectives. So it is difficult to make any sweeping conclusions about the opportunities for women WPAs at public institutions in the first half of the century to know or support one another. Instead, we must look at individual cases from these public colleges, including the Woman's College, to see whether *any* counternarratives emerge—and if so, with what important local caveats. Without faculty specializing in composition and rhetoric on staff, the English department of the Woman's College postwar indeed turned to a literature professor to administer its writing program—in this case, a Milton scholar with several years' experience in teaching, fresh from her doctoral study, Dr. May Delaney Bush. It is her story, alongside the story of poet Randall Jarrell, that I turn to next.

A Tale of Two Promotions
"What would happen if everybody behaved as I do?": May Delaney Bush

Little is known, institutionally speaking, about May Bush, and that in itself is telling. As opposed to the boxes of Randall Jarrell's archival papers housed in the UNCG archives, May Bush has just one slim folder. Bush came to the Woman's College in 1934, having received her AB in 1923 from Hollins College—also a women's college—and her MA in 1928 from Columbia University. She served as a high school English teacher in Greensboro from 1924 to 1926; a faculty member at Finch College (New York) from 1926 to 1932, and, briefly, a department chair at Peace College, a private (and then two-year) women's college in Raleigh, North Carolina, from 1934 to 1935 ("Two to Retire").[9] At the bottom of her 1960–61 biographical information form, dated October 10, 1960, Bush adds a handwritten comment: "Surely you have enough about me!"

Perhaps Bush's frustrated comment here stems from the fact that while she had filled out this same form at least four separate times during her tenure, her answers had hardly changed. Bush had published one article on Milton concomitant with receiving her doctorate, "Rational Proof of a Deity from the Order of Nature," in the 1942 *Journal of English Literary*

History. But curiously, in the space for "titles of published works" on her biographical form, she never lists this article, nor is it mentioned in her January 1968 retirement announcement published in the daily *Greensboro Record*. Between coming to the Woman's College in 1934 and retiring in spring 1968, Bush received her PhD from Johns Hopkins University in 1942, allowing for a promotion to assistant professor after eight years of being in the instructor rank. Ten years later she would be promoted to associate professor, and eight years following that promotion, to full professor. The only extended pieces of prose detailing May Bush as a Woman's College community member come from a brief, published eulogy written by departmental colleague Amy Charles, and a letter written by Robert O. Stephens, head of the English department in 1983, to May Bush's sisters (Mrs. Russell Lyday and Miss Ellen Douglas Bush) on the occasion of her death.

Upon May Bush's retirement from the university in 1968, Amy Charles describes Bush as admired by her colleagues and students alike: "Miss Bush's students have commended her insistence of high scholarly standards for herself and for them, her fair-mindedness, her enthusiasm, and her belief in them. Colleagues have mentioned her unflagging concern for excellence, her courage and integrity, her steadfastness and lack of self-seeking, and her utter honesty. New instructors have had reason to appreciate her friendly welcome, her instinctive kindliness, her grace and dignity, as well as her awareness of practical difficulties that more than once has led to loans to tide over the newcomer awaiting his first pay day" (Charles, "May Delaney Bush"). We can see Bush's feminine traits ("grace and dignity") being highly valued here, in contrast to the sometimes rough or isolationist portrait of the typical (male) writer. Indeed, her apparently outgoing nature and enthusiasm would stand in some contrast to widely accepted portraits of Jarrell, often characterized as a "loner" and supremely private individual, dedicated to his craft. It is ironic that one of Bush's noted traits would be financial generosity toward junior colleagues, given her own difficulty in obtaining raises and advancements in rank throughout her thirty-four years at the Woman's College. Jarrell, in contrast, is not historically characterized as stingy, but is known alternatively for his love of sports cars, bought with his considerable Woman's College salary.

Charles closes her article by recalling Bush's lifelong ethical principle, advanced by her philosophy professor at Hollins College: "What would happen if everybody behaved as I do?" This question seemingly drove her polite acceptance of her lesser status in the department as compared to high-profile faculty such as Jarrell. It also matched neatly with the social and ethical values in place at the Woman's College and promoted to students during Bush's tenure, as discussed in chapters 1 and 2. Further, Bush's question is an interesting meta-inquiry for the focus of this book. What, indeed, *would* have happened if everyone at the Woman's College had "behaved" as Bush did and eschewed the financial and social promises of creative writing postwar? Or, what would have happened if composition and rhetoric had been a more forceful presence in the department against the rise of creative writing, and had been fully recognized as a scholarly field in the 1940s, rather than later, in the 1970s? How would this archival tale of the Woman's College have changed for those of us now reconstructing the field's history through these overlooked narratives of students, faculty, and administrators? These are wistful questions to ponder, both for my own research here, and for the future research of my fellow readers.

Bush's philosophical mantra is repeated by Chairman Robert Stephens in his letter to her surviving sisters, on the occasion of her death in 1983, as he insists,

> It is good now to remember her as she was during her long active career on this campus, as a fine and conscientious teacher and adviser, as a responsible member of this department and this faculty, who set high standards for her students and for herself and really lived by the question asked by her philosophy professor at Hollins: "What would happen if everybody did as I do?" She was a woman of high principle and, when occasion required, a courageous champion. . . . May had a rare quality of thinking of others first. . . . In any effort, she always took more than her share of the responsibility. And though she never sought popularity, she had loyal students who kept in touch with her over the years. (letter, Nov. 7, 1983)

Stephens makes no note of Bush's scholarship—admittedly minimal though it was—and instead focuses, like Charles, on Bush's personality and ethics. She is the good soldier; she is the one who took on "more than her share" while being given far less in return. She is the martyr for a variety of unpopular departmental causes left unstated here, among them the oversight and maintenance of the composition curriculum. While very little in the archives narrates Bush's accomplishments, beyond those regarding the *Yearling,* her presence at department meetings was regular and her contributions always noted respectfully, in a department that had its own personnel tensions and lively personalities, and notable women faculty. Bush is not, for example, in the league of other women faculty such as Nettie Sue Tillett, whose departmental comments in meeting minutes were frequently characterized as disruptive, off-topic, or inflammatory, and whose actions were formally critiqued by Randall Jarrell himself.[10]

Nor is she comparative to Lettie Hamlett Rogers, who resigned over the chancellor's sanction of a published nude sketch in the student literary arts magazine *Coraddi*.[11] Additionally, she cannot by definition have kinship with another group of women on faculty, the "faculty wives"—such as Mrs. James Painter and both the first and second Mrs. Jarrells—whose status was tied to the work of their husbands and thus purely contingent labor, yet who were given pay raises more frequently than was Bush herself.

Instead, Bush's legacy in archival documents is that of a stalwart, nonconfrontational department soldier assigned to a variety of committees—including the afore-discussed Committee on Freshman and Sophomore English; the freshman composition committee; the English 449 (senior seminar) committee; the English A (remedial writing) committee; the committee to select the new department chair of English, in 1961 (on which Jarrell also served); and the Committee on Graduate Work (ironically so, since she was not, at that time, a member of the graduate faculty). Bush was, however, keeping up with the profession outside of her heavy teaching and committee load; within the archival records of Chancellor W. W. Pierson, there is a handwritten note from Bush to Pierson, thanking him for the "authorization of the travel grant toward expenses for the Modern Language Association meeting [of 1956]" (Bush, letter to Pierson, Dec. 18, 1956). Finally, Bush appears (alongside fellow Woman's College colleague Leonard B. Hurley) in several back-matter notes in the *South Atlantic Bulletin,* in recognition of her work for the North Carolina Education Association, which had as its primary charge articulating and refining secondary school English requirements for the state's public schools.

Each of the institutions where Bush was employed—Finch, Peace, and the Woman's College—were single-sex institutions, and her bachelor's degree was also from a women's institution (Hollins). So in her employment record at the very least, Bush had a personal commitment to women's education that was clearly visible. But despite her support of women's education, and perhaps as a deep rationale for her support of others' bids for advancements within the college, May Bush's own road to promotion and tenure was troubled—a trouble not incidentally starkly in contrast to the ease of advancement granted to her colleague, Randall Jarrell.

While a skeptic might point to Bush's lack of scholarly production as a key reason for her lack of regular or timely advancement in rank, and therefore her lack of concomitant pay raises, an archival reading of Bush's situation highlights two issues that undercut this argument. First, a lack of publications in literary history or theory would be a common, if negative, consequence of being assigned heavy administrative (and committee) duties in first-year writing and general education, on top of a four-class-per-semester teaching load; unlike Jarrell's notably lighter teaching load of two courses per semester, on average, there is no indication that Bush had any reassigned time for her administrative or service work. Second, the fact that the English department chairs continually advocated for her advancement—but those words fell on deaf ears at the level of the dean, who denied said requests repeatedly while granting similar requests regarding Professor Jarrell—shows that in fact, Bush's department supported her promotion (and tenure), or at least articulated such support in regular chair's reports and thus held her in a position of some value during her tenure at the college.

Archival department records are thick with a long history of requests for Bush's promotion (and tenure) that were articulated, in some cases, multiple times from department head Leonard B. Hurley to the chancellor and/or dean(s) of the Woman's College. These requests are located in the papers of the chancellors and deans to whom the appeals were made, and are also alluded to in some departmental documents related to personnel matters and faculty accomplishments. The first notable request comes on March 23, 1948, when Leonard Hurley wrote to Chancellor Jackson to appeal for two "urgent cases"—one of which was May Bush. Hurley categorized these requested increases in salary as *the* two to be made "if *any*" should be funded for fall 1948. Hurley writes:

> Dr. May Bush is completing her fourteenth year at the Woman's College. Since coming here she has spent two years in graduate study at Johns Hopkins University and has been awarded her Ph.D. degree with distinction by that great university. She is an extremely hard and conscientious worker and an excellent scholar. She is very highly regarded in the English department and throughout the College and the community. She serves as Chairman of the Freshman English work—a taxing job. She teaches Freshmen, Sophomores, Juniors, and Seniors. . . . Dr. Bush is on the Board of Trustees of Hollins College and could go there to teach at any time she made known her desire to do so. (I know that there is an opening there for her next year). Dr. Bush wishes to stay at Woman's College, but I think that she is becoming pretty thoroughly discouraged because she has had no promotion in rank during the past eight years.

This would be the first of many requests from Hurley, a staunch classically trained and traditional thinking literature professor who (as previously noted in the alumnae interviews) kept a firm leash on the department and an even firmer leash on the women students and faculty. Despite Hurley's predilections as chair, however, he defends Bush's work and her value to the department and college, recognizing the personal toll the numerous denied promotions have taken on her. His advocacy for Bush in these archival documents is undeniable.

On June 9, 1948, Hurley sent a follow-up memo to Jackson, noting that Bush receives $3,360 in salary, and that "if nothing more can be done at this time, [her salary] *must* be brought to at least $3500.00 . . . $140.00 to do this." In this same memo, Hurley clarifies Randall Jarrell's status for 1948–49: that he would, in fact, desire part-time teaching in the department, and his wife—normally a part-time instructor—would consequently teach full time, with each receiving $2,400 for the year for their work. Jarrell had been granted "special permission by the directors of the Guggenheim Fellowships to remain here while holding the fellowship and continue to conduct his part of the Writing Workshop. But in order to meet the need for teachers of sophomore sections, etc., we would have to have Mrs. Jarrell for full-time during this one year." Hurley adds, "Mr. Jarrell has recently been offered an Associate Professorship elsewhere at $4100.00. In view of the arrangement outlined above, he has elected to remain here" (memo, June 9, 1948).

A few notable threads emerge from these two related memos. First, it is clear that Hurley had been a regular advocate for May Bush's advancement for some time, by the time of this 1948 correspondence. It is also clear that Hurley appreciated Bush's work in the department. Yet he framed Bush's requested advancement as first, a desperate plea for increase in rank and status—linking the lack thereof to Bush's noted "frustration" with the department. But later, Hurley was willing to take a lesser prize for Bush: a meager increase in salary, simply to save face, as it were, when holding her salary against much younger assistant professors in the department.

In contrast, Hurley's appeal for Jarrell's replacement is far less dire, more framed as a matter-of-fact request. It goes without much saying that a replacement for Jarrell (and Taylor) is needed, due to their important work in creative writing within the department. It also goes without saying that Jarrell is sought after; his explicit counteroffer from an outside institution carries with it a $4,100 salary; hence, Hurley's request for the equivalent of a $4,800 salary for Jarrell's half-time work in the coming year. There is no desperate pleading; in fact, there is an assumption on Jarrell's part that said offer would be forthcoming, as indicated by his decision to turn down the $4,100 counteroffer. In fact, Hurley uses the "saved" $600 in Jarrell's salary for next year, owing to his half-time status, to budget projected funds for Bush as well as Professors Spivey, Thayer, and England's raises. So, in very direct terms, Jarrell's good fortune of receiving a Guggenheim—for being a renowned poet—is seen as a way to pay May Bush for her continuing, dedicated employment in the comparatively "taxing" work of administering freshman composition at the Woman's College.

Despite these compelling pleas for an increase in Bush's standing and salary, Hurley's requests go unanswered, as evidenced in a memo to Jackson dated April 30, 1949. Hurley opens his memo with an initial category of "necessary adjustments." These adjustments are primarily for Randall and (first wife) Mackie Jarrell, as follows:

> Mr. Jarrell (Associate Professor) was on half-time this year at a salary of $2400.00, while holding a Guggenheim Fellowship. He is to go back on full time salary and work next year. (In this connection may I call to your remembrance our understanding of last spring: When Mr. Jarrell was offered a position at Bard College, New York, at a salary of $4200.00,[12] a sum in excess of what he was receiving here, I was authorized to point out to him that in all likelihood his salary here would be larger than that, beginning with the fall of 1949. . . . We wish Mrs. Mackie Jarrell to continue on a full-time schedule next year. If she were not to do so, we should have to cut the number of freshman sections below what they have been for the past two years; and the number of students in each of the sections that we have is already too large. (We shall be attempting to begin our graduate program with no increase in personnel; hence, we cannot spare any teacher for an increased number of Freshman sections).

Whereas these requests are framed rhetorically as "necessary adjustments"—including the hiring of Mackie Jarrell on a full-time basis, with the clear argument that to do so would severely compromise the composition (freshman) program—the repeated request for May Bush is anything but a minor "adjustment," nor is it assumed to be met. Whereas a failure to hire Mackie Jarrell full-time would result in a loss of composition sections—implicitly, because no one else could possibly teach these courses, and because the department could not (or would not?) seek another temporary hire to replace her—no such argument of value is made for composition, at least not for May Bush, the director of composition. Hurley instead reiterates his previous request of spring 1948 word-for-word, and adds that in the case of both Bush and Spivey, "I have been urging these promotions for four years," pointing out that he does not believe "there are two more urgent cases in the college" (Hurley memo to Jackson, Apr. 30, 1949). In this memo, he also re-articulates the need for promotion to full professor for Professors Tillett and Bridgers, as well as Rowley and

Gould—the latter of whom were women associate professors who had been at this rank for twenty-six and twenty-two years, respectively.

At this point in the documentation provided by Hurley's memos, it seems prudent to ask: to what degree was the lack of promotion and advancement for Bush due to her gender, as well as her lesser status as a teacher and director of composition? Given the lingering "terminal associate" status of Rowley, Tillett, and Gould, it seems pertinent to question whether the progressive view of the Woman's College toward its students, and their intellectual advancement and success, was in fact not adequately reflected in its views toward women *faculty*. The answer seems to be that both gender and teaching or administrative area may have been a factor, if later records from the department, as it eased into its new standing as a coeducational university, are any indication.

In an English department report for the year 1964–65—an academic year of transition just a few months before Randall Jarrell's untimely death, three years before Bush's retirement, and the first year of the college's forced coeducational enrollments—an accounting of current departmental faculty by rank is spelled out in detail. Embedded in this report is an articulation of new lines needed in the future, and a brief discussion of current faculty in relation to graduate student work, in particular theses directions. The report also comments on upcoming promotions and their potential effect on the graduate program. This report was written for then-dean of the college, Otis Singletary.

In this staffing report, May Bush is listed as one of the five full professors in the English department, having finally achieved this rank in 1960–61. However, Bush and her previously noted colleague in denied promotions, Dr. John Bridgers—a faculty member whose vocal concerns for first-year and basic writing are noted in numerous department meeting minutes, and whose teaching was primarily at the freshman and sophomore levels only—are simultaneously singled out as those who "cannot be qualified to direct theses in the graduate program," and are relegated, in the chart-by-rank, as for "undergraduate" teaching only. Because, as noted in the report, Bush and Bridgers are not able to direct MA theses, this leaves only two professors—Bryant and Watson—eligible to potentially do so at the full professor level. Hence, an embedded secondary request in this memo is the immediate promotion of an incoming faculty member, T. C. Rumble, to full professor to ensure that there be "professorial strength for the M.A. program." A third associate professor, Dr. Jean Gagen, is described as having published her first book, a revision of her dissertation, through a "vanity press"; the report notes that she may come up for promotion to full professor on the strength of a second book "now nearing completion" at the same time as Watson. However, the report makes clear that Watson would be the preferred choice when the two are put side-by-side, as "putting him [Watson] in competition for a position with Miss Gagen would [be] for many reasons . . . unfortunate" as his "value to the Department is considerably greater."

A reading of the departmental politics concerning tenure and promotion, based on this document alone, evidences some disturbing truths: that not only were composition-heavy faculty (those responsible for the first-year writing courses, such as Bush and Bridgers) valued less than the literature-primary, and especially the creative writing, faculty, as weighted by their perceived ability to direct graduate theses, but also the less kind truth that male faculty were being valued over women faculty. An allied reading would argue that the new coeducational status of the college led to increased promotion and tenure expectations, in terms of publishing, in order to keep pace with the campuses at Raleigh and Chapel Hill. But in either scenario, the value of women's education as offered by *women faculty* and administrators—noted as those who most encouraged leadership and success among the undergraduates in chapter 2's alumnae interviews—seemed to be taking a backseat to the lure of prestigious hires, in this case men, that would bring the college a new, national attention.

A review of general standards for promotion and tenure during this postwar era (*prior* to the coeducational merger of 1964) reveals no specifics on these two cases, however—as such matters are typically not part of the public record and, as those readers who have served on promotion and tenure committees know, such details on individual cases are rarely put in writing. But the evaluation sheet for faculty, signed by the department head and submitted to the dean and above for review, is somewhat telling in its categories, categories that may privilege men over women, certain personalities over others. In addition to the rank, salary, and years in service, faculty are rated as excellent, superior, average, or inferior based on the following:

1. teaching ability (with no subheadings);

2. personal traits, with the subheadings of intellectual integrity, breadth of interests, emotional balance, cooperation, and open-mindness. There are also two blank spots for additional write-in subheadings within this category;

3. administrative ability (again, with no subheadings);

4. professional growth, with subheadings of research, creative work, professional activities, and further study; and

5. service to campus, community, state, and nation.

While teaching is the first category in the list, personal traits ranks second—above administrative ability, professional growth, and service. It is hard to ignore that this nebulous category includes one consideration—"emotional balance"—that surely could have been used to single out women from men. May Bush—by all indications—resisted this "emotional" profile in her departmental work and was implicitly rewarded for this resistance by Hurley, while faculty such as Nettie Tillett did not. In addition, "cooperation" serves as an early term for the oft-contested current notion of "collegiality," another point in which gendered power relations within a department could certainly result in a low ranking in this category. It is hard to know how "open-mindness" is to be read, but one possible interpretation is the ability to accept new (and/or unwanted) duties without complaint, or accept departmental decisions that did not fit one's views with acceptance. Within an institution that valued women's abilities—as *students*—to enter into society with a range of knowledge and a keen sense of self and community, it seems ironic that such standards would exist in the review of women *faculty*.

Further, it seems odd that given the low status of "research" in this paradigm—a subheading under "professional growth" that is second-to-last in the evaluation form—certain faculty would be singled out for their lack of scholarly production in the English department, as if this component of their job were first or second in importance for tenure and promotion (such as Bush, barred from directing MA theses, and Jean Gagen[13]). Here, we begin to see discordant evidence: even though the teaching load was quite high, and heavy scholarship thus not necessarily expected (if one is to use the ordered criteria on the evaluation form as a rank of importance), the creative writing faculty were significantly—perhaps inordinately—valued *for* this production of work, work that was not only part of their "professional growth" but also public evidence of their standing as productive artists. Their high production level also allowed the department to excel in one corner of its scholarly production—the publication of poetry and fiction—and thus overachieve within the typical framework of, and public expectations for, a teaching-centered, regional college for women, wherein the woman WPA had one of the highest work burdens of all faculty on salary.

May Bush would carry the legacy of her WPA workload through her career at the Woman's College, staying on faculty despite her disappointing road to full professor. In a memo to Dean Mereb Mossman, dated April 12, 1957, Hurley outlines Bush's venerable track record in his larger request for Bush's promotion to full professor, the sole subject of the memo. He recalls her many accomplishments inside and outside the college, including her work as "chairman" of freshman English (again labeled as "taxing"); her departmental committee work; and her university service on the College Chapel Committee, the war bond drive, and the Committee on Humanities in General Education. Hurley also notes Bush's service to local organizations such as the Guilford County Mental Hygiene Society and her membership in the MLA, South Atlantic MLA (SAMLA), American Association of University Women (AAUW), and other regional professional organizations. He concludes that she is a "well prepared, scholarly, and most conscientious teacher . . . something of a leader in the intellectual life of the community. I think she deserves the promotion requested."

But the promotion for 1957–58 was not to be, as evident by Hurley's subsequent memo to Gordon Blackwell, chancellor, on March 5, 1958. Hurley writes in wake of Randall Jarrell's acceptance of an offer of employment from Kenyon College for 1958–59, noting that "the department budget as we saw it then [spring 1957] has been sharply changed." Hurley articulates his past request for May Bush's promotion to full professor, and later in the memo more fully spells out his underlying concerns surrounding the lack of promotion for Bush, in the context of the Woman's College as an institution:

> The Department of English at the Woman's College has had for many years at least one woman at full professorial rank (See attached material of sample years, taken at random, back to the period at which full professorships became a part of our arrangements here at the Woman's College). In recent years we have had two women professors. Both retire this year. I think that in a women's college, in every department staff that includes a number of women, as the English department here does, there should be at least one woman with the rank of Professor. Dr. May D. Bush will be the top ranking woman in the department. . . .
>
> I hope that she may be promoted at this time.

Hurley's archived material on rankings and gender indicates exactly the proportion that he here broadly describes. The latest (randomly selected) year charted was 1951–52, in which two of the nine full professors were women; in both 1943–44 and 1946–47, one of the eight full professors (Jane Summerall) was a woman. In earlier years of the college, there was consistently one woman full professor among the five to eight full professors listed (in 1925–26, 1929–30, 1934–35, and 1938–39). Such disparity is evident in one of the last salary comparison sheets for the Woman's College during May Bush's employment. In 1960–61, Randall Jarrell's salary is $10,500. Leonard Hurley's salary—as department head—is only $9,200 by comparison. May Bush, having finally achieved the rank of full professor in fall 1960, is listed at a salary of $7,500. Bush's salary is the lowest of all the full professors, including John Bridgers, another colleague whose promotion bids were frequently denied. Robert Watson, an associate professor, is listed as receiving a salary of $6,700—just $800 behind May Bush, despite Bush's service record that extended more than sixteen years prior to Watson's in the department. Add to this final salary accounting the fact that Bush went with *no* raises of any kind from her appointment to assistant professor in 1940 through 1945, and one can see a demoralizing frame around her Woman's College career.

The two main creative writing faculty in the department at this time— Randall Jarrell and Peter Taylor—were available for and assigned to the primary direction of MFA theses, though Taylor was anticipated, in the 1964–65 report on requested promotions and appointments, to be "away on leave, a semester at a time, with relative frequency." The report also carefully notes that "neither [Taylor nor Jarrell] can direct the MFA program," likely due to their semiregular absences from campus in the form of these leaves, temporary appointments, and general calls for readings and lectures at institutions throughout the country. Jarrell's personal papers alone contain at least twenty letters from universities and colleges pleading for a moment of his time with their students and faculty. These requests were frequently lucrative; in 1956, Oglethorpe College, on the promise of collecting admission fees of one dollar per person for his public reading, offered Jarrell $750 for one day's work—one-tenth of his then-current yearly salary at the Woman's College.[14] May Bush would receive no such offers or public recognition, her supposed standing offer of employment from Hollins College notwithstanding. As a WPA and faculty member associated with service and, arguably, servitude, Bush would never be singled out as obviously valuable to the *prestige* of the college—a factor important, no doubt, in higher-level promotion and retention decisions. Jarrell, in contrast, would spend his nineteen on-and-off years at the Woman's College living a celebrated life known only to a small circle of midcentury poets and fiction writers, and would find himself conflicted over where he ultimately belonged, as a writer, teacher, and community member in the college he would come to call "Sleeping Beauty."

"They leave you to yourself extraordinarily": Randall Jarrell

Compared to the lack of personal and professional information available on May Bush, a woman who appears to have lived her life in relative anonymity, quietly soldiering on in the face of frequent disappointment where promotion and advancement are concerned, much is obviously known about Randall Jarrell as both a man and a writer. It is neither the aim of this book to recapitulate that public knowledge, nor to make value judgments about Jarrell's work or life, or to undertake analysis of his poetry or prose. I leave that to his biographers and literary critics. Instead, I wish to briefly discuss some campus-based perspectives on Jarrell, including those that come from himself, his colleague Robert Watson, and Jarrell's second wife, Mary, so as to set the stage for a detailing of his own successful and financially lucrative career at the Woman's College. In briefly presenting this Woman's College–centered portrait of Jarrell, I hope to illuminate his institutional standing compared to that of May Bush, thereby highlighting the human differences between being a creative writer and being a compositionist (or a faculty member charged with the enterprise of composition) during the postwar era, and to add to the sometimes contradictory messages about literacy, professionalism, and writing education that the Woman's College sent to its students and faculty during the postwar era.

In an eight-page essay written on the occasion of Jarrell's death, and archived in Robert Watson's personal papers at the university, Watson reflects at length about his colleague and friend. In addition to admiring his intelligence and his interest in all things literary (including German and Russian literature), Watson characterizes Jarrell as a thoughtful, careful individual who "always won an argument—even when he was wrong, which was not often—because he knew his subject in more detail, had a marvelous memory, and had a mind that worked with a matchless velocity" ("Randall Jarrell," 5). Watson describes Jarrell's relationship with his students as stemming from this marvelous mind, and as mutually respectful, noting, "What endeared his writing students to him was the seriousness with which he took their writing; he spoke to them as if they were all potential Homers" (4). Watson remembers that Jarrell felt "the best teachers of writing he always claimed were the best works of the best writers. He knew that imaginative writing could not be taught; he knew too that only rarely would he have students who could really write" (4). Jarrell's view of creative writing instruction would match perfectly with the larger views of organizations such as the AWP, and of graduate programs in creative writing around the country, which were designed to locate and cultivate talent rather than create it. Such a view stands in stark contrast to the daunting charge of a course such as first-year writing—whose implicit (and often explicit) aim is to "fix" students into good (or great) writers and to create language-perfect writers of any and all students required to enroll in the course.

Watson also remembers Jarrell as a willing servant to the department, someone who was "very conscientious about both committee meetings and faculty meetings," using as primary example Jarrell's two-time service on the committee to revise freshman and sophomore English. Yet Watson also paints a picture of Jarrell as an intensely private and critical person, both of his colleagues' creative work and of his own. Watson recalls, "Randall was awkward at parties attended by more than a few people even though he could address a thousand from the platform with ease. At parties many interpreted his silence and apparent indifference to disdain of the company. Actually he was shy and uncomfortable" (5). Watson's lasting memories of Jarrell do much to illuminate his significant presence on a campus wherein women deeply desired to be recognized as intellectual equals and students of promise, and where writing was becoming an art form of distinct study rather than a utility, or tool, in rote learning at the undergraduate, and soon graduate, levels. Jarrell saw writing as a deeply intellectual activity, rather than a system by which mass amounts of students were acculturated into the university. His private profile matched that of the stereotypical writer—or perhaps, one might argue, helped to *shape* that eventual stereotype: the intensely private, inwardly focused individual who is at once a public superstar and private recluse, ultimately characterized by Watson as "like many children, [having] sometimes . . . little grasp of the practical world" (6).

In addition to Watson's essay, one of the most comprehensive sources of personal reflection by Jarrell is found in the volume *Randall Jarrell's Letters,* edited by his second wife and widow, Mary Jarrell. One notices herein a marked contrast between the much-lauded English department member Jarrell and the private Jarrell, who often questioned his comfort with the South and with the Woman's College, as noted more obliquely in Watson's remembrance. Particularly early in the letters, in his first period of residency in Greensboro, Jarrell remarks on the college not altogether favorably and articulates his position primarily in terms of financial rather than intellectual gains.

Jarrell's first impression of the Woman's College was in April 1947, during his campus visit—a visit that had been arranged by soon-to-be colleague and close friend Peter Taylor. In a practice rooted in personal connections and small-field networking that continues, to a great extent, in graduate creative writing departments and units today, Taylor served as a chief architect for Jarrell's hire, just as Allen Tate had arranged for Jarrell's close friend Robert Lowell to have a half-year position in residence at the University of Iowa Writers' Workshop in 1953 (Mary Jarrell, *Letters* 376).[15] Mary Jarrell writes that Randall was hired as an associate professor, and his first wife Mackie as an instructor, as noted previously. The letters make evident that Mackie's appointment was not based on any particular qualifications besides being a faculty wife, and that Randall's associate rank was barely justifiable, given that he had only taught for three years at the University of Texas at Austin, and for one year at Sarah Lawrence prior to coming to the Woman's College. This profile illustrates his critical material differences from May Bush, who had to wait eight years for a promotion to associate professor, even with her PhD (versus Jarrell's master's degree) in hand.

Indeed, Jarrell's early correspondence with fellow writers such as Robert Lowell characterizes university teaching as an especially good financial "gig" for a writer, with fairly light work expectations. Jarrell writes to Lowell in October 1947:

> I have seven girls in my writing-poetry and fifteen in my modern poetry
> . . . two have done nice slight poems, one a very clever imitation of your
> couplets—I'll bring it when I come up. The classes are better than I thought
> they'd be—quite serious and overjoyed with the poetry. . . . Wouldn't you
> like to come next year to take my job for a year while I do the Guggenheim
> here? (Rhyme, Rhyme!) You'd have a job with the rank of associate professor, a good bargaining point from which to arrange for another job; there'd
> be very little work and $3600; they leave you to yourself extraordinarily; and
> a number of the girls you'd have to teach would be ones I'd already done
> for a year, so it wouldn't be starting in a desert. I think it could be arranged
> without any trouble, if you'd like to. I believe it would be a good way to
> spend nine months—you could get a great deal of writing done here. (Jarrell,
> *Letters*, 182)

Jarrell's letter to Lowell evidences his low teaching load (two courses) and lack of other firm or compulsory commitments to the department or college. Indeed, Leonard Hurley agreed, as a term of Jarrell's initial appointment, that he would not teach freshman courses (that is, composition), nor would Peter Taylor.[16] A comparative look at Jarrell's load against other faculty, in particular May Bush, shows in spring 1955 a great difference: Jarrell had 11 students total, all in upper-division courses, whereas May Bush had 80 students total, 70 of whom were lower-division (freshmen and sophomores). Hurley's own accounting for the "average" faculty load in the department from this same semester indicates a figure of 79.5 students, nearly identical to Bush's load, but far above Jarrell's (Hurley, "Report on English Department Enrollments"). Later in his letters, Jarrell mentions that he teaches for two hours on Monday, Wednesday, and Friday afternoons—again a two-course load, representing only one-half of the regular four-course load held by other departmental faculty during this era of the college.[17]

Jarrell's differential teaching load status seems somewhat shocking in retrospect, especially considering other contemporary factors at the college, such as too-high enrollment caps of twenty-five to twenty-eight students in the first-year composition sections and heavy lower-division student loads carried by Bush and other women and junior faculty in the department. But Jarrell's lesser teaching responsibilities became a standard by which many graduate faculty in creative writing MFA programs today are hired and retained, under the (understandable) argument that teaching writing is highly time-consuming. No such argument, interestingly, was or is made for composition-primary faculty, by comparison, even at the Woman's College, where literacy and eloquence were, as previously discussed, highly valued by both faculty and students, and where full-time faculty regularly taught first-year writing, often in multiple sections.

Jarrell writes again to Lowell in December 1947, in part to again communicate his surprise at these overall good conditions in place at the Woman's College, in this case regarding the students themselves. He notes that his modern poetry class all wrote "paraphrases of 'Of Nature Considered as a Heraclitean Fire,'" despite having not read this particular piece as a class; he also notes that his workload remains light—as "in six weeks of school we've had one meeting of any kind. At Sarah Lawrence they wanted you to go to some meeting every other day. I confess I didn't go to *any*" (*Letters* 185). Yet in letters to others, such as close confidante and possible romantic interest Elizabeth Eisler, Jarrell expresses simultaneously a contentment with the setting of Greensboro for his life and writing, and a somewhat less gracious attitude toward the students and faculty at the college. He writes in October 1948, "[Greensboro] is pastoral, with trees and pleasant country around. The campus of the college is very quiet, mild, and pleasant, too. It is a wonderful place to write. . . . The faculty of the college are very much like the city of Greensboro, though this is doing an injustice to several trees which are cleverer than several of this faculty. But there are four or five pleasant ones who are quite fun, and usually there are several students who are fun, too" (202). Jarrell's general disposition was reflected, perhaps, in this statement to Eisler, above, as he notes in a later letter dated November 1948,

> I lead an odd, independent, unsocial life remarkably unlike most other people's lives, the life of someone whose principal work-and-amusement is writing, and reading and thinking about things. . . . I like the feeling of being taken care of, of having decisions made for me, of being saved bother . . . for ten years I've been (1) teaching, or being in the army, or being on *The Nation*, (2) writing poetry, and (3) writing criticism, answering letters from magazines, etc. Having all these going on at once means one feels distracted, and harassed, especially if one is lazy and easily gets feelings of guilt. (204–5)

Jarrell's self-description is worth noting, as it fits nearly perfectly, again, with the description of the stereotypical creative writer, or creative writing faculty: his primary activity is writing (and reading), and unlike other colleagues in the English department who see teaching and scholarship as highly interrelated activities, Jarrell sees teaching as one of many distractions, equivalent to working for a journal or being in the army. Clearly he is not what we would today call a good "multitasker," but his statement is more revealing than that, in terms of how creative writing faculty would go on to significantly shape English departments, including that of the Woman's College, in the mid- to late twentieth century. Seeing creative writing faculty as writers *first*, teachers second—or as private citizens who write and also *happen* to be teaching, to pay bills, in lieu of another temporary vocation—is a far cry from the more traditional image of college faculty as being connected (or even chained) to their institution through a community of scholarship and teaching. The contrast between Jarrell's description and Leonard Hurley's descriptions of May Bush as a tireless departmental and college citizen reveals some substantial differences in how work and the roles of faculty are defined for a writing program administrator and teacher of first- and second-year writing versus a poet and teacher of creative writing exclusively, even within a closely knit, teaching-centered college such as the Woman's College.

This is not to say that Jarrell did not enjoy his teaching; if his letters are any evidence (in conjunction with his very detailed and copious lecture notes housed in his college papers in the UNCG archives), and if Watson's memories are at all accurate, Jarrell often enjoyed and usually took time with his teaching throughout his years at the Woman's College. Mary Jarrell notes that he was often quoted as saying "I'm crazy about teaching. If I were a rich man, I'd pay to teach" (*Letters,* 434). This view might be seen as an example of Mary Jarrell's biases in presentation if it were not for Randall Jarrell's many other recorded comments supporting this view. For example, in his public acceptance of an award at the Woman's College in 1961, he stated that, "Teaching is something that I would pay to do; to make my living by doing it, here at the University of North Carolina, with the colleagues I have and the students my colleagues have, seems to me a piece of good luck I don't deserve but am immensely grateful for" (453). It is possible that Jarrell, who comes across in his letters as fairly needy of personal attention and loyal friendships—friendships that would be characterized by frequent travel between and among others' homes, and across countries—simply enjoyed the intellect and devotion of his poetry students, who by all indications idolized him as much as did the college as a whole.

Yet, Jarrell writes to his New York–based friend Margaret Marshall in February 1949 that, "We'll probably be going north next year (we're sick of North Carolina—the average North Carolina girl talks as if she were an imbecile with an ambition to be an idiot) and then won't be able to offer you any weather but your own" (*Letters,* 219). In this comment, he seems to contradict his earlier classification of his female students as highly intelligent (regarding the Hopkins paraphrase), and his later expressed love of teaching these very girls, but also evidences his need to pull himself in and out of North Carolina frequently during his early years of employment, mainly to be near northern colleagues and far-flung friends, and to experience new teaching and writing situations when he seemingly grew tired of Greensboro.

Again, this characterization of Jarrell's wanderlust is significant in the context of the creative writing program at the Woman's College. Perceived as a mainstay and a means by which the college could broaden its influence in the education of women both in the South and beyond, the program was really only as secure as the social life of its primary actors—Jarrell and, to a lesser extent, Taylor. This is in contrast to the college's role in May Bush's life, as she seems to have worked in some social isolation and with firm commitment to the institution—through and despite her promotion denials—as opposed to choosing to move to a more hospitable social location, or to be in proximity with like-minded scholars of her area, English literature. While the Woman's College successfully secured Jarrell's residency through many monetary counteroffers and incentives, one can only see Jarrell's acquiescence as being in keeping with his social desires.

Still, Jarrell's letters are evidence of an evolving affection for the students, which grows with his time on campus. While he notes in another letter to Lowell in December 1949 that, "It's pretty much unchanged here [in Greensboro]—but what with Peter's being back, our no longer noticing the dull features, and making lots of money, it's quite pleasant" (*Letters* 235), he also notes upon his return to the college in 1953, after a two-year absence, "Gee, I'm glad to be back here. This college is like Sleeping Beauty" (387). In this characterization, Jarrell continues to paint a "pastoral" and even fantastic picture of the college—and one wonders if this was meant to cloud his occasional dissatisfaction with the students and faculty. In his second and third (and final) stints at the Woman's College, Jarrell indeed seems more settled and less critical of the students and campus overall. He notes in September 1954 that, "We have a big house we're crazy about; we've never been so well settled in our lives. . . . My life is so happy and blissful" (402).

But Mary Jarrell also notes that in 1954–55, Jarrell was a key player in resolving the "wars" between factions created over the general education reform proposal. Instead of characterizing the proposal as Graham's singular vision, Mary Jarrell argues,

> After making an inspection of General Education in California, Friedlander had enlisted a group of younger faculty members and the susceptible chancellor, Eddie Graham, to instigate a General Education takeover at Woman's College, at the expense of funds and faculty in art, music, and the humanities. "How can Marc fall for that?" Jarrell said; but Friedlander did, at the cost of his friends—Hooke in French, Frank Laine in classics, Jarrell in English, and others. Friedlander and his young allies were in active combat with Hooke and the curriculum committee. Jarrell sided with Hooke, but he was preoccupied with his *Selected Poems* and did not involve himself in the controversy at that time. (402–3)

Yet just a few pages later in the *Letters,* Mary Jarrell provides an extensive follow-up to the general education saga, as she describes, with some salacious details,

> The power struggle between the administration and the curriculum committee had become a nightmare. The campus was split in two, friend was pitted against friend, and both sides frantically recruited from the uncommitted while the committed frantically scuttled to avoid them (only the librarian maintained his neutrality). Week after week, the fat faculty got fatter, the thin got thinner, and stress-related ills swept the ranks. Hoping to halt this, Gordon Gray, former Secretary of the Army and now president of

the consolidated university, called a meeting . . . he advised any and all who were not happy with current administrative policies that they were "free to go elsewhere." . . . Outraged by what they called this "slap on the wrist," malcontents from the psychology, philosophy, music, history, and English departments chose Jarrell for their spokesman, knowing he would not be intimidated by institutional authorities. (405)

Mary Jarrell notes that when all was said and done, following a hearing in which Jarrell "attacked Friedlander and Graham with all the logic, ridicule, and brilliance for which he was known," Jarrell never again spoke to either of these men (406).

What rings curious about this account is its complete absence of supporting, or related, documentation in the larger university archives. Jarrell is certainly never characterized, in any of the general education documents, as a hero, or leader of the counterculture on campus, though he clearly did author some of the documents related to the initiative, as discussed in the previous chapter. Further, the fact that Jarrell was, by his own admission, not particularly invested in university politics makes this accounting seem uncharacteristic of his typical campus behavior, especially in his earlier years at the institution. But Mary Jarrell's assertion that given Randall's status, he need not worry about institutional authorities—that his job, implicitly, was not only safe, but also quite critical to the success of the English department and the college as a whole—does seem quite believable. Thus, the curious position of the creative writing faculty member as innately powerful leads to a surprising—if, in fact, true—turn of events for larger discussions of writing and general education on the Woman's College campus, as Graham's later resignation and the failure of the general education proposal are both tied intimately to Randall Jarrell, in Mary's characterizations (408).

From Jarrell's personal writings and Mary Jarrell's editorial comments on these writings, as well as Watson's recollections, the portrait of Jarrell as restless, introverted, and conflicted regarding teaching (versus) writing emerges. We cannot know these kind of intimate details about May Bush; because she was not a famous writer, or public figure, no biography of her life, nor letters to her colleagues or friends, has been published. Such is often the conscripted fate of the WPA in the earlier twentieth century. But seeing Jarrell as a markedly contrasting figure against Bush's more prototypical self—the selfless and dedicated faculty member who is teacher and community member first, scholar and writer later (or, not at all)—helps one to better conceptualize the human dimensions of writing and literacy at the Woman's College postwar. Given the college's already important emphasis on writing and the arts, and Jarrell's willingness to be wooed—indeed, his enthusiasm for it, both financially and socially speaking—this image of writing as *creative* and *artistic* is an easy postwar sell.

This portrait of Jarrell also helps to explain his frequent, short-term faculty visits to other campuses, emerging from his status as a successful poet. Jarrell enjoyed semester and year-long positions at several other colleges, and upon his return from each, enjoyed either a bump in pay or some other perk (such as guaranteed employment for his spouse, or promotion to full professor) designed to keep him in good stead at the college, as discussed above. The starting salary for Jarrell at the Woman's College, as noted by the then department chair, Leonard Hurley, was at the top of the associate professor scale: $3,600. Still, Jarrell was apparently wondering, even at this early point, about future salary increases and promotion in rank, as articulated in Hurley's letter, addressed progressively to both "Mr. and Mrs. Jarrell." This letter also evidences Hurley's explicit promise to make money not an object in future negotiations with Jarrell:

> You will note that those who fixed the salary for the newly created position which we have offered Mr. Jarrell fixed the salary at the top of the bracket for Associate Professors according to the old [contract]. . . . it is pretty well fixed for next year. . . . Hence I have attempted to see to it that the figure for Mrs. Jarrell's salary is near the top [$2,400] . . . so as to even this up as much as possible. I cannot make definite commitments for the future; all that I can say is that we are most eager to build up our writing group within the department and that *I will do all within my power toward this end.* (Hurley, letter to Randall and Mackie Jarrell, Apr. 18, 1947; emphasis added)

If archival evidence is at all reliable, Hurley made good on his promise to do "all in his power" to keep Jarrell, and creative writing, first and foremost in the English department through the 1950s, and in the face of many other competing offers that promised to both lure away Jarrell and, by extension, jeopardize the future of creative writing at the Woman's College. The last archived offer of these was from Smith College, who had asked Jarrell to be their writer-in-residence for the fall semester of 1966. Mary Jarrell, his second wife, corresponded with Thomas Mendenhall in May 1965 and confirmed Jarrell's interest in the position—as noted in a return letter that same month from Mendenhall that promises "very flexible kinds of arrangements" that would allow both the Jarrells to live and work at Smith during this semester of residency (Mendenhall, letter to

Mary Jarrell, May 15, 1965). Unfortunately, Jarrell died before he could take this position.

As feverish as Hurley had advocated for Bush's pay raises, his tone is clearly more laced with desperation in his pleas for Jarrell's financial standing in the college. He even is willing to argue for a top-flight pay scale for Jarrell's wife, who seemingly brought nothing more specific or special to the department than any other contingent faculty member in writing, save her status as the spouse of a coveted writer. The archives reveal that Hurley made good on his promise to "do all within [his] power," thereby safeguarding, in the department's view, the future of creative writing at the Woman's College. In the years between his 1947 appointment and his untimely 1965 death, Jarrell was wooed from the outside with great rigor, and the English department at the Woman's College struck back repeatedly, at the expense of other personnel. One such strike from Hurley to Dean Walter B. Jackson came on May 10, 1949, as part of a dual-request memo for salary increases for both Peter Taylor and Jarrell. Hurley notes that, "If $4200.00 could be provided for Mr. Peter Taylor, we could bring him back" next year, and that "Mr. Taylor was receiving $3500.00. . . . A 15% increase on this would bring the sum to $4025.00. An additional sum of only $175.00 would provide the necessary $4200.00." It is notable that the salary increase is construed as somewhat of a bargain, and granted; similar "bargain" requests for Bush during this same era were repeatedly denied.

Despite these pleas for pay raises—which were granted, by all accounts—Jarrell still secured a two-year leave from fall 1951 to spring 1953, teaching first for one year at Princeton University, and then at the University of Illinois. But the most striking example of sheer desperation on the part of the English department regarding Jarrell's employment comes in a handwritten letter from Leonard Hurley to Chancellor Gordon Blackwell on January 25, 1958—addressed to Blackwell's vacation home in Ithaca, New York, where he was staying during a brief holiday from campus. The letter, which details Jarrell's offer of continuing employment from Kenyon College, where he was a visiting writer, exemplifies the truly frantic feelings of Hurley and the department toward Jarrell's always-imminent departure from the Woman's College, and the subsequent demise of the creative writing program.

After spending about one and one-half pages rather nervously explaining the timeline of Jarrell's receipt of the offer, his phone call to Hurley, his subsequent call to Dean Mossman, and the impending proposed meeting of all of these individuals together on January 29, Hurley explains the terms of the Kenyon offer, highlighting therein the financial, material, and other factors leveraging the situation. To illustrate, I quote here from the letter, at length:

> When Randall arrived at Kenyon a few days ago, he was told by [John Crowe] that they wanted to offer [the editorship of the *Kenyon Review*]. The salary stated was $10,000—but I believe John Crowe told Randall that they might go slightly higher. He was to teach one class, to work with the young writers, and to edit the *Review*. Mr. Jarrell . . . felt that he must give the offer very serious consideration, but is apparently not too eager to accept it. He spoke of how much he liked his work and his associations here in Greensboro. . . . I gather the idea, too, that he feels that desirable as it would seem in many ways to be at the head of the influential *Kenyon Review,* [but] the editorial work involved . . . would leave him less free for his own writing than the work here has done. . . . I would like to emphasize: I think Randall Jarrell is in all probability the person of greatest national reputation and distinction in our teaching faculty, and one imminently suited to working in our faculty. He very much likes teaching young women, and his students like him. . . . We should not lose Jarrell if any means can be found by which he can be kept here as a center around which we can rebuild our writing program.

As evidenced in Hurley's letter, Jarrell was explicitly the present and future of the English department of the Woman's College—and, implicitly, the future of the college *itself.* Hurley draws a portrait of a nearly beatific writer and man who resists uprooting himself and his family, but is torn by the professional opportunities. In today's university, of course, careers are made and broken over competing offers of employment. But Hurley makes it completely clear that Jarrell's future is not simply his own: his national reputation is to the benefit of the department, and is the cornerstone of the creative writing program itself. He *must not* leave. The Woman's College—somewhat marginalized by the larger state system, hamstrung by its otherwise high teaching load, and desirous of a better station in (national) university life, especially if it is to remain a women's-only institution—*must not* lose its standing as a center for creative writing. Ultimately, Hurley's harried and frantic appeal was successful; Jarrell remained at the Woman's College, with a substantial bump in pay.

In retrospect, what was a coup for the Woman's College and for Jarrell personally was the beginning of a successful narrative of creative writing in the university that exists to this day, and a local example of the pressing cultural forces that pushed composition and rhetoric out of the leadership role in college-level writing postwar, and for arguably the remaining years of the twentieth century. This contrasts with our current conceptions, particularly in rhetoric and composition circles, of creative writing as a symbiotic field with expository writing and rhetoric, changing in harmony with one another and breeding similar pedagogies—such as the workshop model and the notion of peer review (at the Woman's College also shown to be in place in first-year writing well before creative writing held dominance over the English department). This portrait of Bush and Jarrell also contradicts the notion that the feminization of composition, in Miller and Holbrook's terms, and even in portraits drawn by Crowley, rose in isolation from other fields of writing. Examining the Woman's College as, ironically, a site of writing wherein one would expect the *most* solidarity among and support for women's faculty in rhetoric and composition studies but where there existed far less support than was desirable, allows for a locally based rereading of one of the other master narratives of composition, namely that which sees creative writing as a discipline copacetic with composition, and women's labor struggles as independent of competing writing pedagogy resources within English departments.

May Bush's story—of a local, shoulder-to-the-wheel nobody who would never aspire, or be selected, to appear in a large-scale history of composition—might be viewed as an isolated narrative in history, neither representative of the trajectory of women's labor in composition studies nor the cultural valuation of creative writing over composition. This is an easy argument to make, since at the moment, no other WPA narratives or histories that I have found contextualize this work in terms of the rise of creative writing in the academy, particularly at public women's colleges where such rises were less avidly documented, and where public support for such programs was highly dependent upon local community values and the loyalty of alumnae. Yet such unearthing of May Bush's story is exactly the reason for more local archival research of the kind undertaken in this book. In delving into the histories of our home institutions, especially those positioned lower in the general academic hierarchy, we can further interrogate the "academic" versus "artistic" labors of fields of writing that put them historically in competition with one another. The Woman's College cannot stand for *all* instantiations of midcentury writing program administration (composition or creative writing). But it can illustrate the consequences that one extremely prominent creative writing faculty member had, without likely even knowing it, on an arguably "average" WPA and her career trajectory, even in a department generally supportive of and beholden to the endeavor of first-year composition.

We are, in fact, still more likely in our field histories to catalogue individual stories of success than of failure—wherein "individual" may be defined as a person or an institution. Uncovering Linde's "noisy silences" in local histories of women's colleges complicates, but also enriches, how we see both the surface and the undercurrent of composition studies in the twentieth century. A brief look at the demise of the mission of the institution, vis-à-vis its forced conversion to a coeducational university in 1964, in my next and final chapter reveals that while creative writing promised to bring the Woman's College to the national forefront in English studies—and in fact, did raise its profile in creative writing, extant to this day—the impetus to make young women into creative writers, which took center stage over the allied impulse to make said women into *rhetorically savvy* writers of prose and criticism, was not enough to be sustained as a single-sex educational enterprise into the 1970s. If anything, the Woman's College stands as a contradictory model of literacy education for women, particularly in the creative arts. I argue for the value of articulating field counternarratives such as those of the Woman's College—even if those stories leave us with lingering questions as much as, or more than, satisfying historiographic answers.

5

What's in a Name?

Women's Writing Histories and Archival
Research in Composition Studies

Historians of rhetoric and composition are . . . more sensitive than are many
professional historians to the fact that histories are constructed narratives,
that there exists no objective means of finding, interpreting, or assembling
historical data which could guarantee the truth of the resulting narrative.

Sharon Crowley, "Octalog"

IN THE PRECEDING chapters, I have attempted to paint an archives-based
portrait of the postwar Woman's College of the University of North Carolina by analyzing how its progressive writing pedagogies worked with,
and against, its conservative social structure; how its valuation of student
expository and creative writing extended to venues outside the classroom,
and to the lifelong habits of some of its alumnae; and how its steadfast embrace of local curricular traditions held strong in the face of sweeping national education reforms that assumed the value of a common curriculum
for the greater pedagogical good. I have also examined the people behind
these literacy-based happenings at the Woman's College, specifically the
students who helped to create and sustain the first-year magazine, and
the faculty whose careers personified the intellectual and material struggles between creative writing and composition in the Woman's College
English department. In bringing forward these multifaceted narratives
of the Woman's College's postwar English department, I have made the
argument that investigating the literacy practices of an overlooked insti-

tutional type such as the Woman's College—a normal school turned small public women's-only college—is a valuable way to expand and even revise the master narratives of composition studies that have been written, read, and subsequently employed in graduate classrooms and other settings of our field for the past thirty years.

"Octalog: The Politics of Historiography," presented at the CCCC in 1988 and published in *Rhetoric Review* that same year (Murphy et al.), posits the historian as an ethical vehicle—or ideally so—defined by powers of interpretation, narrative abilities, and responsibilities divided between finding the "truth" and finding the "answer"—which may or may not be, to the recipient/reader, the best or most attractive version of historical reality.

Nan Johnson's conception of archival work is distinctly archeological in nature: "I proceed on the assumption that historical research and writing are archaeological *and* rhetorical activities. As an historian, I am responsible both to the claims of historical evidence *and* to the burden of proclaiming my enterprise as an attempt to tell 'true stories'" (Murphy et al. 8). James Berlin, however, underwrites "a version of the normal" and the "proper arrangement" of delineated groups: "The difficulty for the historian is that, even when evidence is available and extensive, the writing of history is itself a rhetorical act. The historian is herself underwriting a version of the normal, of the proper arrangement of classes, races, and genders. History does not write itself, having in itself no inherent pattern of development. Historians cannot escape this play of power, inherent in all signifying practices" (11).

Berlin's observation poses a problem for me, in practical application. If archival historians are archeologists, how much can they be expected to "underwrite" this historical normal when the prevailing archeological evidence privileges anything but the mainstream, or master narrative? What are the responsibilities of the archeologist to call attention to the gaps and even misdeeds that question a history of the "normal" or the proper ordering of events and people? Where and when do Johnson's "true stories" and Berlin's "power play" collide, and with what social and material consequences for those to whom history is narrated, or narrated *about*? Certainly these debates over the historian's representative responsibility were also emergent long before this 1988 dialogue, and in academic venues outside of composition and rhetoric. But these questions and debates comprise an unavoidable chorus of voices behind my reading and interpretation of the highly contradictory archival materials that make up the (or a) history of literacy instruction at the Woman's College postwar. They accentuate both its larger value to the field of composition studies research and its own inner contradictions that might compel some to give it less status in that field research.

My case study of the Woman's College makes clear, for example, that the social and cultural attitudes of this college sometimes worked in direct opposition to the literacy goals presented, and ultimately enacted, in the writing classrooms. It also exposes the contradiction that existed between the progressive benefits offered to the women students—including a campus that treated them as intellectual equals to men and celebrated rather than discouraged their academic interests as separate from men's in a variety of ways—and the sometimes stifling treatment of the women faculty and administrators concerning tenure, promotion, and departmental leadership expectations and associated benefits. Additionally, my research lays bare the material contradictions at play in the rise of creative writing over composition in the college's English department, those that brought fame and (arguably, faculty) fortune to the college, but that also failed to save it from a generally hostile takeover by the North Carolina university system in 1964. Each of these contradictions is important to recognize if we are to begin widespread investigations into local narratives of composition studies' history. Glossing the sometimes messy aspects of writing instruction, and English department politics thereof, keeps us from recognizing when these contradictions reemerge in our own programs and departments, and make us (wrongly) believe that history is simple, whereas the present is complicated. As Robert Connors remarks, also in the "Octalog," "Meaningful historical writing must teach us what people in the past have wanted from literacy so that we may come to understand what *we* want" (Murphy et al. 7). Included in this understanding is knowing what we want to avoid, in our pedagogies and other departmental practices, as well as what we want to replicate.

Any reading of the archives is ultimately, in these respects, an act of narrative privileging—to recall Charlotte Linde's assertion in the introduction to this book—as well as a weighty act of truth-telling, insofar as one can be "truthful" to a community of which he or she was never a part. With these considerations, I offer the case of the Woman's College as a starting point for how we might augment, advance, or otherwise rearticulate the trajectory of our collective and disparate composing histories in the twentieth and twenty-first centuries. To end my study in the spirit of narrative closure, therefore, I examine in this final chapter archival documents related to the end of the Woman's College as a single-sex institution, with particular attention to the ways in which its former and current stakeholders in 1962–63 used the institution's rich history of educating women to argue against its merge with the larger North Carolina state system. The renaming affected more than the title of the institution; it deeply affected the core identity of the Woman's College community.

This end of the Woman's College is an important, if obvious, closing issue for this book, as the loss of the college's identity—what made it a "special" institution among so many others postwar, including those whose stories are more typically told in composition studies' history—even more strongly makes the argument for recovering heretofore forgotten voices and practices in our field histories, and using this data to better understand what should, and must, continue in order to make individual sites of composing, and composition instruction, equally "special" to students and faculty today. As we face increasing pressure to elide our traditions of college writing through various means—dual-credit, exam equivalencies, and mass-produced online for-profit education—we need to better document and promote what makes composition studies a *local* and *unique* endeavor among other postsecondary subjects. We must, in the spirit of current projects such as the NCTE-sponsored National Gallery of Writing, pay homage not only to our current students and faculty, and their writing, but also to the students and faculty who came before them—and who struggled to remain intellectually and materially independent of sweeping national trends that would elide local values, such as did the populace of the Woman's College. I hope to reflect on how local case studies should be used as a starting point for recovering lost composition histories. This may benefit other writing program administrators seeking to uncover their own institutional histories, and add to our aggregate knowledge base of composing practices (both expository and creative) in the United States, spotlighting the demise of the Woman's College as one cautionary historical tale, among many.

"An Exercise in Semantics": The Fight to Save Women's-Only Education

Throughout chapter 4, I argued that the Woman's College prioritized the subject area of creative writing in its faculty retention, promotion, and payroll decisions, as represented chiefly through the figure of Randall Jarrell. I contended that the English department viewed its embrace of creative writing as being a marker of excellence and uniqueness among the other branches of the University of North Carolina state system. It saw the artistic aims and public appeal of creative writing, and creative *writers* as faculty, as well aligned with the larger aims of the department and college to produce well-rounded, intelligent women who were broadly educated in the merits of the fine arts, in addition to other more vocational disciplines and subjects. The visibility of first-year composition and rhetoric and those directing the course (for these postwar years, May Bush) was minimized in the fervor surrounding the primacy of creative writing as *the* profile of writing instruction embraced by the department, and more importantly, the college, within the context of a larger focus on the fine arts. As a public women's institution facing possible extinction at the end of the 1950s, the Woman's College clung tightly to its reputation as a center for creative writing, as a permanent home for Randall Jarrell and the colleagues he had brought in to join him in the program, and as a foothold for premier public women's literacy education.

Yet as fiercely well planned and wise as this endeavor may have been politically, resulting in a full complement of creative writing courses at the undergraduate and graduate levels and successful published writers on faculty to guide students and oversee an MFA program, the college only partly succeeded in its dual desire to be preeminent in writing *and* in women's-only education. While the college today, as the University of North Carolina–Greensboro, is still home to a leading MFA program in creative writing and still is considered a strong and vital location for writing instruction and the arts within North Carolina and the southern United States (and, perhaps ironically, houses a thriving doctoral program in rhetoric and composition, in which I teach), it is no longer a women's college. Like many other single-sex public institutions originally chartered as normal schools, the Woman's College met its demise at the end of the postwar era, only to rise again in renewed form as a coeducational, research-intensive university.

What are the root questions that emerge from a consideration of this demise of the Woman's College, which was only one in a litany of similar specialized institutions that were fated to be absorbed by larger university systems throughout the country? What can we now say about the success of writing instruction as an historical enterprise—including the uncomfortable relations of creative writing and composition in many English departments—in light of its inability to "save" a special college such as the Woman's College? Or should we alternatively see the creative writing program at the Woman's College as a *savior* of the institution, given that its continuation into the coeducational University of North Carolina–Greensboro only cemented its national reputation for writing and the arts and elevated the college to a "known" quantity in literacy education? Or is it better still to see creative writing in this case as a Goliath, stomping across composition and its champions, including May Bush, in order to get in the national spotlight, only to then be woeful of receiving what it had wished for? What, indeed, does it mean to see such a dedicated plan for writing and the arts for women students collapse into the background of yet another large, generic university? And what does this collapse mean, further, for the history of composition as an interwoven history of people and places, often described in sweeping, unifying, and successful—rather than discordant, divisive, and failed—terms?

Despite the rise to prominence accomplished by retaining Randall Jarrell as the core of the creative writing program at the Woman's College, its "Sleeping Beauty" social and material conditions were not destined to continue past the close of the postwar era. The monetary signs driving college sustainability—in the form of enrollment figures—had foretold the eventual demise of the college as a single-sex institution for several years prior and illustrated a fluctuating optimism toward how many women students in North Carolina (and elsewhere) would continue to value and choose a public, sex-segregated education. The Woman's College was one of a dying group of institutions nationwide that were no longer seen as financially or practically appealing to the expanding postwar workforce—or so was the rationale for the rise of the comprehensive university from the ashes of the former and current normal schools in existence at the start of the 1960s.

As Norward J. Brooks notes in a 1980 report on the "Future of Comprehensive Colleges and Universities," published by the National Institute of Education, these institutions, nearly all former normal schools, began to dot the national landscape in the 1960s as a result of their "credibility as training institutions for teachers and many other skilled occupations in our economy. Resources were plentiful, and staff were added in unprecedented numbers to build new programs or improve existing ones. . . . faculty and administrators came to believe that all emerging needs could be met by constantly expanding financial resources" (5). This view of "plentiful" resources certainly pervades the rhetoric of the University of North Carolina system merger, in which the Woman's College would become a branch campus at Greensboro, and would serve a regional co-educational populace, just as a new proposed campus at Charlotte would. William Friday, chancellor of the University of North Carolina system, wrote to Thomas Pearsall[1] in October 1962: "we should proceed with the proposed statutory definition of the University, our judgment being that the State can really have but one state university, with multiple campuses. . . . that in the foreseeable future we should accelerate graduate work in the humanities and social sciences at the Greensboro campus . . . [and] that we should have a common undergraduate program in the arts and sciences open to both men and women on all three campuses" (letter, Oct. 9, 1962). Friday's letter is notable for its adherence to the idea of one university with multiple campuses that would characterize the bulk of comprehensive universities from the 1960s forward, while maintaining the Greensboro campus's existing "special" identity as a liberal arts outpost. The classic definition of the comprehensive university, as described by Brooks, above, does not particularly fit this model. But Friday articulates this as a kind of compromise between what the Woman's College *was* and what it must *become*.

Enrollments throughout the 1950s were just barely steady, perhaps alarmingly so, given all the work the English department and the college had put into building a strong program in writing and the arts. A *Greensboro Daily News* piece dated October 16, 1957, notes that enrollment at the Woman's College had dipped from 2,306 students in 1956 to 2,276 students in 1957. Also in October 1957, the registrar's office charted the number of students in the freshmen–senior classes, and showed that while 535 freshmen were enrolled, there were only 344 seniors—evidencing a retention problem between the lower and upper classes of undergraduates. In another document from the registrar's office, dated December 1960, longer term enrollment projections for the Woman's College were cautiously positive, but not strikingly so: in 1959–60 there were 2,118 students enrolled; in 1964–65, the projected enrollment total was 2,338, for an approximate 10 percent expected growth over five years, which would only just meet the enrollment figures of 1956—for little ground gained in nearly a decade. These 1960 projections, based on an assumption of a steady freshman enrollment with no significant losses from year to year, were far under earlier projections, calculated in December 1957 for the North Carolina system as a whole, which showed that of the 11,310 students expected to be enrolled systemwide, a full 3,387 of these would be at the Woman's College. Clearly, the math was internally contradictory, but in any case did not add up to a boom in enrollment for the college, despite its assertions that single-sex education was still valuable and desirable in North Carolina ("Woman's College Budget," Dec. 1960).

These enrollment figures were a symptom of problems facing the great number of women's-only colleges that shut their doors in one manner or another starting in the late 1950s. The report "Women's Colleges in the United States," sponsored by the National Women's College Coalition, notes many women's colleges became coeducational or merged with all-male or coeducational institutions, while others closed based on falling enrollments and their general inability to compete with the larger (growing) college market. As a result, "the number of women's colleges shrank from over 200 in 1960 to 83 in 1993" (Harwarth, Maline, and DeBra 1–2). This was a significant decline, considering the steady number of women's colleges at both the two- and four-year levels in the United States. Again according to the coalition, "from the late 1800s to the early 1960s, there were an estimated 270 women's colleges in 1935, 276 in 1945, 248 in 1955, and 252 in 1960" (9). The coalition report adds, "One historian of women's colleges estimates that 81 women's colleges closed their doors between 1960 and 1986" (qtd. in Harwarth, Maline, and DeBra 27). Others, including elite private colleges Goucher (Maryland) and Connecticut College, became coeducational.

Today, the vast majority of women's colleges are private, with some having religious affiliations; the only three women's public institutions still operational in 2011 are Mississippi College for Women, Douglass College of Rutgers University, and Texas Women's University, all of which admit some male students to particular programs. The paradox facing these publicly supported women's colleges is exemplified in the 1982 lawsuit brought against the Mississippi University for Women, in which a male applicant sued for admission to the nursing program; the applicant's request was granted, due to the court's finding that denying this man admission "not only violated the Equal Protection Clause of the Fourteenth Amendment, but also was not beneficial to women because this policy furthered the image of nursing as 'women's work'" (Harwarth, Maline, and DeBra 2).

It is entirely possible that had the Woman's College of North Carolina remained single-sex in enrollment, a similar lawsuit may have arisen—particularly given its prominent creative writing program—and the student public's desire to work closely with writers such as Jarrell. This public desire may be why in 1957 the college reported an enrollment of ten male graduate students within the fairly tiny number of total enrolled graduate students on campus (sixty); in the area of graduate education, the college was willing to admit some "day" students (nonresidential), but was unwilling to open up the gates entirely to male applicants. Yet, even as late as 1967 and 1968, one can skim UNCG yearbooks and find just a handful of male students—on average, five to ten—in each class of several hundred women. This was a longstanding culture that was difficult to overturn even for several years after the coeducational merger took place.

But the Woman's College was not alone in its problems. According to a memo from the Office of Admissions director Sayde Dunn to Chancellor Singletary, dated October 18, 1962, North Carolina as a whole was experiencing a drop in first-year enrollments. Dunn notes that State College in Raleigh experienced a total drop of 1,000 applications that current fall term alone, and Chapel Hill, 223 fewer first-year applications. Duke, comparatively, was doing about as badly, with 1,000 fewer applications—400 of those lost being women applicants, in comparison to the previous year. The Woman's College lost only 108 first-year applications over the previous year's class, and actually *gained* transfer applications—a rise of 43.2 percent over 1961. Additionally, Dunn points out that "we had *better* applicants than in the previous years. I am not sure what accounts for this . . . [perhaps] more realistic counseling is going on . . . [to] discourage the applications of less qualified students who normally would have applied." Dunn also asserts that while the quality of applicants went up, the admission standards held firm.

So, as in other narratives describing the history of the Woman's College postwar, the demise of it as an all-women's institution also exposes troubling contradictions. Women's colleges around the country were beginning to suffer, but the Woman's College of North Carolina appeared to be holding its own, particularly in the context of statewide enrollments. Seeing such a surge in *transfer* admissions might also lead one to conclude that students were hearing about the college some time after they had completed coursework elsewhere—whether it was at coed or single-sex colleges, the data do not reveal. It seems that on this ripple-effect reputation alone the college could have made a strong case for continuation, especially as a cost-saving alternative to those "missing" four hundred women students who did not apply to Duke in the fall of 1962. But in fall 1964, due to a variety of political and legislative pressures, and despite a veritable storm of protests from alumnae, current students, and faculty, the Woman's College, upon orders of system chancellor William Friday, became the University of North Carolina–Greensboro.

In a written address to students, faculty, and alumni on November 23, 1962, John T. Caldwell, chancellor of North Carolina State University, put his own administrative perspective on the name change for the three individual campuses:

> The proposal to make the Woman's College coeducational requires a change
> in its name. The proposal to extend the university role to some additional
> campuses requires the finding of a name. The emerging pattern, therefore,
> inevitably suggests a different nomenclature from the earlier one for *all* the
> campuses. It is now necessary to seize upon a name for the State's University
> including its components which will fully represent its nature and its role.
> . . . Much is at stake for North Carolina; much is at stake for this college. It
> is heart-warming that the members of this great and loyal family of "State"
> should not wish suddenly to lose the name which has identified the object
> of its affections and the source of its pride. . . . Feelings about these mat-
> ters cannot be overcome by persuasion alone or in a short time. But I feel
> it a duty to appeal to you members of this wonderful family to grasp the
> full meaning of the State's whole university to its people and the positive

advantages to this College of our moving up with a giant step into a new era of service and recognition.

Caldwell's rhetoric was laced with optimism; the merger was an opportunity, not a burden, for State's continuing status as an institution. But if North Carolina State University was at all excited at the prospect of merging formally with Chapel Hill, and in the process gaining a higher—and research-based—university status while "finding" a name, the feelings at the Woman's College, whose identity would be lost rather than found, were far more troubled. A working document titled "Miscellaneous Thoughts re Coeducation at Woman's College" and authored by Otis Singletary, chancellor of the Woman's College from 1961 to 1967, for the Pearsall Committee, outlines several facts in evidence just prior to the establishment of the college as the University of North Carolina–Greensboro, and his own views, in contrast to those of Caldwell. While undated, this document is likely from mid-1962, near the beginning of Singletary's term as chancellor.

Through a litany of numbered items, Singletary identifies the issues, or "miscellaneous thoughts," pertaining to the impending coeducational shift, a shift he notes in personal terms: "I did not come here with any commitment to lead a movement for making W.C. a coeducational institution [and] I would be happy to continue things as they are, if this were possible. I do not believe this is possible because our traditional protective tariff is disintegrating before our eyes" (4). The "tariff" that Singletary invokes is regarding the agreement within the University of North Carolina system that "few women [are] admitted to State or Chapel Hill, therefore if they wanted to attend a branch of the state university they came to W.C." (1). Singletary surmises that "in the rest of [the] South, [there are] no first-rate state supported women's colleges. Reason: they never enjoyed this protective tariff, hence were unable to compete with coeducational institutions" (1).

Facing the fact that the tariff was about to dissolve—and thus women would be geographically and financially (insofar as this would open up their public college options) free to choose their college of attendance, Singletary asked himself, what will happen when the tariff is finally eroded? His answers were, "increasing admission of women at Chapel Hill . . . [and] State College" and "perhaps, creating a fourth branch of the University at Charlotte" (1). Since a large percentage of incoming first-year women had historically come from a suburb of Charlotte (Mecklenberg), as Singletary notes, this new, added campus would "directly affect our enrollment." In short, the Woman's College would no longer be special—by design, or by state or governmental default. Singletary ultimately proposed that if men needed to be admitted, they should be admitted as day students only, not as residential students. This would help to both preserve the campus culture and limit the number of men who would be interested in attending the college.[2] He also notes, with implied frustration, that the impending name change (to UNC-Greensboro)—which apparently was a proposed change regardless of whether the college became coeducational—only made sense "if men are going to be admitted. Otherwise, it becomes an exercise in semantics" (Singletary, "Miscellaneous Thoughts," 3).

But titles are critical to stakeholders in any organization, let alone academic communities who are already at the margins, and are far from an exercise in semantics on such critical occasions. Woman's College alumnae flooded the chancellor's office, and the offices of the board of trustees, with letters of protest over the move to admit men to the college.[3] Indeed, as archived in Otis Singletary's records on the coeducational merger, board of trustees member C. M. Vanstory Jr. wrote to the president of Citizens Bank and Trust in Andrews, North Carolina, on October 26, 1962, cautiously agreeing that the forthcoming merger and change in status for the Woman's College was sound, yet he was fearful of the community's reaction:

> Percy, as you well know I am not a fence-straddler and have an open mind as to Woman's College being made a coeducational institution, but I would like to hear some discussion or comments from the ladies or the alumnae. I honestly don't know how they would react but conceivably they could violently oppose such a move. If Woman's College is made coeducational would you advocate having an equal number of men and women or would it still be predominantly a woman's college? If it became predominantly a college for men where would the incoming crop of young women go? (Vanstory, letter to Ferebee, Oct. 26, 1962)

Vanstory's fears, to say nothing of the logical questions that drove them, proved to be quite accurate. Excerpts from four of the piles of alumnae and community letters archived in Singletary's records illustrate the ferocity with which Woman's College graduates and stakeholders defended the value and purpose of their alma mater, and the long-lasting value of the education they received in Greensboro. To put these letters in greater context, however, it is helpful to first examine a sample exchange between an alumna and then Woman's College president Julius Foust from the *first* name change for the college—back in 1919.

Apparently some students and alumnae vocally objected to the (not yet finalized) name change proposed in 1919, from the State Normal and Industrial College to the North Carolina College for Women. These women preferred instead the name "McIver College," in honor of the college's esteemed founder. These women collectively sought the opportunity to both pay homage to McIver and perhaps give the college a more lofty title that did not immediately communicate the generic rhetorical import of "state college," or that gave the impression of, perhaps, a small private college instead. In a February 5, 1919, letter to Julia Dameron, an alumna of the State Normal and Industrial College and member of the college's board of trustees, President Julius Foust notes that "some members of the board are in favor of McIver College and that other members, while not opposed to the name of McIver College, are equally decided in their views that the name should indicate that the college belongs to the state." Miss Dameron's letter to Foust had noted that, "As you know, most of the central and western states have universities, normal schools, and state colleges, [as do] a great many of the eastern and southern states. The result is that the words 'State College' connote vocational education. . . . Our liberal arts work is part of the college work that has suffered from the present name [of State Normal and Industrial College]" (Feb. 9, 1919). This exchange clearly illustrates the discordance between the college's label and its curricular content and scope, as well as the fears of state (and system) ownership of the college as it evolved in name and therefore public identity throughout the early twentieth century. It also reveals an awareness on the part of the college's alumnae that the selection of labels, and their underlying definitions, is critical for already marginalized groups within larger operational systems, including higher education.

Such fears about what a name truly signifies—in this case, a shift to vocational education and away from the liberal arts, which was the perspective that made the college unique among public women's institutions—was re-reflected, in no uncertain terms, when the college was about to go coeducational and become just another geographically designated branch campus of Chapel Hill some forty-five years later. A letter from Mattie Erma Edwards Parker, Woman's College class of 1925 (and thus, coincidentally, member of one of the first graduating classes under the North Carolina College for Women moniker) articulates her opposition to the proposed change to coeducational status in terms of the longstanding comparisons between the Woman's College and elite women's institutions of the Northeast. Parker notes that she attended UNC–Chapel Hill and Radcliffe college following her graduation from the Woman's College, and went on to teach at Vassar, North Carolina State, and Meredith College thereafter. One of Parker's most salient points about coeducational colleges is in her assertion that,

> Through these associations, I have learned that the educational opportunities afforded women at coeducational institutions are not equal to those afforded men at the same institutions, nor to those offered in colleges for women. One reason for this may derive from a fact which I discovered in teaching, namely, that the emphases and teaching methods effective with men students, who are chiefly motivated by professional goals, do not stimulate the minds of women students, whose interests are broader and less utilitarian than those of college men. At Carolina [Chapel Hill] and in Radcliffe-Harvard classes, instruction was directed to men, not women. This, I think, would be true in any coeducational institution. Admitting men to Woman's College would necessarily result in classes that were not designed to train women to think, but were designed instead to train men to earn a living. (Dec. 5, 1962)

Parker's letter reinforces some points made earlier in this book, noted by educational historians: that elite women's colleges such as Radcliffe—born of men's educational traditions—did not always speak to women students as well as public institutions created *for* women at their inception, such as the Woman's College. Further, Mrs. Parker's letter reiterates that the alliance between the larger aims of the Woman's College and those of special programs such as creative writing were strongly built, attending to the "broader and less utilitarian interests" that these students held. Creative writing may be many things, but utilitarian or "professional," in the sense invoked by Parker, it is not. Finally, Parker's letter reinforces the lineage often found in the Woman's College graduates—further education plus a career devoted, in some measure, to women's education, here illustrated by her teaching stints at Vassar and Meredith.

As noted elsewhere in her letter, to make the Woman's College coeducational would be to "deprive women students of most of their present opportunities for contact with able women teachers." Parker was of the mind of her Northeast elite counterparts, who saw women's colleges as a primary opportunity for young women to learn from their same-gender role models. While Parker's fear did not come to pass—UNC–Greensboro continued to hire and retain a good proportion of women faculty post-conversion to a coed school—her concerns are valid, especially given the research emphasis and associated increased need for prestige that would logically attract many ambitious male faculty previously not interested in teaching "girls," in the terms of the Radcliffe-Harvard divide of decades past. Parker represents, in these ways, a classic Woman's College alumna, the kind most angered by the proposed change to the college's mission and population.

Another letter from a woman with strong ties to the college—her mother was from the Normal School class of 1898, her daughter was a current student (in 1962) nearing graduation, and she herself graduated from the Woman's College in the 1940s—articulates similar objections to those above, responding to "rumors I've been hearing" of a future coeducational status change. Mrs. Mary Bailey Williams (Thomas H.) Davis notes that a friend's daughter in New Orleans had recently been told to "look for a college commensurate with her abilities, three having been recommended: first was Woman's College, and the second and third were 'name' colleges in the North" (letter, Nov. 12, 1962). She goes on to note that in the case of her own daughter, "scholarship help at our Church colleges" would have made private education as feasible as Woman's College, but "we wanted our daughter to have exactly what W.C. can offer." Mrs. Davis sums up what the "exceptionally fine Woman's College" can offer, if it were to remain a single-sex college: "1. Academic excellence second to none in the state. 2. Means of training women in leadership which can never be aspired to by a coeducational institution. 3. A tradition which schools everywhere could have reason to envy. . . . I would like to see the legislature give the financial and moral support to make it the strong Woman's College it can and should become." Davis's letter reinforces Parker's letter in its comparison of the Woman's College to "named" northeastern colleges and its elevation of the Woman's College to a status known by those far outside the Carolinas. It further brings up the notion of women's leadership—a point articulated by my interview subjects Jacqueline and Lucy, in chapter 2. Davis notes the danger of reducing women's confidence in academic excellence and curricular and extracurricular leadership within coeducational settings, and in doing so articulates a real rationale for some of the student enrollment at the Woman's College. Where else in the state could one find a reasonably priced public institution that not only did not enroll men, but did not require that women compete with men for intellectual and social leadership roles? Certainly this level of engagement was something noted by Randall Jarrell in his own teaching of poetry to young women students, as well as a factor in the development of so many outlets for literary and expository writing throughout the college—including the *Yearling* but also *Coraddi,* and earlier versions of both of these publications. Such opportunities for engagement that thrived without the presence of dominant male classmates were also remembered fondly by my interview subjects Jacqueline and Lucy.

A third representative letter from Mrs. J. B. (Elizabeth Hinton) Kittrell—notably a member of the board of trustees for the state system—voices yet additional and different concerns, and does so in direct correspondence with William Friday, UNC system chancellor—or "Bill," as she calls him. Kittrell is a persuasive rhetor of considerable situated ethos, noting in her letter's opening that, "You know in our past nine years of association on the Board of Trustees I have always backed you, Gordon Gray, and Dr. Purks one hundred percent in your forthright plans for the University, and I regret now that on this present Woman's College issue I feel differently." Kittrell continues:

> I have heard three full presentations of the present plans for the University.
> I have read every report and every newspaper article and editorial in "The
> Greensboro Daily News" and "The News and Observer" and our local paper.
> I have completely analyzed my feelings of loyalty and sentiment and have re-
> moved them as a cause for my two conclusive reasons for wanting Woman's
> College to continue as a *University* for *Women*. You can be assured that I
> feel that I am a "lone voice crying in the wilderness," but I would be less a
> woman if I did not speak for the present and future womanhood in North
> Carolina. What Woman's College has to offer is the kind of education and
> training in leadership and homemaking that a large majority of the young
> girls I talk to want—even in this modern year of 1962. It is what 90% of the
> enrolled students at Woman's College want. It is what the largest majority of
> alumnae want. (letter, Nov. 21, 1962; emphasis in original)

Kittrell articulates a perhaps unprogressive reasoning for keeping the college single-sex in nature: a need for training in leadership, but also "homemaking." An uncomfortable reality could have been the vision of Kittrell as the public face of the college—despite its great strides in areas such as literacy education and leadership, many community members, including the board, may have seen the college as something a step removed from a finishing school, or a training site for wholly domestic careers. Yet Kittrell's eloquent stance as an otherwise avid reader and follower of local political events—including her own membership on the board—communicates the other side of the Woman's College, wherein women were, in fact, trained to be independent thinkers and intelligent citizens in the public sphere rather than simply writers of "good form" or generic society correspondence.

Kittrell ultimately fears that the Woman's College will acquire "fraternities and sororities [and that] a winning football team will be demanded by Greensboro citizens." But she also recognizes that "few can go to Vassar

[and] Duke, Salem, Meredith, St. Mary's, and Queens can take care of very few," noting again the college's allegiance with both northern and southern elite private institutions serving women, including those with segregated status (Duke). In short, Kittrell perfectly articulates the paradox present at Woman's College, as discussed previously in this book: a split-at-the-root mission to both educate and empower (though without using that word) women to be leaders, intellectuals, and—in the case of the English department—writers, alongside a historical mission to provide proper social training for young ladies within the confines of the socially appropriate South, and outside the negative influences of, in Kittrell's estimation, the Greek tradition, or intercollegiate men's athletics.[4]

Finally, a handwritten letter from Gladys Benbow repeats some of the other arguments above—regarding quality (comparing the Woman's College to "Smith, Vassar, and Wellesley") and social mores ("weekends can be kept for dating at a girls' school"). But Benbow also makes a financial and enrollment-based argument and is unabashedly direct in doing so: "In a single dormitory at Woman's College this year there are girls from fifteen different states. These girls are coming to Woman's College because it is a *woman's college.* Change that and, in my humble opinion, your out-of-state enrollments will drop tremendously thus lowering the vitality and variety of your student body. Many Northern girls at the WC are already saying that if it is made coeducational they will not come back. . . . Let's keep Woman's College as it is!" (letter, Nov. 26, 1962 letter; emphasis in original). Benbow closes her letter with an effective appeal to tradition, noting, "Is there no respect for tradition in North Carolina? Change for the sake of change isn't always progress—certainly not in this case."

Benbow raises a valid point that cuts at the very core of the college's desired reputation: for the institution to be truly revered beyond the Carolinas, or even the South, it relied upon a small but steady influx of northern girls among its ranks. Benbow realizes this, and appeals to the chancellor's own likely desire for the Woman's College to continue to prosper at the national level, in a way that no other public women's institution could. She locates this rationale in tradition; her "if it ain't broke, don't fix it" attitude is thereby compelling. There are no supporting pieces of evidence in the archives that would indicate the college was in *significant* financial trouble, and as the admissions officer noted, the *quality* of its enrollees was appropriately consistent, and high-level. So, Benbow—and these other women—ask, in modern colloquial terms, what gives?

These collective objections are evidence of not only a strong (and extremely eloquent) alumnae united against the desecration of their image and memories of the college, but also a deeper philosophical stance against the power of naming—and the seemingly arbitrary reconstitution of an institution that, in their eyes and the eyes of any and all represented in the university archives, did no academic or community wrong. To lose the status of a single-sex public college was one (terrible) thing; to also lose the name that had been associated with the college for so many successful and legacy-building years was yet another. Of course, Singletary is right in his observation that the title meant nothing once the merger to coeducation was complete, and vice versa. But the fierce hold that these women want over what they were *called,* which means everything in terms of how they were collectively *regarded,* is an important footnote to women's rhetorical histories. They were less invested, in practical terms, in the status of the college among its peers—including the success or failure of individual programs—than they were in the continuing legacy of women's education as represented in the institution as a singular, and quasi-independent, whole. Even though the enrollment at the Woman's College would continue to be overwhelmingly female for many years, as noted previously, and even though in 2010 the UNCG total enrollment is, on average, 65–68 percent female, these alumnae had no confidence in a majority female enrollment on its own, without singular naming status, being anything like the atmosphere, spirit, or tradition of the Woman's College itself.

A Useable Past

One lesson that might be taken away from my retelling and representation of the aggregate postwar experiences in literacy education at the Woman's College is to preserve the local and resist the unifying principles of the national. Part of what made the Woman's College unique was its fierce resistance to outside pressures to be something that it was not, and its refusal to bow to stereotypical, often limited notions of how women should or should not be educated in modern American culture. This resistance should perhaps be a model for all our institutions on a large scale: reject the pressure to conform to, for example, governmental standards for common curricula, and/or national modes of standardized testing at the college level, two imminent motions facing campuses nationwide. Since the Woman's College was only able to hold their local-values line for a limited amount of time, however, being forced to succumb to the financial and other material pressures of the North Carolina system, we must also view their demise with caution and keep an eye toward preserving the narratives and artifacts of our individual campuses for as long as they remain unique sites of literacy education, especially those of us who are charged with educating individuals outside the mainstream, however those boundaries are locally or regionally defined. While I would argue that the story of the Woman's College teaches us to privilege individual histories in the construction and maintenance of institutional curricula, it also may teach us that on occasion autonomy is an unforeseen casualty of institutional solvency and even prestige. As such, we need to carefully balance our disciplinary values in writing pedagogy and our larger institutional values that sometimes come into conflict with the discipline in order to decide where and when to relent and join the master narratives, and accompanying communities, made available (or even attractive) to us.

Such lessons provided by the Woman's College postwar are also important for scholars of the archives to consider as tales of failure—or success tempered by failure—and have as much if not more to tell readers in our field as those tales of institutional triumph. As Dana Harrington and Heather Shearer argue, the history of rhetoric and composition—particularly the subhistory of writing program administration—is "inevitably fragmented, partial, and [prone to the] 'interested' nature of all histories" (348). Harrington and Shearer advocate for an unveiling of our "unspoken assumptions" about the history of composition studies as a whole in our future historiographic work. To my mind, this includes our assumptions about the purpose and definition of our very methodologies, which include what sites of research we select, and for what purposes. Composition studies scholars, I would argue, occupy a unique position in terms of researching their field's history, as we have undergone as many waves of theory and practice in the last sixty years as many other fields have in much longer spans of time. We can reclaim those pasts for future use, employing, in many cases, oral histories and other human-based artifacts to augment the traditional scope of archival research and data collection relied upon by scholars of much older, if not more dynamic, academic fields. But we cannot do so without taking great pains to document individual case histories of our field, even and especially those that do not give us neat or tidy narratives with which to work, or provide easy solutions to current curricular, material, and sociocultural difficulties in writing instruction.

For readers who are fellow WPAs, this selection process in researching our institutional histories is akin to the practice of directing a program. Both require a careful selection of the most relevant, important, timely (or timeless) data for immediate use, as well as future consideration. Both WPA work and archival research require that one individual stand in for a collective—for the WPA, his or her composition students and faculty, and for the archival researcher, the subjects represented by and voiced through historical materials. Recovering "gaps" left by previous WPAs, or as extant within the institutional narrative as a whole, is part of the challenge of constructing and maintaining a program characterized by coherence and, above all, attentiveness to institutional, departmental, and disciplinary memory. Sometimes those gaps expose problems to solve in the future; sometimes they expose failures of imagination or collaboration. Recovering similar gaps in field histories requires the same valuation of coherence, memory, and attention to problem solving. The writing program administrator who thus elects to be a (or *the*) program historian for his or her institution—the local archival "voice," as it were, becomes responsible for lending lasting agency to complex and often obscured program history needs, whether the WPA formally creates a physical or electronic archive of the department's program on the local (private) level, or the full-scale history of the program's past on a national (public) level, as I have attempted to do in this book.

The WPA's stance in undertaking this sort of research is in many ways ethnographic by nature, but his or her meaning-making where the representation of that community is concerned, both at the local and national levels, even if necessarily out of time and space, is every bit as ethically situated and publicly high-stakes as that of the ethnographer living and/or working among research subjects. If we begin to regard WPA archival research as a significant opportunity to re-present and bring to light one's own programmatic histories in the context of existing field histories—particularly for lesser-researched settings such as women's public colleges—we can *readily* see it as an ethnographic practice, one necessarily limited by time and space but as rich in complexity and interpretation as the work produced by our more traditionally defined ethnographer colleagues. We could further begin to make standard the work of the WPA as participatory in a culture that not only values, but *prioritizes* documentation of not only daily work, but also historical practices that give voice to the students, faculty, and community members whose literacy practices fall outside the elite, the mainstream, or the frequently told narratives of our discipline, and whose stories are made most meaningful positioned beside one another.

In the case of the Woman's College, what remains for the telling, and what I have tried my best to represent in this book, is a portrait of a socially conservative, yet educationally progressive college that came to redefine writing—and literacy—in terms of artistic and creative pursuits, accepting of the consequences for literacy education and the people who participated in that education—students, faculty, and administrators. This redefinition was in line historically with the growing creative arts movement sweeping the country postwar, but it is out of line with our current accepted archival narratives of writing instruction as current-traditional and ideologically reactionary in these same postwar years. Further, what remains in the archives at the Woman's College is a veritable storehouse of perspectives on, and experiences with, women's writing in public institutions that only begins to narrate the story told by silenced voices in other institutional archives, voices waiting for other scholars to re-present them in new field histories.

This overall struggle—to represent people and moments of significance in absentia, and to do so in order to keep the historical lessons of the Woman's College, and other public colleges like it nationwide, alive for future scholars—is a daunting task that relies on the goodwill of archival material representations to guide us, as the authors and owners of these materials are no longer present to do so. Even though, in my case, I was fortunate enough to speak with three individuals for this book, in order to represent their individual histories in their own voices as much as possible, these encounters were limited by time and its effects. My subject pool of Woman's College alumnae is now entering their eighties, and as a result is conscripted, in many cases, by these individuals' own physicality and sometimes mortality. The faculty from this era, including, most problematically, May Bush and Randall Jarrell, and their heirs, are all long since deceased.

Yet studies such as this one can still broaden the ways in which we find archival work useful and purposeful to our aggregate histories of women's writing, and other marginalized sites of literacy education. As Cheryl Glenn and Jessica Enoch, both seasoned archival researchers, argue in a recent issue of *CCC*, "Rather than simply applying theory to what they find in the archive, researchers should allow for a reciprocal process—one that lets the archives speak back to the theory and allows the findings there to push against, open up, question, extend, constrict, or even disregard the theoretical frame altogether. Neither the theoretical approach nor the archival reading is predominant: the reading and theory work together, informing each other as well as the researcher" (334).

I share a concern for agency and purpose—and researcher-to-text collaboration—as I present this archival narrative of the people and actions of the Woman's College postwar, and want to see, in turn, our archival research "talk back" to myself and other archival scholars. I also want to see the lessons of historiography occupy a useful and even prominent place in our development of current best practices in college and university writing programs, especially those found within institutional types, and specialized learning communities that remain on the margins of higher education. As such, I present this book as one local articulation of the history of women's writing and literacy education postwar, in the sincere hope that it will not be the last of its kind. I call for other scholars, and particularly WPAs, to enjoin this history to their own, and retell the narrative of composition studies in human terms, with all of its fallibility and unsettling—if now settled—compromises.

Notes

Introduction: The History of Composition Is the History of Its People

1. I thank Tonya Hassell for introducing me to Linde's work.

2. See, for example, as a microcosm of this phenomenon, the following articles, all appearing within the last five years in *College Composition and Communication*: Lerner, "Rejecting the Remedial Brand"; Spring, "Seemingly Uncouth Forms"; Gold, "'Nothing Educates Us Like a Shock'" and "Eve Did No Wrong"; and my own "Before Mina Shaughnessy."

3. See, for example, Tate, "A Place for Literature in Freshman Composition," and Lindemann, "Freshman Composition," both of which first appeared in *College English* (March 1993) and became known, in shorthand, as the Tate-Lindemann Debate." Since the appearance of this pair of articles, other composition scholars have also taken up the question of whether literature is an appropriate textual type for first-year writing. For a recent, extended discussion of this lingering issue, see Anderson and Farris, *Integrating Literature and Writing Instruction*.

4. Mayers's *(Re)Writing Craft* is one exception to this general oversight in our

scholarship, yet his work is not archival and does not fully interrogate the specific and pivotal historical moments in which creative writing and composition came to coexist, especially in smaller women's colleges and other less-studied settings.

1. Her History Matters: The United States Normal School and the Roots of Women's Public Education

1. See Christine Ogren's comprehensive appendix in *The American Normal School* for the full list of institutions.

2. One thinks here of the Ivy League schools' relatively recent decision to admit women (excluding the absorption of women's colleges into their existing counterpart universities, for example, Barnard College women into the general population of Columbia University in 1983). While Cornell began to admit women in 1872, following the general trend of coeducational admissions for public colleges and universities in the western states, Yale began to admit women only in 1968, Princeton in 1969, and Dartmouth in 1972.

3. In 1891, University of North Carolina–Greensboro (UNCG) was founded as the State Normal and Industrial School. It was designated as the North Carolina College for Women in 1919. In 1931, it was consolidated by the North Carolina General Assembly, along with the University of North Carolina–Chapel Hill, and the North Carolina College of Agriculture and Engineering, into "one state university with three distinct missions" (Gallien 67). At that time, it was renamed the Woman's College of the University of North Carolina. In 1964, the Woman's College became the University of North Carolina–Greensboro, a coeducational, research-intensive institution.

4. It seems far more than coincidence that the Woman's College of the University of North Carolina would bear the same name as the Woman's College of Duke University, and that these universities would appear as freestanding institutions divorced, to a great extent, from their all-male parent institution, within one year of each other. While there is no explicit reference in the archives to the naming of the Woman's College of the University of North Carolina as homage or as mimicry of the Woman's College at Duke, it seems highly unlikely that these two moves were being done in isolation, or without each other's knowledge. Especially given the Woman's College's apparent ambitions to be the preeminent public women's college in the South, the identical naming appears deliberate, at least at some sociopsychological level.

5. For readers interested in the intersections of race and gender politics in women's colleges in the twentieth century specifically, or within women's education in the South more generally, see Christina Greene's *Our Separate Ways;* Adam Fairclough's *A Class of Their Own;* Susan K. Cahn's *Sexual Reckonings: Southern Girls in a Troubling Age;* and my own colleague Hephzibah Roskelly's

forthcoming project on the collaborative social activism of black and white female students at the Woman's College and at Bennett College in the early to mid-twentieth century.

6. The Native American population at UNCP numbered only 16 percent in 2010, which still seems relatively significant, given the overall population of Native Americans in the United States. African American students numbered just over 30 percent, and white students 40 percent ("What Makes Pembroke Pembroke?").

7. Such was the case within the Guilford County School District in Greensboro, North Carolina, where teachers were required to abandon their duties upon their fifth month of pregnancy. This regulation continued through the mid-1960s, according to a former teacher at Grimsley High School in Greensboro, Jim Ballance, whom I interviewed for another project. Ballance observed this tradition in practice among his Grimsley female colleagues as well as in the career of his own sister, a teacher at another school in the district during this time.

8. In the tradition of uniform-based education in the parochial schools and in boarding schools for both men and women, the Woman's College required that all women wear their "class jacket" with an appropriate accompanying skirt or dress to classes each day, and to class assemblies and gatherings. Each class had a distinctive color combination, as noted by one of my interview subjects in chapter 2. Such standardization, one may argue, resulted in either a leveling of class or economic standing, as is the goal of the public school uniform today, implying a kind of campus equality for the women, or in a hampering of individual or stylistic freedoms, often highly desired by young adult women (and men), especially as they begin a life away from home, signaling a more maternalistic chokehold on the students (since housemothers were the frequent enforcers of social rules and regulations, including dress codes).

9. At the Woman's College, activism and rhetoric were also married from the start of the twentieth century. For a discussion of the intersections of the Woman's College students and key social movements (and protests) of the twentieth century, see Ava De Almedia, *Lifting the Veil of Sisterhood.*

10. Adding to the pressure on gender equity and social considerations for women on campus was the transformation of Radcliffe from "a heavily commuter college, not a more expensive residential one" postwar (Synott 199). Despite the obvious change in residential climate during this era, Harvard still insisted on marginalizing the Radcliffe students to the point of denying them regular admission to morning prayers, barring a "special vote of the Harvard Corporation" (Synott 200). Such a lack of social as well as religious freedom stood in sharp contrast to the many religious and social societies found on the campus of the Woman's College of the University of North Carolina during the 1940s and 1950s.

11. Despite Hughes's protests, an examination of the 1930–31 Wellesley Col-

lege Department of English's *Manual of Instructions* for composition reveals very little that would distinguish it from similar documents at the Woman's College. Perhaps the only notable difference is its emphasis on acquiring familiarity with the college library. My thanks to the Wellesley archives staff for duplicating this document and sending it to me, free of charge, here in North Carolina.

12. One of Barnes's co-authors was Herbert Fowler of the Lewiston Normal School. Interestingly, however, none of the authors of this survey was from any of the southern states. The closest—Walter Barnes—hailed from Fairmont, West Virginia; the other authors taught in the Midwest or on the eastern seaboard.

13. The descriptions stayed the same except for an addition to the Rhetoric and Composition I and II sequence description, which states that, "One hour a week is devoted to oral composition and interpretive reading."

2. In Her Own Words: The *Yearling* and First-Year Writing, 1948–51

1. Though the preponderance of students at the Woman's College was from the Carolinas and Virginia, students also came from other geographical areas, following the college's reputation for educating women. For example, the class of 1952—from which my alumnae interviews were taken—included 12 students from Maryland, Pennsylvania, Delaware, New York, New Jersey, and Massachusetts, and four from Florida and Georgia, of the 390 graduating seniors (*Pine Needles 1952*).

2. In the 1949–50, 1950–51, and 1951–52 editions of the *Bulletin,* the following writing courses are offered in addition to first-year composition (English 101 and 102): English 221 and 222, Advanced Composition (with the former being on essays and exposition, and the latter on the short story); English 223 and 224, Journalism I and II; English 325 and 326, Writing Workshop I and II; English 329, Playwriting; and English 525 and 526, Writing—Advanced (also open to graduate students). In addition, English 319, English Grammar, and English 321, Grammar and Composition, are offered. While the conflation with journalism offerings evidences the early curricular structuring of many state colleges or normal colleges, this variety of writing courses allowed students of the Woman's College to be exposed to many different writing genres and to move through various writing course sequences along the way.

3. Elizabeth Stanfield-Maddox, personal interview.

4. While there are a handful of pieces that discuss magazines for *high school* writers, the only college-focused piece I could locate from the early part of the twentieth century is the September 1920 "Speaking of College Papers," written by Frances Wentworth Cutler in *English Journal,* which profiles the literary magazine at Vassar College. Vassar's magazine seems to be one of the longest sustained

publications of its type, as it was still in publication—as noted in other articles—some forty years later.

5. In total, eleven state teachers colleges were represented and one city-based teachers college (Milwaukee Teachers College).

6. This typically included wives of tenure-line male faculty members, such as both wives of the poet Randall Jarrell at the Woman's College. At the Woman's College, ten of the sixteen instructors of English 101 and 102 in the year 1949–50 were women, one of whom was listed as "Mrs. James Painter" in that year's *Manual of Instruction.* Coincidentally, *Mr.* James Painter was also English faculty at the time.

7. It is interesting to note that neither Bryn Mawr nor Converse College is listed in Edith Wells's 1950 survey of institutions regarding freshman magazine publications. While she may have read Edgar Stanton's piece on Converse College, I assume that Bush had personal knowledge of the status of these institutions' publications through her own networking as a woman's college faculty member and alumna of a women's college (Hollins College, Virginia). Certainly models at that institution included the early 1900s literary magazine *Tipyn O'Bob,* in which Marianne Moore's work was famously published, or the student magazine of the summer school, *Shop and School,* published annually in the 1920s and 1930s (see the work of Karyn Hollis for more on this particular publication).

8. Since the manual did not visibly change in design or content between 1948 and 1951, the years in which the *Yearling* was published, I only refer to one year of its publication here.

9. Because my interviews for this chapter were from alumnae of the class of 1952, I have not found any information on this writing club for the class of 1953, nor have I found any reference to it elsewhere in the archives, the Woman's College yearbook, or other documents; hence, I cannot further investigate its construction or purpose. Its mention here, however, is yet another indicator of the wide interest in literacy-based and writing-centered activities at the Woman's College during this time, and the role of publications such as the *Yearling* in promoting interest in expository and creative writing among the first-year student body.

10. I say "unintentional" because among the stated various purposes of first-year magazines both midcentury and today, rarely (if ever) do we hear these publications being considered archival collections, or historical snapshots, of a program and/or its students, a purpose that the *Yearling* clearly serves in my research on the Woman's College.

11. Mandatory desegregation could have been a hot topic on campus in spring 1948, given President Truman's executive order regarding the desegregation of the U.S. armed forces earlier that year.

12. While it is not the aim of this chapter to recapitulate the difficult position

for Jewish men and women in higher education during this era, I can point out that anti-Semitism was not the province of southern colleges by any means, as Jerome Karabel elegantly analyzes in his book *The Chosen*. This *Yearling* author seems cognizant of these cross-cultural and often contradictory biases that existed nationwide.

13. I originally contacted seven possible interview subjects, using the editorial staff listings of the *Yearling* as my initial guide, and matching these up with records provided to me by the alumni relations office at UNCG. Of the seven requests I sent, three women responded and agreed to be interviewed.

14. Elizabeth provided me with a copy of her latest article in the *United Daughters of the Confederacy* monthly magazine; Jacqueline sent me her original copy of the 1949 *Yearling*; Lucy gave me her autographed copy of *Coraddi*—signed by Robert Penn Warren—and a copy of her sophomore writing project, "Page's Pages." My heartfelt thanks go out to these three fascinating and generous women for their time as well as these valuable artifacts of their work, and of the Woman's College.

15. Indeed, many of the students whose work was published in the *Yearling* were active in other literacy-based organizations on campus. Of the women I interviewed, Elizabeth was a staff member of *Coraddi* in her junior and senior years; Lucy was also on the *Coraddi* staff her sophomore through senior years, and on the staff of the student newspaper, the *Carolinian*, her junior year; Jacqueline was the senior year editor of the yearbook, *Pine Needles*. Two other women whose work I cite also held positions in other literacy-based organizations, according to their biographies in the 1952 issue of *Pine Needles*. These are Sally Beaver, who worked on the *Carolinian*, and Jean Hollinger, who worked on the Arts Forum and Lecture Series (for drama, art, music, writing, and dance).

16. To put this in a regional context, it is also important to note that the University of North Carolina–Chapel Hill did not routinely admit women in their first or second years; women could be considered for admission only if they had junior or senior standing, as transfer students; hence the importance of the Woman's College as a "feeder" school for some. This issue reenters my discussion in chapter 5, where I discuss the demise of the Woman's College as related significantly to the loss of its "protective tariff" that brought women to Greensboro but kept them almost completely out of Chapel Hill (and Raleigh, or North Carolina State University).

17. As Elizabeth and I discussed during her interview, the Hope Scholarship—an award of free tuition available to all Georgia residents who maintain a minimum GPA during their years at any Georgia public college or university—often leads to first-year students deliberately doing poorly on entrance exams in order to place themselves lower in English and math courses than they otherwise would. This lower placement ensures that they will start below their actual abil-

ity levels, thereby ensuring a higher likelihood of meeting the minimum GPA required to keep the Hope Scholarship. Considering that Georgia state system officials lament the fairly high level of "remedial" coursework needed as indicated upon examination at the state colleges, this well-known strategy among in-state students is an important (and oddly nontheorized) footnote.

18. This contrasts with Lucy's memory of Robert Penn Warren, who served as a guest judge for an issue of work that had been published in *Coraddi*, and who responded to Lucy's story (in that issue of the magazine) as "worthless—not very good, throw it out." Lucy commented that this was not as discouraging as it sounds, since she "didn't think it was very good either."

19. Lucy describes her situation as such: "I came from a background that was very different from everyone else's. Everyone else had a momma and a daddy, and a home. I'm not knocking it, I'm just saying that's how it was." She wrote about a visit to her father in the hospital as the topic of her essay in the *Yearling*, "They Also Serve," a point she raised at the start of our interview, emphasizing that the situation she describes with the patients and visitors seems "apropos of any veterans' hospital," even today. In Lucy's case, her publication in the magazine seems to have more personal significance, and lasting value, in comparison to the pieces published by Elizabeth and Jacqueline, who have less immediate memories of their counterparts' work.

20. Jane Summerall is notable for asking her women students to enact their political and rhetorical agencies in the space of her writing classes, most visibly in her in-class writing assignment on the occasion of V-E Day. These essays, handwritten and preserved in the university archives, illustrate some forward thinking about world politics and the position of the United States in, and after, wartime, thinking not altogether foreign to the student writers profiled in the *Sample Case* and the *Yearling*. These essays, like the work in the first-year writing magazine, stand in structural and rhetorical contrast to what might be expected at a "typical" public women's college. The fact that these essays were also carefully preserved and archived indicates that Summerall—or someone in the English department at the time—recognized the need to document this type of student writing for future generations. I do not incorporate a discussion of these essays within this book because I feel the archive is worthy of its own separate analysis, perhaps in the context of wartime women's rhetoric at the college.

3. Revisionist History: General Education Reform from Harvard University to the Woman's College, 1943–56

1. A brief article in the *Crimson* characterizes Morrison as "not a tyrant who broods in a Warren House office over new ways to torture Freshmen and take the joy out of their bright young lives." The article quotes Morrison's directorial view

of English A, a program he took over in 1937: "Everyone," he says, "has a right to grouse about English A because too few people have been let in on the secret of its aim. It seeks to improve not only writing but also reading and thinking, with which writing must be inevitably connected. English A is therefore a synthesis of literary and non-literary elements. As the sole course in the humanities that is directly specified for a degree, it must especially emphasize its literary side in wartime when science and technology are beamed upon and the 'liberal tradition' is shunned. That is why English A section men discuss Shakespeare's sonnets to a dark lady when two-thirds of their students are worrying about long white envelopes from the War Department" ("Faculty Profile"). It would be difficult to know about Morrison's work with English A or the remedial English courses from his public profiles, however. His 1987 obituary in the *New York Times* makes no mention of it, only his Bread Loaf work and creative writing teaching and publishing while at Harvard ("Theodore Morrison, Poet and Professor").

2. For a compelling archives-based discussion of the endeavor of first-year composition at the University of Chicago in the late 1940s and early 1950s, see Beardsley.

3. Others reviewing the final Redbook report took a more nuanced view of the practical needs behind the report, including Claude Moore Fuess, headmaster of Phillips Academy (Andover), who commented—perhaps with unintended irony, given his institution's own generally elite student population, "Without a trace of intellectual snobbery or even of condescension, the Report displays an intimate acquaintance with the needs of the common man" ("A Précis," 2).

4. Kuhn would later become a Harvard fellow, a protégé of James B. Conant, and an important figure in the history of science, as readers likely know, earning both a Guggenheim fellowship and a George B. Sarton medal for his work.

5. Two articles from the Harvard *Crimson* provide some additional student insight into the English A requirement in relation to general education initiatives. First, in "New Look for English A," from February 28, 1949, the unnamed student author notes the possible pros and cons of aligning English A writing assignments with other general education courses:

> This re-evaluation of Harvard's English instruction can have some good results if well handled. Certainly the idea of teaching writing along lines useful in later life is a welcome change from the "What I Did This Summer" themes of English A. But this brings up problems which are going to have to be licked to make the program work out. The GE announcement implies that the course papers will be read for writing skill as well as context, and that the student who fails to meet basic standards will be required to take the corrective course: an eminently constructive approach and well in line with the whole idea of the program. It entails, however, the ability of the man

reading the papers to compare them on the basis of English skill as well as knowledge of course material, an ability that may very well be absent in many specialized instructors and section men. ("New Look for English A")

A second article in the *Crimson,* dated February 9, 1951, describes the new English A experimental course now in action, "General Education A," or GEA, as taught by I. A. Richards and critiqued by Theodore Morrison. Citing its origins in the principles of the Redbook report, which found fault with the segregated nature of English A as opposed to the rest of the general education curriculum, the article explains that the GEA course

has two weekly lectures and no compulsory section meetings. Written work consists entirely of six 150-word essays called "protocols." Done on one side of a 5" by 8" card, the essays can be projected on a screen in the lecture hall by a system of reflectors. Using this system, Richards can discuss and criticize as many as fifteen protocols at each lecture. Essay topics range from "How would you define a square knot?" to "Why do you believe 2 plus 2 equals 4?" The system of concise answers to these abstract questions eliminates the huge quantity of written work required in English A. Theodore Morrison '23, director of English A, yesterday described Richards' course as an attempt to "short-cut" the old system, but Morrison is doubtful whether any "miracle" can simplify the difficult problem of improving writing style. One hundred and ninety-two Yardlings and Radcliffe girls signed up for the G.E. course in the fall, and roughly the same number has enrolled for the spring term, Student reaction to the course is generally favorable, despite low grades. Many freshmen consider Richards' course "less work and more fun" than English A, while a disgruntled minority finds it "over our heads." One Yardling commented, "If it lasts anywhere, it'll last at Harvard." ("General Education A Finishes First Term")

6. It is clear from available archives at Radcliffe and Harvard that the institution was eagerly reading and logging in peer reviews of the Redbook. As Dean Paul Buck of Harvard wrote to President W. K. Jordan at Radcliffe on July 7, 1945: "A good many extremely favorable and I fear flattering letters have poured into Mr. Conant's and my offices about the report. . . . You will be interested to learn that the advance orders of the book had reached the point where ten days ago it was necessary to go into a second edition—as this is a full month before the date of publication." Buck also notes that, "The President of Emory University and the Chancellor of Vanderbilt think the report is an historic document. No comment yet from Yale or Princeton. So it goes . . . God save us all when the reviews appear next month." This call for advance copies, and possibly the quickly published re-

views of the study, were likely due to the mailing (at Jordan and others' request) of the Redbook to organizations including the *Boston Globe,* the Record Newspapers, the University of Chicago Press, and the Rockefeller Foundation.

7. This despite an explicit statement at one of the committee's first meetings that, "It was agreed our guests should represent an adequate geographical spread; a spread between the different types of schools; and that we should be sure to include those who represent the extreme views in the liberal arts and vocational education" (Harvard Committee on General Education, minutes, Sept. 28, 1943). Perhaps "adequate" was determined to not include the South.

8. I find it interesting that this description is akin to the description of a jury and its deliberations—down to the "twelve men" that comprise the group.

9. Though Gerald Graff noted in *Professing Literature* that Richards's views of literary criticism, articulated in his *Practical Criticism,* and the views of general education in the Redbook were overlapping—in that these works shared "an assumption that great literary works are independent of history and culture and that literary education must henceforth base itself on 'direct' experience of those works, unmediated by history" (177)—I find little physical, noted evidence of Richards's participation in, or material contribution to, the final findings of the committee where expository writing and rhetorical literacy were concerned.

10. *Basic English I* (1952) and *Basic English II* (1952) were short films of about fifteen minutes in duration, produced by the March of Time documentary series, with scripts written by Richards himself that drew from his text *The Pocket Book of Basic English.* Many of the dialogues, actually rote demonstrations of basic English phrases, are situated in rural surroundings (or, more accurately, sets replicating these surroundings), with actors dressed as farmers or farmers' wives, perhaps to represent prototypical American life. These films have been archived online by HBO, and are available for viewing at http://www.hboarchives.com/apps/searchlibrary/ctl/marchoftime.

11. In the archives of the Radcliffe Committee on General Education, included is a document entitled "Points made in presenting 'The Case for Coeducation' at Radcliffe College, October 21, 1944." The document's author, Burton P. Fowler, then-headmaster of Tower Hill School in Wilmington, Delaware, argues six main points: (1) "The education of boys and girls together on a nationwide basis is, like compulsory education, an American development"; (2) "Segregation of the sexes is a European importation which has flourished almost solely on the Eastern Seaboard"; (3) The Quakers "have developed coeducational day and boarding schools, and colleges with marked success"; (4) "Co-education is desirable because it is a natural, healthy association of the sexes on the intellectual as well as the social level"; (5) "While there needs to be some differentiation of courses for boys and girls . . . there should be a common core of studies for both sexes supplemented by a carefully guided choice of electives"; and (6) "The rigid social patterns of our

elite class are probably responsible for the survival of the most segregated second-ary schools in this country" (1–2).

12. Not as in religious education, but as in holding universally appealing prin-ciples, that is, a universal education.

13. It is not clear why Hollinshead chose to read only seventy-two of the sub-mitted surveys. Archival documents seem to indicate, however, that he was disin-clined to read and/or tabulate the entire data set.

14. This survey was built, in part, upon the template of an earlier alumnae survey sent to Radcliffe graduates in March 1928. According to the cover note attached to each survey and coauthored by Ada L. Comstock, then president of Radcliffe College, and Dorothy Brewer Blackall, then president of the Radcliffe Alumnae Association, the survey was being conducted to create a database for the new issue of the *Radcliffe Alumnae Directory*, and also represented "a desire to accumulate certain facts about the former students of the College. Some of these facts, such as profession, date of marriage, and names and ages of children, may be included in the Directory. Others may contribute to studies about the part which Radcliffe women play in their communities. . . . May we suggest that the prompter the replies the sooner the Directory can appear?" This earlier questionnaire, how-ever, contained items that may have been helpful to the general education study in 1944, had they been replicated in that later survey. For example, there is in the 1928 survey a space for "published writings" and "creative work (paintings, sculp-ture, musical compositions, etc.)" to be listed—interesting data given the Radcliffe alumnae's apparent desire for more college coursework in just these areas. There is also a question that asks, "which of the following aspects of college life makes the most important contribution to a girl's development? (Number them in the order of importance): Scholastic training; character formation; training in citizenship; contact making." The 1944 survey, by comparison, was far more attuned to the actual curriculum at Harvard, and the vocational successes of the graduates, with little attention to opinions about the nature of women's education or their specific artistic/scholarly contributions to society.

15. As Hollinshead himself notes in a letter to President W. R. Jordan at Rad-cliffe, "since Radcliffe has no faculty of its own, there is less casual personal con-tact with the faculty than there would be at an ordinary college where faculty members were constantly available." Such an arrangement obviously stands in sharp contrast to the faculty assignment at the Woman's College (and any other public women's college of the era), whose duties were not designed as secondary or ancillary to their primary duties instructing the "primary" male students. Ar-chival records show that when Harvard faculty were assigned duties at Radcliffe, for example teaching English A, such requests were not always accepted happily or without complaint.

16. Indeed, a great number of meeting minutes in the archives for the Harvard

committee exhibit considerable attention to the subject of tutoring and individual conferencing. In sum, after exploration of the issue and inconsistent findings as to whether these tutorials were helpful—or whether they were of equivalent quality across various courses—including a separate survey given to Radcliffe graduates on this subject, the recommendation to make tutorials a prominent part of the Redbook report was scrapped. See Harvard Committee on General Education, "Tutorials."

17. He was, in fact, the chairman of a previous Harvard committee, formed in 1939, which published a study titled *The Training of Secondary School Teachers.*

18. Here I see a strong parallel with May Delaney Bush at the Woman's College, also in charge of English composition, who was tenure-track, but who waited many years for a promotion to associate professor, and even longer—some twenty-five years after her hire—for a final promotion to full professor, as I will detail further in chapter 4.

19. According to Allen Trelease's comprehensive study of the history of UNCG, *Making North Carolina Literate,* which includes the postwar Woman's College era, Graham was a leader whose "management style and personal behavior . . . engendered hostility" (218). Trelease characterizes Graham as an ambitious, impetuous, and somewhat embittered leader who sought notoriety for his chancellorship by whatever means necessary, but failed ultimately to secure the trust and acceptance of the faculty—hence his resignation just six years after taking office.

20. See Ritter, *Before Shaughnessy,* chapter 4, for a detailed discussion of this committee's work between 1919 and 1950.

21. Through my reading of the Woman's College archives—including Edward Graham's papers and the documents related to the general education reform—I agree with the common interpretation held by others regarding Graham's vision of general education revision. Mary Jarrell, however, offers a competing version of events that position Marc Friedlander as the instigator of reform, and Graham as an unwitting enabler. See chapter 4 for a brief accounting of Mary Jarrell's version.

22. Ashby was a much-loved faculty member who was openly admired by students, including my own interview subjects, and for whom the honors college was later named. He was noted by my Woman's College interviewees as being the "young" and extremely intelligent faculty member whose work deeply affected their learning outside the English department. Indeed, his use of inclusive language in this passage indicates someone slightly ahead of his time (and observant of the actual subject of his discourse).

23. There is no existing record of meetings for the fall 1955 semester, or August–December 1955.

4. The Double-Helix of Creative/Composition: Randall Jarrell, May Bush, and the Politics of Writing Programs, 1947–63

1. Several curricular proposals put forward in the department between 1952 and 1963 specifically call for the primacy of creative writing within the department and its budget. These include a May 1952 detailed request for several undergraduate tuition scholarships related to creative writing (modeled after the system in place at Kenyon College, one of Jarrell's employment suitors); a graduate fellowship designed to further the MFA program recruitment; a formal creative writing major; and increased publicity for the program in general, both inside and outside North Carolina. As justification for these resource requests, the authors of the memo—then creative writing faculty Lettie Rogers and Robie Macauley—noted, "at present, classes are smaller than they ought to be. The level of student ability is . . . disappointingly low. We feel that there are two possibilities in the future: either the program may go on to become a well-known and vital part of the educational plan here, or it may languish on as a number of courses attended by a few students with vaguely literary interests" (memo to Graham et al., May 28, 1952). Given that just the year prior, the student-run *Yearling* had ended its brief run with no visible advocacy for continued financial or other departmental support, this request for funds for creative writing is especially striking.

Similarly, in November 1952, department meeting minutes note a proposal that suggests "a new course, English 225–226, to be called 'Creative Writing' be set up in addition to English 221–222, which would then be designated 'Expository Writing.' After discussion among the staff, it was agreed that it would probably be a better idea to continue the course as English 221–222 'Advanced Composition,'" designating in the catalogue write-up that one section would stress creative writing and another would emphasize expository writing ("Second Monthly Staff Meeting Minutes," Nov. 10, 1952). Eventually this course would be split as requested into a separate creative writing course sequence of English 223–224, as well as English 325–326 (The Writing Workshop I, II) and English 525–526 (Writing-Advanced, for undergraduate and graduate students). In October 1963, the 500-level courses were formally split into separate sections of 'Writing-Advanced, Fiction,' 'Writing-Advanced, Poetry,' and 'Writing-Advanced, Plays,' with corresponding separate numbers (Bryant, memo to Bridgers et al., Oct. 22, 1963).

2. In the extensive and unusually detailed English department meeting minutes from February 9, 1956, the faculty undertook a protracted discussion of "remedial" writers and the concept of ability grouping. Jarrell is noted as questioning "the wisdom of dividing the more able students from the less able. He said that there was an assumption that the complex works should be studied by the poorer

students, who would study them with a view to human values. Mr. Jarrell felt this assumption to be unreasonable. Mr. Jarrell stated that if this division were made, then there would still be a big difference of ability in his two new sections [which Hurley had asked him to take on for that term]. . . . Mr. Jarrell stated his belief that poorer students profited by being with the better students." One may read this as quite sudden self-interest, given that Jarrell had not taught first-year writing at the Woman's College prior to this semester. But his view is strikingly progressive for its time—given his implication that "better" students were reading and writing for the purposes of acculturation into the ways of the humanities and fine arts, whereas poorer students would read and write potentially the *same* material simply to gain basic literacy skills.

3. This association between creative writing and the campus culture, or its claim to fame, extends to the rhetoric found embedded in the (now UNCG) campus today; at the front door of the Walter Jackson Library, where one might expect to see a dedication or aphorism from a politician, historical figure, or school founder, there is engraved a quote from fiction writer Fred Chappell, who taught at UNCG through the 1990s.

4. It should be noted that although the PhD in creative writing has been in existence since 1975—and has been offered as a degree option at forty or more universities, including, for a time, at the Iowa Writers' Workshop (University of Iowa), the Associated Writing Programs as an organization does not recognize it as the true terminal degree in creative writing. Instead, it continues to call the MFA the "true" terminal degree in this field.

5. R. M. Berry notes that in 1990, "around 3,000 poets and fiction writers" were graduating from creative writing graduate programs each year, compared with 800 doctoral recipients in other fields of English studies (57).

6. See Crowley, chap. 7, "You Can't Write Writing: Norman Foerster and the Battle over Basic Skills at Iowa." Notable, of course, in this example of an early creative writing program director is Foerster's claim to fame: his vision that creative writing would be an organic outgrowth of the English department, rather than a separate (financial and philosophical) arm of the university, divided from department literacy initiatives and scholarly pursuits.

7. See, for example, collections such as Grimes.

8. Connors, in *Composition-Rhetoric,* cites Warner Taylor's famous 1929 survey, which reports that 38 percent of all composition instructors were women, a trend he argues continues into the 1990s (201–2). Connors labels the period 1885–1940 as the era when the "composition underclass" formed. At institutions where men were the predominant or only faculty on campus, male WPAs were the norm. At institutions such as the Woman's College, however, where women faculty were demographically on par with men, these women appeared to take up

these roles instead. In 2010, composition remains widely regarded as a "woman's" field, and a significant number of scholars who have published seminal works on WPA issues—for example, Jeanne Gunner, Alice Gillam, Shirley Rose, Carrie Leverenz, Laura Micciche, and Eileen Schell—are women WPAs.

9. There is an important footnote that must be recorded in relation to Bush's reported time at Peace College. While Bush notes on her personnel file—in her own hand, so this is no administrative error in reporting—that she was "head of the English department, 1933–1934" at Peace, archival research into the official records of Peace College turn up no support for this claim. The records at Peace instead list her as an instructor during the second semester (spring) of 1933–34. As Diane Jenkins, current Peace College archivist, notes, however, there was no "official" head of the English department at Peace until the following year—1934–35—when such titles began to be listed in the catalogue, but at that time the chair was not listed as May Bush. So Jenkins concedes that Bush *could* have acted in an ad hoc administrative capacity at some point, but that her official catalogue listing is that of temporary instructor, and for only one semester of this year (e-mail to the author, May 3, 2010). Here is, perhaps, an early example of unheralded women's administrative work in English departments, if indeed Bush worked as an uncompensated, nonrecognized department chair for this year at Peace College.

10. In the May 14, 1956, minutes, there is an extended statement by Randall Jarrell, which he asked to be added to the previous meeting's minutes (March 12). It reads:

> I spoke briefly about the problem of Miss [Nettie] Tillett's habitual behavior in staff meetings. My tone was serious, objective, and troubled. I did not refer to Miss Tillett by name, but both the content and the department's knowledge of the facts made it plain that it was she to whom I was referring—there is no one else in the department who has behaved in this way. I said that, for as long as I had known it, our department had been faced with an extraordinary problem: the problem of having one member who did not observe, in department meetings, the ordinary rules of social behavior, but who allowed herself to make intemperate or openly insulting remarks about the head of the department, the department as a whole, or individual members of the department. This one member had often questioned the good faith of the head of the department or of the department itself, when its actions and policies had displeased her; she had sometimes interrupted speakers with disapproving and emotional ejaculations. Such conduct had been habitual on this member's part, and the other members of the department had habitually responded by embarrassed silence, by staring uneasily out the window and then going on with the discussion, never making a direct comment on what had happened. Some of us had begun to question the wisdom of our behavior, since it allowed this one member to live in a sort of

social vacuum in which even her most extreme speeches were not checked by any direct comment on them. Perhaps, I said, we should reconsider this habitual behavior of ours; should, by making direct comments on this member's most intemperate remarks, arouse in her the sense of ordinary give-and-take, or ordinary social reality.

As an addendum to Jarrell's remarks—and in implicit support of them—fellow English faculty member Jane Summerall asked that the following statement of her own be entered into the minutes: "I do not subscribe to, or in any way approve of, the criticism of Dr. Hurley, as set forth in the third paragraph of Miss Tillett's statement incorporated in the minutes of April 9." Tillett resigned from the Woman's College at the end of the 1957–58 academic year; in a memo from Mereb E. Mossman, dean of the college, to Chancellor Gordon Blackwell, Mossman notes this resignation alongside Randall Jarrell's return (from leave) to the college for 1958–59, at a projected salary of $7,500—a salary equal to Tillett's final salary for 1957–58. Mossman also asks, "how heavily would we be justified in drawing on [a reserve in romance languages] to add to Mr. Jarrell's salary?" (Mossman, memo to Blackwell, Jan. 26, 1958).

11. In a memo to Edward K. Graham dated January 2, 1955, Rogers offers her resignation, noting, "This resignation is in protest of your administrative action of publicly censuring the *Coraddi* staff. I consider such an action, and the stated reasons for that action, undemocratic in principle and in precedent, and contrary to our tradition here of intellectual freedom." It was widely known that Graham had waited until the issue of *Coraddi* was published to issue the censure, and that the issue had been approved through all other administrative ranks of the university prior to this censure. Such was one more example of Graham's political and intellectual disconnect with the faculty ranks of the Woman's College, as discussed in the context of general education reform in chapter 3.

As a further note, after Lettie Rogers tendered her resignation in 1955, and the terms of her resignation were published in the local newspaper, Nettie Tillett stated, in the January 10, 1955, minutes, that,

> I believe it should be noted that until recently—I would say, without having checked, within the last eight or ten years, at most—the *Coraddi* had an adviser who saw everything that went into the publication. I was that adviser under two administrations, and I have in my possession a letter from Dr. Jackson saying he is releasing me from the appointment only at my own request and thanking me generously for doing good work in it. I mention the letter as proof of his position concerning the matter of freedom. I know no tradition connected with the *Coraddi* that the Chancellor's action has violated. I believe I know more about the *Coraddi*'s past than any other person now associated with the college knows.

Tillett's comments would seem indicative of the kind of interjections—confused in fact and topically tangential to the issues at hand—that Jarrell would in the following year find worthy of formal complaint.

12. I do not know if $4,200 was a revised figure—over the previously agreed upon $4,100—or a typographical error in this particular memo.

13. Gagen's book was published by Twayne Publishers (New York); whether this would be considered "vanity" is somewhat debatable. The press is now an imprint of Gale/Cengage.

14. At Oglethorpe, the economics of creative writing were very clear. As Professor Van K. Brock, himself a recipient of an MFA from the University of Iowa Writers' Workshop and a published poet, writes, "One obvious problem here is that while Oglethorpe is generally interested in poetry, it is assumed that poetry ought to be free or cost very little. In being able to make you this offer, I feel that a breakthrough has been achieved" (Brock, letter to Jarrell, Jan. 19, 1965).

15. The atmosphere at the Iowa Writers' Workshop would seem to have agreed with Jarrell, as he remarked to wife Mary after his visit to the program in 1952, "Well, I've had a wonderful time here at the University of Iowa! I never saw such a pleasant, unspiteful, un-nasty intellectual bunch of writers as here. . . . the people [at the reading] were so *nice* to me, and seemed to like me and what I said so much, that I felt childishly embarrassed and happy" (*Letters* 344–45). If such sentiments were voiced publicly upon his return to the Woman's College, they surely would have only increased the anxiety that Jarrell would find greener (employment) pastures elsewhere.

16. In a lengthy memo to Chancellor Graham July 13, 1951, Leonard Hurley argues for a temporary one-year replacement for Mackie Jarrell, coinciding with her impending leave of absence. Hurley points out that Randall Jarrell took a freshman section at Hurley's "urgent request" in fall 1950, but that Peter Taylor "for several years past has not been expected to teach freshmen"; the combined effect of this and other staffing issues would leave the department in dire need of another composition instructor for the coming fall term.

17. The low load carried by Jarrell did not go unnoticed by higher administration, though it also appears to go unchanged—and in contrast, sanctioned—throughout his career at the Woman's College. In a memo to Chancellor Graham on April 21, 1955—the memo that would precipitate Hurley's accounting of load credits for his faculty the following fall—Dean Mossman communicates that she "talked with Dr. Hurley about Mr. Jarrell's teaching load and implications of such a small load. He is going to work on this problem with the thought that the poetry class might develop into a considerably larger class and also consider the possibility of a sophomore English section for Mr. Jarrell for the coming year." Note that half of this proposed solution hinges upon Jarrell's poetry class increasing in size—that is, the growing of the creative writing concentration—rather than a

load reevaluation beyond the possible sophomore English section. His two-course (six-hour) load continued into the 1960s, as is noted in a November 7, 1961, memo from then department chair J. A. Bryant to Dean Mossman, in which Jarrell's two-course load is referenced in relation to his offering of an advanced graduate seminar at the Chapel Hill campus. Hurley concluded that this seminar should be considered "overload" for Jarrell, and that he thus should be paid "an additional amount equal to one-third of his regular salary for the semester [and] should also be reimbursed for his weekly transportation to and from Chapel Hill." Meanwhile, his fellow colleagues in the English department—those not in creative writing—were teaching a four-course-per-semester load, with no extra pay.

5. What's in a Name? Women's Writing Histories and Archival Research in Composition Studies

1. Thomas Pearsall chaired a committee bearing his name and was the North Carolina House Speaker from the mid-1950s to the early 1960s. This committee was also labeled the Governor's Commission on Education beyond the High School, and it was an interesting political body: it was also in charge of providing vouchers for parents who opposed the mandatory desegregation of the public schools in North Carolina following the *Brown v. Board of Education* decision.

2. An interesting comparative to both the tariff and the general enrollment of men at the Woman's College may be found in the history of remedial writing, or "Subject A," at the University of California at Berkeley, as recovered by Jane Stanley. Stanley cites a 1952 memo from the Special Committee on Educational Policy that expresses concern for the representation of men on campus at Berkeley, given the much higher success rate on the Subject A exam found among women applicants. The committee notes: "Women traditionally do better in the Subject A exam while our male students are brighter on any type of general aptitude test. The reason for this relative brightness of men, incidentally, is that women are more predictable and work more nearly up to capacity, so that when both sexes must meet the same standard, as they must, to be eligible for the University, the men are automatically brighter. . . . Any device that puts restrictions on the entrance of male students at the University of California should be looked at askance" (*The Rhetoric of Remediation*, 91). Such institutional rhetoric favoring male applicants—to the extent of recommending that a literacy test on which women perform with much greater results—should be eliminated is surely the kind of prejudice that the Woman's College students, faculty, and administrators felt might be lurking out there once the institution was subsumed under the UNC heading.

3. Though I could not locate it in the archives, one of my interview subjects from chapter 2, Elizabeth Poplin Stanfield-Maddox, tells me that she, too, sent a

lengthy letter of protest to the college regarding this impending shift in status. She also noted that she fiercely believed in the sanctity of the college as a site for women's only education—a sentiment extremely common among Woman's College graduates, particularly those attending postwar.

4. As a supposed homage to the years of the Woman's College, and despite its status as a medium-sized, coed research university, UNC–Greensboro to this day does not have a football team, though it does have teams in many other sports, both men's and women's.

Works Cited

Adams, Donald J. "College and the Writer." *College Composition and Communication* 7.1 (1956): 5–7.

Adams, Katherine H. *A Group of Their Own: College Writing Courses and American Women Writers, 1880–1940.* Albany, NY: State U of New York P, 2001.

Ammons, Jacqueline Jernigan. Personal interview. Nov. 5, 2008.

Anderson, Judith, and Christine Farris, eds. *Integrating Literature and Writing Instruction: First Year English, Humanities Core Courses, Seminars.* New York: MLA, 2007.

"Annual Report of North Carolina Colleges: Enrollment." Gordon William Blackwell Records. UA 2.6, Box 2. University of North Carolina–Greensboro Archives, Greensboro, NC.

Barnes, Walter, Herbert E. Fowler, Lydia Jones, C. R. Rounds, Florence Skeffington, Elizabeth Tait, and W. H. Wilcox. "Final Report of the Committee on English in the Normal School: A Committee of the National Council of Teachers of English." *English Journal* 7.1 (1918): 29–38.

Basic English I. March of Time Films, 1952. DVD.

Basic English II. March of Time Films, 1952. DVD.

"Basic English Worth $108 a Word." Feb. 25, 1947. Papers of I. A. Richards. HUG(B) R461.10, Box 1. Harvard University Archives, Cambridge, MA.

Beardsley, James. "'Extraordinary Understandings' of Composition at the University of

Chicago: Frederick Champion Ward, Kenneth Burke, and Henry W. Sams." *College Composition and Communication* 59 (2007): 36–52.

Beaver, Sally. "On Baby Brothers and Modern Art." *Yearling* 3.1 (1950): 8–9.

Benbow, Gladys J. Letter to Chancellor Otis Singletary, Nov. 26, 1962. Otis Arnold Singletary Records. UA 2.7, Box 6. University of North Carolina–Greensboro Archives, Greensboro, NC.

Berger, Shirley. "An Approach to Segregation." *Yearling* 1.1 (1948): 22–23.

Berke, Jacqueline. "The Campus Literary Magazine and Composition." *College Composition and Communication* 14.1 (1963): 10–14.

Berlin, James. *Rhetoric and Reality: Writing Instruction in American Colleges, 1900–1985.* Carbondale, IL: Southern Illinois UP, 1987.

———. *Writing Instruction in Nineteenth Century American Colleges.* Carbondale, IL: Southern Illinois UP, 1984.

Berry, R. M. "Theory, Creative Writing, and the Impertinence of History." *Colors of a Different Horse: Rethinking Creative Writing Theory and Pedagogy.* Ed. Wendy Bishop and Hans Ostrom. Urbana, IL: NCTE, 1994. 57–76.

Bishop, Wendy, and David Starkey. *Keywords in Creative Writing.* Logan, UT: Utah State UP, 2006.

Brereton, John. *The Origins of Composition Studies in the American College, 1875–1925.* Pittsburgh: U of Pittsburgh P, 1995.

———. "Rethinking Our Archive: A Beginning." *College English* 61.5 (1999): 574–76.

Bridgers, John, Jean Gagen, Robert Humphrey, Randall Jarrell, and Robert Watson. "Recommendations of the Freshman-Sophomore Committee." May 1956. Department of English Records. UA 4.22, Box 1. University of North Carolina–Greensboro Archives, Greensboro, NC.

Brock, Van K. Letter to Randall Jarrell, Jan. 19, 1965. Randall Jarrell Papers, 1929–69. Mss009, Box 7. University of North Carolina–Greensboro Archives, Greensboro, NC.

Brooks, Norward J. "The Future of Comprehensive Colleges and Universities." Washington, DC: US Department of Health Education and Welfare, National Institute of Education, Feb. 19, 1980.

Brunt, Mildred. "Aunt Emmaline." *Sample Case* 1.2 (1930): 4–5.

Bryant, J. A. Memo to Chancellor Otis A. Singletary, Oct. 29, 1962. Otis A. Singletary Records. UA 2.7, Box 4. University of North Carolina–Greensboro Archives, Greensboro, NC.

———. Memo to Dean Mereb E. Mossman, Nov. 7, 1961. Otis A. Singletary Records. UA 2.7, Box 1. University of North Carolina–Greensboro Archives, Greensboro, NC.

———. Memo to Professors Bridgers, Bush, Charles, Dixon, Ellis, Gagen, Futzel, Stephens, Taylor, and Watson, Oct. 22, 1963. Otis A. Singletary Records. UA 4.22, Box 1. University of North Carolina–Greensboro Archives, Greensboro, NC.

Buck, Paul. Letter to W. K. Jordan, July 7, 1945. Records of the Radcliffe Committee on the Higher Education of Women. RGI Series 14, Box 1, Folder 7. Radcliffe College Archives, Cambridge, MA.

Bush, May Dulaney. Letter to Dr. W. W. Pierson, Chancellor, Dec. 18, 1956. William Whatley Pierson Records, 1956–57. UA 2.5, Box 1. University of North Carolina–Greensboro Archives, Greensboro, NC.

———. Personnel Form for News Bureau, Feb. 1, 1941. May Bush File, Biographical Files of Faculty. UA 202, Box 2. University of North Carolina–Greensboro Archives, Greensboro, NC.

———. Personnel Form for News Bureau, Dec. 2, 1943. May Bush File, Biographical Files of Faculty. UA 202, Box 2. University of North Carolina–Greensboro Archives, Greensboro, NC.

———. Personnel Form for News Bureau, Fall 1960. May Bush File, Biographical Files of Faculty. UA 202, Box 2. University of North Carolina–Greensboro Archives, Greensboro, NC.

———. "Rational Proof of a Deity from the Order of Nature." *Journal of English Literary History* 9.4 (1942): 288–319.

Cahn, Susan K. *Sexual Reckonings: Southern Girls in a Troubling Age.* Cambridge, MA: Harvard UP, 2007.

Caldwell, John T. Letter to Students, Faculty, and Alumni of North Carolina State College, Nov. 23, 1962. Otis Arnold Singletary Records. UA 2.7, Box 6. University of North Carolina–Greensboro Archives, Greensboro, NC.

Campbell, JoAnn. "Controlling Voices: The Legacy of English A at Radcliffe College, 1883–1917." *College Composition and Communication* 43.4 (1992): 472–85.

Carr, Jean Ferguson, Stephen L. Carr, and Lucille M. Schultz. *Archives of Instruction: Nineteenth Century Rhetorics, Readers, and Composition Books in the United States.* Pittsburgh: U of Pittsburgh P, 2005.

CCCC. Workshop on "Administering the Freshman Course." *College Composition and Communication* 15.3 (1964): 197.

"CCCC Bulletin Board." Report of the 1955 Conference on College Composition and Communication. *College Composition and Communication* 6.3 (1955): 180–83.

Charles, Amy. "May Delaney Bush." *Alumni News* (Spring 1968). Biographical files of faculty. UA 202, Box 2. University of North Carolina–Greensboro Archives, Greensboro, NC.

Click, L. L. Letter to Randall Jarrell, July 15, 1946. Randall Jarrell Papers, 1929–69. Mss009, Box 7. University of North Carolina–Greensboro Archives, Greensboro, NC.

Coffman, George R. "A New Order." *South Atlantic Bulletin* 11.2 (1945): 1, 4–5.

College Committee on English in the Normal School, National Council of Teachers of English. "Editorial: Supervisors of English." 3.10 (1914): 661–62.

Comstock, Ada L., and Dorothy Brewer Blackall. Memo, "To the Former Students of Radcliffe College," Mar. 15, 1928. Radcliffe College 1928 alumnae questionnaires. RG1X, Series 14, Carton 1. Radcliffe College Archives, Cambridge, MA.

Connors, Robert. *Composition-Rhetoric: Backgrounds, Theory, Pedagogy.* Pittsburgh: U of Pittsburgh P, 1997.

Conway, Kathryn M. "Woman Suffrage and the History of Rhetoric at the Seven Sisters Colleges, 1865–1919." *Reclaiming Rhetorica: Women in the Rhetorical Tradition.* Ed. Andrea A. Lunsford. Pittsburgh: U of Pittsburgh P, 1995. 203–26.

Coraddi. Woman's College of the University of North Carolina, Greensboro, NC.

Covington, Lois. "On Being Plain." *Sample Case* 1.2 (1930): 10.

Cowan, Mary. Untitled aphorism. *Sample Case* 1.2 (1930): 12.

Crowley, Sharon. *Composition in the University: Historical and Polemical Essays.* Pittsburgh: U of Pittsburgh P, 1998.

Cutler, Frances Wentworth. "Speaking of College Papers." *English Journal* 9.7 (1920): 407–10.

Dameron, Julia. Letter to Julius I. Foust, Feb. 9, 1919. Julius Issac Foust Records, 1855–1906. UA 2.2, Box D. University of North Carolina–Greensboro Archives, Greensboro, NC.

Davies, Ruth. "A Defense of Freshmen." *College English* 12.8 (1951): 440–48.

Davis, Mrs. Mary Bailey (Thomas) Williams. Letter to Chancellor Otis A. Singletary, Nov. 12, 1962. Otis Arnold Singletary Records. UA 2.7, Box 6. University of North Carolina–Greensboro Archives, Greensboro, NC.

De Almedia, Ava. *Lifting the Veil of Sisterhood: Women's Culture and Student Activism at a Southern College, 1920–1940.* Unpublished thesis, 1989. UA Ref 2, c.1. University of North Carolina–Greensboro Archives, Greensboro, NC.

"Department of English Budget Proposal for 1945–1946." Walter C. Jackson Records. UA 2.3, Box 15. University of North Carolina–Greensboro Archives, Greensboro, NC.

Department of English. "A Manual of Instructions for Freshman English," 1930–31, 1949–50. UA 4.22, Box 1. University of North Carolina–Greensboro Archives, Greensboro, NC.

———. Ninth Monthly Meeting Minutes, May 19, 1944. Department of English Records. UA 4.22, Box 1. University of North Carolina–Greensboro Archives, Greensboro, NC.

———. Fourth Monthly Staff Meeting Minutes, Mar. 8, 1948. Department of English Records. UA 4.22, Box 1. University of North Carolina–Greensboro Archives, Greensboro, NC.

———. Second Monthly Staff Meeting Minutes, Dec. 6, 1948. Department of English Records. UA 4.22, Box 1. University of North Carolina–Greensboro Archives, Greensboro, NC.

———. Third Monthly Staff Meeting Minutes, Jan. 10, 1949. Department of English Records. UA 4.22, Box 1. University of North Carolina–Greensboro Archives, Greensboro, NC.

———. Third Monthly Staff Meeting Minutes, Dec. 13, 1950. Department of English Records. UA 4.22, Box 1. University of North Carolina–Greensboro Archives, Greensboro, NC.

———. Sixth Monthly Staff Meeting Minutes, Apr. 11, 1951. Department of English Records. UA 4.22, Box 1. University of North Carolina–Greensboro Archives, Greensboro, NC.

———. Seventh Monthly Staff Meeting Minutes, May 16, 1951. Department of English Records. UA 4.22, Box 1. University of North Carolina–Greensboro Archives, Greensboro, NC.

———. "Second Monthly Staff Meeting Minutes," Nov. 10, 1952. Department of English Records. UA 4.22, Box 1. University of North Carolina–Greensboro University Archives, Greensboro, NC.

———. Third Monthly Staff Meeting Minutes, Jan. 11, 1954. Department of English Records. UA 4.22, Box 1. University of North Carolina–Greensboro University Archives, Greensboro, NC.

———. Minutes of the Meeting of Committee to Examine Freshman and Sophomore English Courses, Feb. 15, 1954. Department of English Records. UA 4.22, Box 1. University of North Carolina–Greensboro University Archives, Greensboro, NC.

———. Minutes of the Meeting of Committee on Freshman and Sophomore English, Feb. 21, 1954. Department of English Records. UA 4.22, Box 1. University of North Carolina–Greensboro University Archives, Greensboro, NC.

———. Minutes of the Committee on Freshman and Sophomore English, Mar. 1, 1954. Department of English Records. UA 4.22, Box 1. University of North Carolina–Greensboro University Archives, Greensboro, NC.

———. "Tentative Language." Memo from Committee on Freshman and Sophomore English, Mar. 1, 1954. Department of English Records. UA 4.22, Box 1. University of North Carolina–Greensboro University Archives, Greensboro, NC.

———. Minutes of the Committee on Freshman and Sophomore English, Mar. 8, 1954. Department of English Records. UA 4.22, Box 1. University of North Carolina–Greensboro University Archives, Greensboro, NC.

———. Minutes of the Committee on Freshman and Sophomore English, Mar. 15, 1954. Department of English Records. UA 4.22, Box 1. University of North Carolina–Greensboro University Archives, Greensboro, NC.

———. Minutes of the Committee on Freshman and Sophomore English, Apr. 22, 1954. Department of English Records. UA 4.22, Box 1. University of North Carolina–Greensboro University Archives, Greensboro, NC.

———. Minutes of the Committee on Freshman and Sophomore English, May 3, 1954. Department of English Records. UA 4.22, Box 1. University of North Carolina–Greensboro University Archives, Greensboro, NC.

———. Minutes of the Committee on Freshman and Sophomore English, May 10, 1954. Department of English Records. UA 4.22, Box 1. University of North Carolina–Greensboro University Archives, Greensboro, NC.

———. Minutes of the Committee on Freshman and Sophomore English, May 25, 1954. Department of English Records. UA 4.22, Box 1. University of North Carolina–Greensboro University Archives, Greensboro, NC.

———. Meeting of the Staff Minutes, May 28, 1954. Department of English Records. UA 4.22, Box 1. University of North Carolina–Greensboro University Archives, Greensboro, NC.

———. Monthly English Staff Meeting, Jan. 10, 1955. Department of English Records. UA 4.22, Box 1. University of North Carolina–Greensboro University Archives, Greensboro, NC.

———. Minutes of the Freshman-Sophomore Study Committee, Feb. 21, 1955. Department of English Records. UA 4.22, Box 1. University of North Carolina–Greensboro University Archives, Greensboro, NC.

———. Minutes of the Freshman-Sophomore Study Committee, Mar. 7, 1955. Department of English Records. UA 4.22, Box 1. University of North Carolina–Greensboro University Archives, Greensboro, NC.

———. Minutes of Staff Meeting, Mar. 14, 1955. Department of English Records. UA 4.22, Box 1. University of North Carolina–Greensboro University Archives, Greensboro, NC.

———. Minutes of the Feb. 9, 1956, Staff Meeting. Department of English Records, UA 4.22, Box 1. University of North Carolina–Greensboro University Archives, Greensboro, NC.

———. Minutes of the English Staff Meeting, May 14, 1956. Department of English Records. UA 4.22, Box 1. University of North Carolina–Greensboro University Archives, Greensboro, NC.

Dillman, Caroline Matheny. "Southern Women: In Continuity or Change?" *Women in the South: An Anthropological Perspective*. Ed. Holly F. Mathews. Athens: U of Georgia P, 1989. 8–17.

Dockray-Miller, Mary. "Feminine Preoccupations: English at the Seven Sisters." *Modern Language Studies* 27.3/4 (1997): 139–57.

Donahue, Patricia, and Gretchen Fleisher Moon, eds. *Local Histories: Reading the Archives of Composition*. Pittsburgh: U of Pittsburgh P, 2007.

Dunn, Sayde, Office of Admissions. Memo to Chancellor Otis Singletary, Oct. 18, 1962. Records of Otis Arnold Singletary. UA 2.7, Box 6. University of North Carolina–Greensboro Archives, Greensboro, NC.

Edwards, Elizabeth. *Women in Teacher Training Colleges, 1900–1960: A Culture of Femininity.* New York: Routledge, 2001.

Edwards, Margaret, Mckee Fisk, James A. Highsmith, Franklin H. McNutt, Lawrence S. Ritchie, Lyda Gordon Shivers, and Eugene Pfaff. "Report of the Curriculum Revision Committee," Mar. 15, 1943. Records of the Woman's College of the North Carolina Curriculum Committee, Ad Hoc Appointed and Elected Committees, 1945–52, Box 27. University of North Carolina–Greensboro Archives, Greensboro, NC.

Eisman, Julia. Untitled summary. Dec. 10, 1923. English A Miscellaneous Correspondence: Sample Themes, Radcliffe, 1923–24. UAV 363.123.6, Harvard University Archives, Cambridge, MA.

Elliott, Harriet. Address to Faculty Council, Apr. 17, 1944. Minutes of the Faculty Council. UA 1.2, Box 3. University of North Carolina–Greensboro Archives, Greensboro, NC.

"English Department Committees 1948–1949." UA 4.22, Box 1. University of North Carolina–Greensboro Archives, Greensboro, NC.

"English Department Staff, 1964–1965." Otis Arnold Singletary Records. UA 2.7, Box 8. University of North Carolina–Greensboro Archives, Greensboro, NC.

English 222 Class. "Papers Written by the English Class in Composition (English 222) Just after Hearing President Truman's Broadcast on V-E Day, May 8, 1945." Jane Summerell, Instructor. CQ P214 c.1. University of North Carolina–Greensboro Archives, Greensboro, NC.

"Enrollment Projections: The Woman's College of the University of North Carolina." Dec. 7, 1960. William Whatley Pierson Records. UA 2.5, Box 5. University of North Carolina–Greensboro Archives, Greensboro, NC.

Faculty Council of the Woman's College of the University of North Carolina. Minutes, Sept. 10, 1934. Faculty Council/General Faculty, Minutes and Related Material, 1895–1996. UA 1.2, Box 3. University of North Carolina–Greensboro Archives, Greensboro, NC.

———. Minutes, Apr. 17, 1944. Faculty Council/General Faculty, Minutes and Related Material, 1895–1996. UA 1.2, Box 3. University of North Carolina–Greensboro Archives, Greensboro, NC.

"Faculty Evaluation Form." Walter C. Jackson Records, UA 2.3, Box 15. University of North Carolina–Greensboro Archives, Greensboro, NC

"Faculty Profile: Theodore Morrison, A.B." *Harvard Crimson* Apr. 21, 1943. Web. http://www.thecrimson.com/article/1943/4/21/faculty-profile-ptheodore-morrison-is-director/.

Fairclough, Adam. *A Class of Their Own: Black Teachers in the Segregated South.* Cambridge, MA: Belknap Press, 2007.

Fenza, Dave. "About AWP: The Growth of Creative Writing Programs." Web. Accessed July 31, 2011. http://www.awpwriter.org/aboutawp/index.htm.

Finkelstein, H. N. "Milton's Hypothesis." English A Miscellaneous Correspondence: Sample Themes, Radcliffe, 1923–24. UAV 363.123.6. Harvard University Archives, Cambridge, MA.

Fitzgerald, Kathryn. "A Rediscovered Tradition: European Pedagogy and Composition in Nineteenth-Century Midwestern Normal Schools." *College Composition and Communication* 53.2 (2001): 224–50.

Foust, Julius Issac. Letter to Miss Julia Dameron, Feb. 5, 1919. Julius Issac Foust Records, 1855–1906. UA 2.2, Box D. University of North Carolina–Greensboro Archives, Greensboro, NC.

Fowler, Burton P. "Points Made in Presenting 'The Case for Coeducation' at Radcliffe Col-

lege, Oct. 21, 1944." Records of the Radcliffe College Committee on the Higher Education of Women. RGI Series 14, Box 1, Folder 3. Radcliffe College Archives, Cambridge,
MA.

Fowler, Herbert E. "English in a Normal School." *English Journal* 4.4 (1915): 244–47.

Friday, William. Letter to Thomas J. Pearsall, Oct. 9, 1962. Otis Arnold Singletary Records.
UA 2.7, Box 6. University of North Carolina–Greensboro Archives, Greensboro, NC.

Friedlander, Marc. "Some Points in the Present Integration of Freshman and Sophomore
English." Feb. 1954. Department of English Records. UA 4.22, Box 1. University of
North Carolina–Greensboro Archives, Greensboro, NC.

Gallien, Louis Bertrand, Jr. *The Coeducational Transition of the Woman's College of the
University of North Carolina: A Case Study in Organizational Change.* Diss. University
of North Carolina–Greensboro, 1987.

"General Education A Finishes First Term; Freshmen 'See' Essays Criticized in Class." *Harvard Crimson* Feb. 9, 1951. Web. Accessed Dec. 8, 2009. http://www.thecrimson.com
/article/1951/2/9/general-education-a-finishes-first-term.

"General Education at Radcliffe College." Governing Boards/Radcliffe College Committee
on the Higher Education of Women. RGI Series 14, Box 1, Folder 6. Radcliffe College
Archives, Cambridge, MA.

General Education Steering Committee. Meeting Minutes, Sept. 24, 1951. Edward Kidder
Graham Records. UA 2.4, Box 4. University of North Carolina–Greensboro Archives,
Greensboro, NC.

———. Meeting Minutes, Oct. 25, 1951. Edward Kidder Graham Records. UA 2.4, Box 4.
University of North Carolina–Greensboro Archives, Greensboro, NC.

———. "Record of Motions to Adopt Humanities, Natural Sciences, and Social Sciences
Statements, and Steering Committee Report." May 19, 1953. Edward Kidder Graham
Records. UA 2.4, Box 4. University of North Carolina–Greensboro Archives, Greens-
boro, NC.

———. "Statement of Objectives," Nov. 20, 1951. Edward Kidder Graham Records. UA 2.4,
Box 4. University of North Carolina–Greensboro Archives, Greensboro, NC.

George, D'Ann. "'Replacing Nice, Thin Bryn Mawr Miss Crandall with Fat, Harvard Sav-
age': WPAs at Bryn Mawr College, 1902–1923." *Historical Studies of Writing Program
Administration.* Ed. Barbara L'Eplattenier and Lisa Mastrangelo. Lafayette, IN: Parlor
Press, 2007. 23–36.

Glenn, Cheryl, and Jessica Enoch. "Drama in the Archives: Rereading Methods, Rewriting
History." *College Composition and Communication* 61.2 (2009): 321–42.

Goggin, Maureen Daly. *Authoring a Discipline: Scholarly Journals and the Post–World War
II Emergence of Rhetoric and Composition.* Mahwah, NJ: Lawrence Erlbaum, 2000.

Gold, David. "Eve Did No Wrong: Effective Literacy at a Public College for Women." *College Composition and Communication* 62.1 (Dec. 2009): W177–W196.

———. "Nothing Educates Us Like a Shock: The Integrated Rhetoric of Melvin B. Tolson."
College Composition and Communication 55 (Dec. 2003).

———. *Rhetoric at the Margins: Revisiting the History of Writing Instruction in American
Colleges, 1873–1947.* Carbondale, IL: Southern Illinois UP, 2008.

Goldin, Claudia. *Understanding the Gender Gap: An Economic History of American Wom-
en.* New York: Oxford UP, 1990.

Graff, Gerald. *Professing Literature: An Institutional History.* Chicago: U of Chicago P, 1987.

Graham, Edward Kidder. "Tentative Statement of Objectives in General Education," Jan.
27, 1951. Edward Kidder Graham Records. UA 2.4, Box 4. University of North Carolina–Greensboro Archives, Greensboro, NC.

———. Letter to Dr. Ralph McDonald, Executive Secretary, Department of Higher Education, Mar. 10, 1951. Edward Kidder Graham Records. UA 2.4, Box 4. University of North Carolina–Greensboro Archives, Greensboro, NC.

———. Letter to Clarence Faust, Ford Foundation, Apr. 7, 1951. Edward Kidder Graham Records. UA 2.4, Box 4. University of North Carolina–Greensboro Archives, Greensboro, NC.

———. Letter to Frank H. Bowles, Apr. 20, 1951. Edward Kidder Graham Records. UA 2.4, Box 4. University of North Carolina–Greensboro Archives, Greensboro, NC.

———. Letter to O. C. Carmichael, Carnegie Foundation, Apr. 24, 1951. Edward Kidder Graham Records. UA 2.4, Box 4. University of North Carolina–Greensboro Archives, Greensboro, NC.

———. Letter to Thomas S. Hall, Dean of Washington University–St. Louis, Apr. 27, 1951. Edward Kidder Graham Records. UA 2.4, Box 4. University of North Carolina–Greensboro Archives, Greensboro, NC.

———. Letter to Clarence Faust, Ford Foundation, May 22, 1951. Edward Kidder Graham Records. UA 2.4, Box 4. University of North Carolina–Greensboro Archives, Greensboro, NC.

———. Letter to Frank H. Bowles, Dec. 19, 1953. Edward Kidder Graham Records. UA 2.4, Box 4, University of North Carolina–Greensboro Archives, NC.

———. "Summary Descriptions of the General Education Program at the Cooperating Institutions." Edward Kidder Graham Records. UA 2.4, Box 4. University of North Carolina–Greensboro Archives, Greensboro, NC.

Greene, Christina. *Our Separate Ways: Women and the Black Freedom Movement in Durham, North Carolina.* Chapel Hill: U of North Carolina P, 2005.

Grey, Gordon. Letter to O. C. Carmichael, Apr. 24, 1951. Edward Kidder Graham Records. VA 2.4, Box 4. University of North Carolina–Greensboro Archives, Greensboro, NC.

Grimes, Tom. *The Workshop: Seven Decades of the Iowa Writers' Workshop. 43 Stories, Essays, and Recollections on Iowa's Place in Twentieth-Century American Literature.* New York: Hyperion, 2001.

Harrington, Dana, and Heather Shearer. "Administrating Ourselves to Death: Historiography and the Ethics of Writing Program Administration Narratives." *The Perils and Promise of Writing Program Administration.* Ed. Shane Borrowman and Theresa Enos. Lafayette, IN: Parlor Press, 2009. 347–61.

Harvard Committee on General Education in a Free Society. "Accepting One's Physique and Accepting a Masculine or Feminine Role." Committee on General Education in a Free Society Records. UA 10.528.10, Box 2, Serial Nos. 47–66. Harvard University Archives, Cambridge, MA.

———. "The Changed Position of Women." Committee on General Education in a Free Society Records. UA 10.528.10, Box 2, Supplements 1–16. Harvard University Archives, Cambridge, MA.

———. Meeting Minutes, Sept. 28, 1943. Committee on General Education in a Free Society Records. UA 10.528.10, Box 2, Serial Nos. 18–29. Harvard University Archives, Cambridge, MA.

———. Meeting Minutes, Nov. 18, 1943. Committee on General Education in a Free Society Records. UA 10.528.10, Box 2, Supplements 1–16. Harvard University Archives, Cambridge, MA.

———. Meeting Minutes, Apr. 25, 1944. Committee on General Education in a Free Society Records. UA 10.528.10, Box 1, Serial Nos. 99–112. Harvard University Archives, Cambridge, MA.

———. "Message from President Franklin D. Roosevelt." Committee on General Education in a Free Society Records. UA 10.528.10, Box 1, Supplements 1–16. Harvard University Archives, Cambridge, MA.

———. "Revised Timing Schedule." Committee on General Education in a Free Society Records. UA 10.528.10, Box 2, Serial Nos. 67–78. Harvard University Archives, Cambridge, MA.

———. "Tutorials." Committee on the Objectives of a General Education in a Free Society, 1943–45. UA 10.528.10, Box 1. Harvard University Archives, Cambridge, MA.

Harvard Committee on the Objectives of a General Education in a Free Society. *General Education in a Free Society*. Cambridge, MA: Harvard UP, 1945.

Harvard University Committee on the Preparation of Teachers. *The Training of Secondary School Teachers: Especially with Reference to English*. Cambridge, MA: Harvard UP, 1943.

Harvard University Student Council. "A Précis of General Education in a Free Society with Commentaries by William Allen Neilson [et al.]." Harvard Student Council, 1945. HUC 8945.132.15. Harvard University Archives, Cambridge, MA.

Harwath, Irene, Mindi Maline, and Elizabeth DeBra. "Women's Colleges in the United States: History, Issues, and Challenges." Hartford, CT: Women's College Coalition, 1993. 1–43.

Hatfield, W. Wilbur. "'General' Education." *English Journal* 34.9 (1945): 523–24.

Heckathorn, Amy. "Moving Toward a Group Identity: WPA Professionalization from the 1940s to the 1970s." *Historical Studies of Writing Program Administration*. Ed. Barbara Eplattenier and Lisa Mastrangelo. Lafayette, IN: Parlor Press, 2007. 191–220.

Henze, Brent, Jack Selzer, and Wendy Sharer. *1977: A Cultural Moment in Composition*. Lafayette, IN: Parlor Press, 2008.

Hitchcock, Frances. "Summary Sentences." English A Miscellaneous Correspondence: Sample Themes, Radcliffe, 1923–24. UAV 363.123.6. Harvard University Archives, Cambridge, MA.

Holbrook, Sue Ellen. "Women's Work: The Feminizing of Composition." *Rhetoric Review* 9.2 (1991): 201–29.

Hollinshead, Byron S. Letter to W. K. Jordan, Oct. 19, 1944. Radcliffe College Committee on the Higher Education of Women. RGI Series 14, Box 1, Folder 4. Radcliffe College Archives, Cambridge, MA.

———. "Memorandum on Radcliffe Questionnaires." Radcliffe College Committee on the Higher Education of Women. RGI Series 14, Box 1, Folder 2. Radcliffe College Archives, Cambridge, MA.

Hollis, Karyn. "Liberating Voices: Autobiographical Writing at the Bryn Mawr Summer School for Women Workers, 1921–1938." *College Composition and Communication* 45.1 (1994): 31–60.

Hughes, Helen Said. "The Prescribed Work in English: Its Relation to Secondary Schools." *English Journal* 11.4 (1922): 199–213.

Hurley, Leonard B. "Annual Report, Department of English, 1952–1953." June 15, 1953. Edward Kidder Graham Records. UA 2.4, Box 9. University of North Carolina–Greensboro Archives, Greensboro, NC.

———. "Faculty Rank by Year for 1925–26, 1929–30, 1934–35, 1938–39, 1943–44, 1946–47, 1951–52." Department of English, the Woman's College. Gordon William Blackwell Records, 1957–60. UA 2.6, Box 6. University of North Carolina–Greensboro Archives, Greensboro, NC.

———. Letter to Gordon W. Blackwell, Chancellor, Jan. 25, 1958. Gordon William Blackwell Records, 1957–60. UA 2.6, Box 6. University of North Carolina–Greensboro Archives, Greensboro, NC.

———. Letter to Gordon W. Blackwell, Chancellor, Mar. 5, 1958. Gordon William Blackwell Records, 1957–60. UA 2.6, Box 6. University of North Carolina–Greensboro Archives, Greensboro, NC.

———. Letter to Randall and Mackie Jarrell, Apr. 18, 1947. Randall Jarrell Papers, 1929–69. Mss009, Box 7. University of North Carolina–Greensboro Archives, Greensboro, NC.

———. Memo to Chancellor Edward K. Graham, May 5, 1951. Edward Kidder Graham Records. UA 2.4, Box 15. University of North Carolina–Greensboro Archives, Greensboro, NC.

———. Memo to Chancellor Edward K. Graham, July 13, 1951. Edward Kidder Graham Records. UA 2.4, Box 15. University of North Carolina–Greensboro Archives, Greensboro, NC.

———. Memo to Chancellor Edward K. Graham, Apr. 21, 1955. Edward Kidder Graham Records. UA 2.4, Box 15. University of North Carolina–Greensboro Archives, Greensboro, NC.

———. Memo to Mereb E. Mossman, Dean, Feb. 9, 1956. Department of English Records. UA 4.22, Box 1. University of North Carolina–Greensboro Archives, Greensboro, NC.

———. Memo to Mereb E. Mossman, Dean, Apr. 12, 1957. Gordon William Blackwell Records, 1957–60. UA 2.6, Box 2. University of North Carolina–Greensboro Archives, Greensboro, NC.

———. Memo to Walter C. Jackson, Dean, Mar. 23, 1948. Walter C. Jackson Records, UA 2.3, Box 20. University of North Carolina–Greensboro Archives, Greensboro, NC.

———. Memo to Walter C. Jackson, Dean, June 9, 1948. Walter C. Jackson Records, UA 2.3, Box 20. University of North Carolina–Greensboro Archives, Greensboro, NC.

———. Memo to Walter C. Jackson, Dean, Apr. 30, 1949. Walter C. Jackson Records, UA 2.3, Box 22. University of North Carolina–Greensboro Archives, Greensboro, NC.

———. Memo to Walter C. Jackson, Dean, May 10, 1949. Walter B. Jackson Records, UA 2.3, Box 22. University of North Carolina–Greensboro Archives, Greensboro, NC.

———. Memo to Walter C. Jackson, Dean, undated (ca. Spring 1949). Walter B. Jackson Records, UA 2.3, Box 22. University of North Carolina–Greensboro Archives, Greensboro, NC.

———. "Report on English Department Enrollments and Teacher-Student Loads," to Mereb E. Mossman, Dean, Oct. 27, 1955. Edward Kidder Graham Records. UA 2.4, Box 15. University of North Carolina–Greensboro Archives, Greensboro, NC.

"Information for Servicewomen." Walter C. Jackson Records, UA 2.3, Box 15. University of North Carolina–Greensboro Archives, Greensboro, NC.

Isenberg, M. Letter to Marc Friedlander, May 11, 1953. Edward Kidder Graham Records. UA 2.4, Box 10. University of North Carolina–Greensboro Archives, Greensboro, NC.

Jacobs, Timothy. *An Oasis of Order: The Core Curriculum at Columbia College.* Office of the Dean, Columbia College, 1995. Web. Accessed Nov. 1, 2009. http://www.college.columbia.edu/core/oasis/history4.php.

Jarrell, Mary, Ed. *Randall Jarrell's Letters.* New York: Houghton Mifflin, 1985.

Jewett, Ida A. "English in State Teachers' Colleges." *English Journal* 19.4 (1930): 321–29.

Jordan, W. K. "Radcliffe's Newest Committee." *Radcliffe Quarterly* 29.1 (1944): 7–8.

Karabel, Jerome. *The Chosen: The Hidden History of Admission and Exclusion at Harvard, Yale, and Princeton.* New York: Houghton Mifflin, 2005.

Kittrell, Mrs. Elizabeth Hinton (J. B.). Letter to Chancellor Otis A. Singletary, Nov. 26,

1962. Otis Arnold Singletary Records. UA 2.7, Box 6. University of North Carolina–Greensboro Archives, Greensboro, NC.

Learned, William S., and William C. Bagley. *The Professional Preparation of Teachers for American Public Schools: A Study Based upon an Examination of Tax-Supported Normal Schools in the State of Missouri*. New York: The Carnegie Foundation, 1920.

L'Eplattenier, Barbara, and Lisa Mastrangelo, eds. *Historical Studies of Writing Program Administration: Individuals, Communities, and the Formation of a Discipline*. Lafayette, IN: Parlor Press, 2004.

Lerner, Neal. "Rejecting the Remedial Brand: The Rise and Fall of the Dartmouth Writing Clinic." *College Composition and Communication* 59.1 (Sept. 2007): 13–35.

Linde, Charlotte. *Working the Past: Narrative and Institutional Memory*. Oxford: Oxford UP, 2008.

Lindemann, Erika. "Freshman Composition: No Place for Literature." *College English* 55 (Mar. 1993): 311–16.

Lockhart, John C. "Report of the Committee on Post War Planning." Walter C. Jackson Records, UA 2.3, Box 15. University of North Carolina–Greensboro Archives, Greensboro, NC.

Mandel, Andrew K. "Feminism and Femininity in Almost Equal Balance." *Yards and Gates: Gender in Harvard and Radcliffe History*. Ed. Laurel Thatcher Ulrich. New York: Palgrave MacMillan, 2004. 215–26.

Masters, Thomas. *Practicing Writing: Postwar Discourse of Freshman English*. Pittsburgh: U of Pittsburgh P, 2004.

Mathews, Holly F. "Introduction: What Does It Mean to Be a Woman in the South Today?" *Women in the South: An Anthropological Perspective*. Ed. Holly F. Mathews. Athens: U of Georgia P, 1989. 1–7.

Mayers, Timothy. *(Re)Writing Craft: Composition, Creative Writing, and the Future of English Studies*. Pittsburgh: U of Pittsburgh P, 2005.

McCandless, Amy Thompson. *The Past in the Present: Women's Higher Education in the Twentieth-Century American South*. Tuscaloosa, AL: U of Alabama P, 1999.

McConnell, T. R. "Review: Education for Citizenship in a Democracy." *School Review* 53.8 (1945): 495–97.

McCutchen, Hannah. "Early Ambitions." *Sample Case*. 1.1 (1929): 18.

McDowell, Tremaine. "General Education and College English." *College English* 7.6 (1946): 351–57.

McGurl, Mark. *The Program Era: Postwar Fiction and the Rise of Creative Writing*. Cambridge, MA: Harvard UP, 2009.

Mendenhall, Thomas C. Letter to Mary Jarrell. May 15, 1965. Randall Jarrell Papers, 1929–69. Mss009, Box 7. University of North Carolina–Greensboro Archives, Greensboro, NC.

Miller, Susan. *The Norton Book of Composition Studies*. New York: W. W. Norton, 2009.

———. *Textual Carnivals: The Politics of Composition*. Carbondale, IL: Southern Illinois UP, 1993.

Miller-Bernal, Leslie. "Single-Sex Versus Coeducational Environments: A Comparison of Women Students' Experiences at Four Colleges." *American Journal of Education* 102.1 (1993): 23–54.

Moore, Elizabeth, Dora Gilbert Tompkins, and Mildred MacLean. *English Composition for College Women*. New York: Macmillan, 1914.

Morrison, Theodore. "English Composition in the High School." Feb. 1944. Records of the

Committee on General Education in a Free Society. UA 10.528.10, Box 2, Supplement 15. Harvard University Archives, Cambridge, MA.

Mossman, Mereb E. Memo to Gordon W. Blackwell, Chancellor, Jan. 26, 1958. Gordon William Blackwell Records, 1957–60. UA 2.6, Box 6. University of North Carolina–Greensboro Archives, Greensboro, NC.

Murphy, James J, James Berlin, Robert J. Connors, Sharon Crowley, Richard Leo Enos, Victor J. Vitanza, Susan C. Jarrett, Nan Johnson, and Jan Swearingen. "Octalog: The Politics of Historiography." *Rhetoric Review* 7.1 (1988): 5–49.

Myers, D. G. *The Elephants Teach: Creative Writing Since 1880*. Englewood Cliffs, NJ: Prentice Hall, 1996.

Napier, T. H. "The Southern State College for Women." *Peabody Journal of Education* 18.5 (1941): 268–75.

Newkirk, Thomas. "The Dogma of Transformation." *College Composition and Communication* 56.2 (2004): 251–71.

"New Look for English A." *Harvard Crimson* Feb. 28, 1949. Web. Accessed May 25, 2007. http://www.thecrimson.com/article/1949/2/28/new-look-for-english-a-penglish.

North Carolina College for Women. *Annual Catalogue, 1922–23*. Greensboro, NC.

North Carolina State Normal and Industrial College. *Bulletin of the State Normal and Industrial College, 1913–14*. Greensboro, NC.

——. *Bulletin of the State Normal and Industrial College, 1917–18*. Greensboro, NC.

——. *State Normal Magazine* 20.2 (Nov. 1917). CN N86co 1. University of North Carolina–Greensboro Archives, Greensboro, NC.

Ogren, Christine A. *The American State Normal School: "An Instrument of Great Good."* New York: Palgrave MacMillan, 2005.

Page, Lucy, ed. "Pages's Pages." Student essays. Greensboro, NC: The Woman's College of the University of North Carolina, 1950.

Parcell, Blanche. "On Such Stuff." *Sample Case* 1.2 (1930): 10–12.

Parker, Mattie Erma Edwards. Letter to Chancellor Otis A. Singletary, Dec. 6, 1962. Otis Arnold Singletary Records. UA 2.7, Box 6. University of North Carolina–Greensboro Archives, Greensboro, NC.

"Petition for an Allocation of Graduate Function in the Creative Arts and for the Establishment of a Creative Arts Program at the Woman's College." 1948. Walter C. Jackson Records, UA 2.3, Box 21. University of North Carolina–Greensboro Archives, Greensboro, NC.

Pine Needles 1952. Woman's College of the University of North Carolina, Greensboro, NC, 1952.

Pine Needles 1963. Woman's College of the University of North Carolina, Greensboro, NC, 1963.

Popken, Randall. "The WPA as Publishing Scholar: Edwin Hopkins and the Labor and the Cost of the Teaching of English." *Historical Studies of Writing Program Administration*. Ed. Barbara Eplattenier and Lisa Mastrangelo. Lafayette, IN: Parlor Press, 2007. 5–22.

"Précis of General Education in a Free Society, A." Cambridge, MA: Harvard Student Council, 1945. Reprinted from *Harvard Alumni Bulletin*, Sept. 22, 1945.

"Radcliffe Alumnae Information Questionnaire." Radcliffe College 1928 Alumnae Questionnaires. RG1X, Series 14, Carton 1. Radcliffe College Archives, Cambridge, MA.

Radcliffe College Committee on the Higher Education of Women. Agenda for College Conference for Women, Williamstown, MA, Nov. 4–5, 1944. Records of the Radcliffe

College Committee on the Higher Education of Women, RGI Series 14, Box 1, Folder 2. Radcliffe College Archives, Cambridge, MA.

———. Alumnae Survey, 1944. Records of the Radcliffe College Committee on the Higher Education of Women. RGI Series 14, Box 2, Folder 30. Radcliffe College Archives, Cambridge, MA.

Richards, I. A. "Basic English." Papers of Ivor Armstrong Richards, 1940–81 (inclusive). HUGB R461.10, Box 1. Harvard University Archives, Cambridge, MA.

Ritter, Kelly. "Before Mina Shaughnessy: Basic Writing at Yale, 1920–1960." *College Composition and Communication* 60.1 (Sept. 2008): 12–45.

———. *Before Shaughnessy: Basic Writing at Yale and Harvard, 1920–1960.* Studies in Writing and Rhetoric Series. Carbondale, IL: Southern Illinois UP, 2009.

Rogers, Lettie. Memo to Edward K. Graham, Chancellor, Jan. 2, 1955. Edward Kidder Graham Records. UA 2.4, Box 16. University of North Carolina–Greensboro Archives, Greensboro, NC.

Rogers, Lettie, and Robie Macauley. Memo to Edward K. Graham, Leonard B. Hurley, Mereb E. Mossman, Marc Friedlander, and Jane Summerell, May 28, 1959. Edward Kidder Graham Records. UA 2.4, Box 6. University of North Carolina–Greensboro Archives, Greensboro, NC.

Rose, Mike. "The Language of Exclusion: Writing Instruction at the University." *College English* 47.4 (1985): 341–59.

Rose, Shirley. "Representing the Intellectual Work of Writing Program Administration: Professional Narratives of George Wykoff at Purdue, 1933–1967." *Historical Studies of Writing Program Administration.* Ed. Barbara L'Epplantenier and Lisa Mastrangelo. Lafayette, IN: Parlor Press, 2007. 221–40.

Rose, Shirley K., and Irwin Weiser. "The WPA as Researcher and Archivist." *The Writing Program Administrator's Resource: A Guide to Reflective Institutional Practice.* Ed. Theresa Enos and Stuart Brown. Hillsdale, NJ: Erlbaum, 2002. 275–90.

Rounds, C. R. "English in the Normal School." *English Journal* 3.9 (1914): 553–57.

Russell, David. *Writing in the Academic Disciplines: A Curricular History.* Carbondale, IL: Southern Illinois UP, 2002.

Sample Case, The. Freshman English Class of the Woman's College of the University of North Carolina. CN S26 V 1.1, 2.1 (May 1929–May 1930). University of North Carolina–Greensboro Archives, Greensboro, NC.

Schell, Eileen. *Gypsy Academics and Mother-Teachers: Gender, Contingent Labor, and Writing Instruction.* Portsmouth, NH: Boynton Cook, 1997.

"School Ma'ams' Marriages Statistically Analyzed." *Science News Letter* Aug. 25, 1940: 125.

Schwager, Sally. "Educating Women in America." *Signs* 12.2 (1987): 333–72.

"Senate Bill 1509: Serviceman's Education and Training Act of 1943." Committee on General Education in a Free Society Records. UA 10.528.10, Box 3. Harvard University Archives, Cambridge, MA.

Singletary, Otis Arnold. "Miscellaneous Thoughts re: Co-education at Woman's College," 1962. Otis Arnold Singletary Records. UA 2.7, Box 6. University of North Carolina–Greensboro Archives, Greensboro, NC.

Soliday, Mary. *The Politics of Remediation: Institutional and Student Needs in Higher Education.* Pittsburgh: U of Pittsburgh P, 2002.

"Some Characteristics of the General Education Movement in the U.S." Edward Kidder Graham Records. UA 2.4, Box 4. University of North Carolina–Greensboro Archives, Greensboro, NC.

Spring, Suzanne. "Seemingly Uncouth Forms: Letters at Mount Holyoke Seminary." *College Composition and Communication* 59.4 (June 2008): 633–75.

Stanfield-Maddox, Elizabeth. Personal interview. Oct. 17, 2008.

Stanley, Jane. *The Rhetoric of Remediation: Negotiating Entitlement and Access to Higher Education.* Pittsburgh: U of Pittsburgh P, 2010.

Stanton, Edgar E., Jr. "Motivating Freshman Composition: The Freshman Magazine." *College English* 12.1 (1950): 41–42.

Stephens, Robert O. Letter to Mrs. Russell Lyday and Miss Ellen Douglas Bush, Nov. 7, 1983. Biographical files of faculty. UA 202, Box 2. University of North Carolina–Greensboro Archives, Greensboro, NC.

Stevens, Anne. "The Philosophy of General Education and Its Contradictions: The Influence of Hutchins." *Journal of General Education* 50.3 (2001): 165–91.

Synott, Marcia. "The Changing 'Harvard Student': Ethnicity, Race, and Gender." *Yards and Gates: Gender in Harvard and Radcliffe History.* Ed. Laurel Thatcher Ulrich. New York: Palgrave MacMillan, 2004. 195–214.

Tate, Gary. "A Place for Literature in Freshman Composition." *College English* 55 (Mar. 1993): 303–09.

Thames, Elisabeth Moffitt. "The Poetry of John Charles McNeill." Elisabeth Moffitt Thames scrapbook, 1915–19. Mss307. University of North Carolina–Greensboro Archives, Greensboro, NC.

"Theodore Morrison, Poet and Professor, 87." Obituary. *New York Times,* Nov. 29, 1988. Web. Accessed Dec. 8, 2009. http://www.nytimes.com/1988/11/29/obituaries/theodore-morrison-poet-and-professor-87.html.

Thomas, Pat. "Make Mine Southern Style." *Yearling* 4.1 (1951): 3–5.

Townsend, J. Benjamin. Memo to Leonard B. Hurley, Dec. 29, 1953. Department of English Records. UA 4.22, Box 1. University of North Carolina–Greensboro Archives, Greensboro, NC.

Trelease, Allen W. *Making North Carolina Literate: The University of North Carolina at Greensboro from Normal School to Metropolitan University.* Durham, NC: Carolina Academic P, 2004.

"Two to Retire." May Bush File, Biographical Files of Faculty. UA 202, Box 2. University of North Carolina–Greensboro Archives, Greensboro, NC.

University Testing Service. "Survey of Student Opinion on General Education at Woman's College, University of North Carolina, May 1953." Edward Kidder Graham Jr. Records, 1951–56. UA 2.4, Box 10. University of North Carolina–Greensboro Archives, Greensboro, NC.

Vanstory, C. M. Letter to Percy B. Ferebee, Oct. 26, 1962. Otis Arnold Singletary Records. UA 2.7, Box 6. University of North Carolina–Greensboro Archives, Greensboro, NC.

Varnum, Robin. *Fencing with Words: A History of Writing Instruction at Amherst College during the Era of Theodore Baird, 1938–1966.* Urbana, IL: NCTE, 1996.

Wagner, Lucy Page. Personal interview. Nov. 7, 2008.

Watson, Robert W. "Randall Jarrell: The Last Dozen Years." Robert W. Watson Papers, 1948–80. Mss084, Box 9. University of North Carolina–Greensboro Archives, Greensboro, NC.

Wellesley College Department of English. *Manual of Instructions, 1930–1931.* Records of the Department of English Composition. Record 3L, Box 4. Wellesley College Archives, Wellesley, MA.

Wells, Edith. "College Publications of Freshman Writing." *College Composition and Communication* 1.1 (1950): 3–11.

Weneck, Betty. "Social and Cultural Stratification in Women's Higher Education: Barnard College and Teachers College, 1898–1912." *History of Education Quarterly* 31.1 (1991): 1–25.

"What Makes Pembroke Pembroke?" Web. Accessed July 31, 2011. www.uncp.edu/uncp /about/quick-facts.htm.

Willing, M. H. "Review (Untitled)." *Journal of Educational Research* 40.2 (1946): 148–49.

Woman's College of the University of North Carolina. *Bulletin of the Woman's College of the University of North Carolina* (1949–50): 116–25.

———. *Bulletin of the Woman's College of the University of North Carolina* (1950–51): 119–23.

———. *Bulletin of the Woman's College of the University of North Carolina* (1952–53): 117–26.

———. Faculty, 1955. UA 4.22, Box 1. University of North Carolina–Greensboro Archives, Greensboro, NC.

"Woman's College of the University of North Carolina Budget for Year 1960–1961." Dec. 1960. Gordon William Blackwell Records, 1957–60. UA 2.6, Box 20. University of North Carolina–Greensboro Archives, Greensboro, NC.

Woods, Donald Z. "The Department Magazine." *College English* 16.2 (1954): 123–25.

Yearling, The. Freshman English Class of the Woman's College of the University of North Carolina. CN Y39 V 1.1–4.1 (Spring 1948–Spring 1951). University of North Carolina–Greensboro Archives, Greensboro, NC.

Index

249